MAKING SPACE
FOR JUSTICE

MAKING SPACE FOR JUSTICE

SOCIAL MOVEMENTS, COLLECTIVE IMAGINATION, AND POLITICAL HOPE

MICHELE MOODY-ADAMS

Columbia University Press   *New York*

publication supported by a grant from
The Community Foundation *for* Greater New Haven
as part of the Urban Haven Project

Columbia University Press
Publishers Since 1893
New York   Chichester, West Sussex
cup.columbia.edu

Library of Congress Cataloging-in-Publication Data
Names: Moody-Adams, Michele M., author.
Title: Making space for justice : social movements, collective imagination, and political hope / Michele Moody-Adams.
Description: New York : Columbia University Press, [2022] | Includes bibliographical references and index.
Identifiers: LCCN 2021048822 (print) | LCCN 2021048823 (ebook) | ISBN 9780231201360 (hardback) | ISBN 9780231201377 (trade paperback) | ISBN 9780231554060 (ebook)
Subjects: LCSH: Social movements—Philosophy. | Social justice—Philosophy. | Social change—Philosophy.
Classification: LCC HM881 .M666 2022 (print) | LCC HM881 (ebook) | DDC 303.48/4—dc23/eng/20220120
LC record available at https://lccn.loc.gov/2021048822
LC ebook record available at https://lccn.loc.gov/2021048823

Cover image: Aaron Douglas, *Harriet Tubman*, 1931.
© 2022 heirs of Aaron Douglas / licensed by VAGA at Artists Rights Society (ARS), New York.

Cover design: Julia Kushnirsky

CONTENTS

Acknowledgments   vii

Introduction   1

I UNDERSTANDING SOCIAL MOVEMENTS

1 What Is a Social Movement?   13

2 Social Movements and the Task of Democracy   47

3 Social Movements and the Moral Life   79

II SOCIAL MOVEMENTS AND THE POWER OF COLLECTIVE IMAGINATION

4 Taking Imagination Seriously   117

5 Language Matters   155

6 Justice and the Narrative Imagination   187

III THE IMPORTANCE OF
POLITICAL HOPE

7 The Empire of Affect and the Challenge
of Collective Hope 225

8 Hope and History 255

Notes *275*
Bibliography *309*
Index *329*

ACKNOWLEDGMENTS

M   *aking Space for Justice* builds on my long-standing interest in moral progress, by which I mean progress toward producing a more just social world. My work on the topic began with my paper "The Idea of Moral Progress" (1999), defending the idea against various skeptical challenges. In a series of public talks and exchanges, many of which led to further publications, I then turned to consider how we produce moral progress. I first explored the role of social movements in "Moral Progress and Human Agency," for a conference organized in 2015 by Bert Musschenga at Vrije Universität in Amsterdam. I reflected on the emergence of social movements in "Democracy, Identity and Politics" for a conference organized by Colleen McCluskey and sponsored by *Res Philosophica* at St. Louis University in 2017. In spring 2019 I joined Myisha Cherry for an episode of her philosophy podcast, *UnMute*, to discuss monuments, memorials, and the social activism that was challenging monuments to colonialism and the Confederacy. Later in 2019 I spoke on the role of imagination in social movements at a conference on "Imagination and Social Change" organized by Amy Kind at Claremont-McKenna College. I am grateful to the philosophers who invited me to take part in these projects. Professor Kind also provided helpful commentary on this manuscript.

My colleagues in the Columbia Department of Philosophy offered a supportive environment in which to develop central elements of this project. Philip Kitcher encouraged my interest in John Dewey. Bob Gooding-Williams and Carol Rovane were generous interlocutors on a range of topics concerning democracy and ideology. David Albert, Fred Neuhouser, and Chris Peacocke offered helpful comments on my work on "Civic Art of Remembrance and the Democratic Imagination." As *Making Space for Justice* unfolded, Jenann Ismael and Wolfgang Mann provided incisive comments on significant portions of the manuscript.

Philosophers and political theorists from many other departments helped me refine central arguments for the book. In 2018 Jeremy Waldron and Samuel Scheffler invited me to talk about Confederate monuments and political aesthetics for the NYU Colloquium in Legal, Political, and Social Philosophy, which they were then coleading. In addition to in-depth discussions with them, I profited from conversation with Samuel Freeman, Ekow Yankow, and Daniel Viehoff. I also presented portions of the argument to philosophy departments at MIT, Harvard, Amherst, Cal State Bakersfield, and Brooklyn College thanks to Sally Haslanger, Rachel Goodyer, Rafeeq Hasan, Michael Burroughs, and Serene Khader. This led to many productive exchanges about how art, imagination, history, and hope might help to drive progress. In 2020, at the invitation of Robbie Kubala and Elizabeth Scarborough, I was challenged to clarify connections between justice and political aesthetics in "Why Monuments Matter" for a session at a meeting of the American Society of Aesthetics.

Participating in law school workshops at UCLA in 2018 and the University of Virginia in 2019 challenged me to think more deeply about the legal implications of my views. Mark Greenberg, Barbara Herman, and Seana Shiffrin provided collegiality and stimulating conversation during my UCLA visit, as did Micah Schwartzman and Gregg Strauss during my visit to Charlottesville. While in Charlottesville I made an unexpectedly quiet but remarkably instructive visit to the park that, at the time, still contained the statue of Robert E. Lee that had generated controversy and violence in August 2017.

At a pivotal moment in my thinking about social movements, Tommie Shelby and Brandon Terry invited me to contribute to their edited volume, *To Shape a New World* (2018), on Martin Luther King Jr.'s political thought. Working on "The Path of Conscientious Citizenship" for that volume transformed my understanding of the power of collective action. This led me to develop a seminar on "Dissent, Protest and Disobedience" that required the study of social movements in several national contexts and increased my comprehension of what social movements do.

I am deeply indebted to those who encouraged my work during the difficult days and months of the COVID-19 pandemic and lockdown. My husband, James Eli Adams, is a brilliant interlocutor and a demanding reader who consistently challenged me to write in a way that might speak to a broad audience. He was an unflagging source of intellectual sustenance and emotional strength. Our daughter, Katherine Adams, helped to make me a more nuanced observer of the links between art, memory, and political life. She was also an inspiring example of resilience and determination in a time of great uncertainty. I thank Wendy Lochner, my editor at Columbia University Press, whose unfailing support and wise counsel helped me persist through challenging times. Two anonymous reviewers for the press provided commentary that I hope has helped me produce a book that they will want to read anew.

My effort to understand the social and political upheaval of the summer of 2020 played a special role in shaping this project. Like many, I initially reacted to the murder of George Floyd with profound anger and deep despair. But as the summer progressed, I saw that national and global protests spurred by the Black Lives Matter Movement were helping to transform widespread despair into a politically potent, socially constructive hope. I realized that it was more important than ever to provide philosophically informed reflection on social movements, and I thank the hundreds of thousands of protesters who helped to restore hope by bravely demonstrating what it takes to make space for justice.

MAKING SPACE
FOR JUSTICE

INTRODUCTION

Great streams are not easily turned from channels, worn deep in the course of ages.

—Frederick Douglass

*M*aking Space for Justice poses a question rarely asked by philosophers: How might understanding the activities and methods of social movements seeking justice help to answer fundamental questions about the demands of justice and advance important debates about what it takes to satisfy those demands? This book argues that what we learn from progressive social movements could be transformative for philosophical theory as well as for political practice.[1] From the abolitionist movement of the nineteenth century to twenty-first-century movements such as #MeToo and Black Lives Matter, progressive social movements have been wellsprings of constructive moral inquiry as well as transformative political action. Indeed, as Michael Walzer urged in *Interpretation and Social Criticism*, "In so far as we can recognize it, moral progress is more a matter of (workmanlike) social criticism and political struggle, than (paradigm shattering) philosophical

speculation."[2] My book articulates some of the most consequential insights to emerge from the criticism and struggles
conducted by progressive social movements. My aim is to show
what those insights mean for theoretical reflection about the
nature of justice, as well as how they might inform new and
ongoing movements seeking to promote justice.

Philosophers can certainly help to create space for justice by
means of careful theorizing about the nature and sources of justice, critical analyses of moral and political thinkers and traditions, and constructing inspiring visions of political life. But this
book presupposes a way of thinking about the role of philosophers that has been mostly unwelcome in philosophy since the
idea of the "philosopher-king" emerged in Plato's *Republic*. My
argument draws on John Dewey's pragmatism, with its insistence
that the philosopher's critical reflections—however valuable—
have no special authority in the pursuit of social justice. Dewey's refusal to claim such authority led him to argue, in a book
on *Ethics* jointly authored with James Tufts, that the ethical theories produced by philosophers are not "incompatible rival systems which must be accepted or rejected *en bloc*, but . . . more or
less adequate methods for surveying the problems of conduct."
Dewey and Tufts went on to contend that the aim of any comprehensive review of such theories should be the intellectual
"emancipation" of the student of ethics, a process that will put
the student in a position to "judge the problems of conduct for
himself."[3] *Making Space for Justice* is rooted in the philosophical
humility that underlies this Deweyan stance.

In this context, philosophical humility involves acknowledging that social movements frequently produce knowledge that
makes indispensable contributions to social and political thought.
As sociologists Ron Eyerman and Andrew Jamison have argued,
social movements "are best conceived of as temporary public

spaces, as movements of collective creation that provide societies with ideas, identities, and even ideals."[4] On this view, social movements are essentially "forms of cognitive praxis." Eyerman and Jamison focus on the "socially conditioned" and locally valuable knowledge that social movements produce. But I will urge that the value and validity of at least some insights emerging from the criticism and struggle of social movements cannot be limited by social or cultural boundaries. This is particularly true of the moral insights social movements produce through what I call "engaged moral inquiry." Here, I follow William James in holding that "we all help to determine the content of ethical philosophy so far as we contribute to the [human] race's moral life."[5] Yet I also explore the insights that social movements have generated about how to *realize* justice, since such insights are critical to bridging the gap between intelligent theory and effective practice. Some insights in this category will necessarily be socially conditioned and mainly relevant to particular locales.

This book is not the first contribution to political philosophy to take social movements seriously. Philosophers such as David Lyons (on confronting historical injustice), Sally Haslanger (on social movements and ideology), Candace Delmas (on the duty to resist), and Chris Lebron (on Black Lives Matter) have made important contributions to our understanding of the work that many social movements do.[6] Moreover, central theories defended by John Rawls, on civil disobedience, and Iris Young, on the "politics of difference," seek to construct philosophical arguments by relying on important ideas and ideals associated with social movements. I discuss the relevant aspects of Rawls's views in chapters 1 and 4, and important themes from Young's work in chapters 2, 3, and 7. But *Making Space for Justice* is the first book to approach the criticism and struggle carried out by social movements with robust philosophical humility. I am claiming that some of the knowledge generated by social movements is as critical to understanding the nature and sources of justice, and the nature and content of core democratic values, as to determining how collective action might help to promote justice and preserve democracy.

Progressive social movements are often driven by the conviction that those on whose behalf they struggle have been wrongly denied access to valuable elements of "universal citizenship," such as substantive equal rights, equal protection of the laws, and equal liberty.[7] But these movements also teach us that justice ultimately demands what I have labeled *humane regard*—a combination of compassionate concern and robust respect—and that we can remedy injustice only when we properly expand the reach of society's concern and respect. Regrettably, some of the most important elements of humane regard have never been adequately understood by familiar philosophical moral conceptions—whether utilitarian, Kantian, virtue-based, care-focused, or libertarian. I will urge that moral and political philosophy cannot defensibly remain unchanged in light of this fact.

Two changes will be critical. First, we need a deeper understanding of compassionate concern, including better accounts of how it can be developed in individuals and sustainably embodied in social institutions and practices. Second, although there is already a rich literature on the social and institutional requirements of respect, we need to better understand how respect for the moral separateness of autonomous agents can be constructively combined with compassionate concern, which emphasizes moral connectedness. Progressive social movements have consistently challenged us to reject the assumption that compassionate concern and robust respect might be inherently incompatible. This means that we need more sustained reflection, within philosophy and other disciplines, about how to constructively combine compassion and respect in service of humane regard. I argue, here, that social movements convincingly show that imagination in its various uses—especially sympathetic, aesthetic, epistemic, and narrative—is critical to developing our capacity for humane regard.

Social movements have also shown that even if we meet the theoretical challenges associated with understanding justice as humane regard, it can still be extremely difficult to transform societies to meet the demands of justice. As Frederick Douglass argues in "What to the Slave Is the Fourth of July?," long-standing social orders are like "great streams" that are not easily turned from channels of injustice "worn deep in the course of ages."[8] This means that in contemporary political societies, social movements must often devote much of their effort to making cultural and political "space" for justice. That effort typically involves three related tasks: First, social movements must convince people that a given set of circumstances actually constitutes injustice and that the harms experienced by those who are subject to it ought to be addressed. Second, people must be persuaded that there is a reasonable remedy for that injustice and that is sensible to hope for its realization. Finally, they must be convinced that it is humanly and politically possible to realize the objects of that hope in practice. *Making Space for Justice* will explore the methods and tools by which social movements have taken on these tasks and frequently succeeded. The book will show that social movements have often found ways of expanding conceptual and perceptual space for justice by drawing on the transformative powers of imagination, but also that they have often strengthened the motivation to pursue justice by helping to inspire genuine political hope.

Part 1, "Understanding Social Movements," comprises three chapters that explain the nature of social movements and explore several processes by which the constructive social change that they often enable takes place. Chapter 1 contends that constructive social movements are collective, noninstitutional endeavors in "contentious politics" (in Charles Tilly's phrase) through which a social group asserts unaddressed needs, demands attention to insufficiently acknowledged interests, or seeks respect for the worth of some marginalized or excluded group or project. Although some theorists have feared that extra-institutional collective action is always a dangerous expression of collective irrationality, this chapter shows that the contentious politics of constructive social movements often provide invaluable lessons about the moral obligations of citizenship. One of the most important such lessons is that dissent, protest, and even collective disobedience to law can be fully justifiable expressions of conscientious citizenship. The chapter also shows that social movements are complex communities of concern and action characterized by a "division of labor." That labor includes (a) the material sacrifice and political struggle of those who actively assert justice-claims in activities such as sit-ins, marches, boycotts, or strikes; (b) the social criticism produced by people such as philosophers, religious thinkers, historians, and artists; and, finally, (c) the leadership of moral visionaries and social innovators who, in many social movements, become public symbols of the movements' values and goals. Constructive change sometimes takes a long time because successfully coordinating all the necessary labor of social movements is a daunting task.

Chapter 2 argues that many social movements have yielded valuable lessons about the institutions, practices, and habits of mind that are crucial supports of democratic cooperation. They have provided critical insights about the norms of public discussion that are most likely to promote democratic communication and about the kinds of reasons most likely to shape inclusive political deliberation. They have also helped us understand how people who begin by seeing themselves as powerless can become capable of vigorous democratic citizenship: developing confidence in their capacity for effective political agency and a robust sense of why they ought to exercise it. The chapter shows that social movements help make space for justice by affirming the rationality of what Young calls a "communicative" conception (or a "discussion-based" conception) of democracy, and by offering convincing examples of the processes by which democratic activism can produce the "stirrings" of dignity and destiny described by movement intellectuals such as Martin Luther King, Jr., and Vaclav Havel. Chapter 2 concludes by carefully distinguishing progressive from regressive social movements, showing that regressive movements frequently originate as backlash to progressive movements and often reflect the influence of xenophobic populism driven by panic and fear.

Chapter 3 shows that social movements often become invaluable participants in the human community of moral inquirers. I have long maintained that "ordinary" people can have standing to contribute to serious moral inquiry.[9] One aim of *Making Space for Justice* is to extend this account of moral inquiry. Social movements have made two vital contributions to moral and political thought: They have shown, first, that injustice is never simply the "absence of justice" but a very distinctive social phenomenon that can be illuminated only by examining experiences of injustice very closely. Second, a central element of the moral knowledge generated by social movements is that justice is never simply a matter of "respect for persons" but also demands compassionate concern for others' vulnerability to suffering. The combination of respect and compassionate concern is what I call humane regard, and injustice consists in a society's failure to extend humane regard to all those to whom it is due. Chapter 3 considers a range of experiences of injustice—including the injustices done by the terrible murder of Emmitt Till in 1955—that help to deepen our knowledge of how to justly combine respect and compassion. The chapter also reflects on the role of art in helping to ensure that we are not able to simply turn away from the facts and faces of injustice.

The chapters that make up part 2, "Social Movements and the Power of Collective Imagination," explore the ways in which social movements can—and must—harness the constructive powers of imagination to make space for justice. Chapter 4 begins by showing that imagination is critical to the work of social movements because it helps to constitute political societies as communities of collective memory and shared social understanding. This chapter thus builds on the work of anthropologist Benedict Anderson to argue that political societies are "imagined communities." The chapter also draws on the arguments of philosopher Charles Taylor regarding the role of the "social imaginary" in constituting shared social understandings and generating consensus on the legitimacy of basic institutions and practices. The chapter then explores the complex relationships among art, memory, and politics by reflecting on the political iconoclasm of many recent social movements, showing that social movements sometimes need to challenge art and artifacts that symbolically sustain narratives which objectify, stigmatize, and even dehumanize members of socially nondominant groups. When social movements mount such challenges, they engage in *aesthetic activism*.

Chapter 5 considers the role of epistemic imagination in challenging linguistic forms that, as Kenneth Burke argues, select, reflect, and deflect important aspects of reality in potentially unjust ways. Once we understand the power of language to function as a socially and politically consequential filter, it becomes clear that social movements must sometimes engage in *language activism* if they are to create space for social justice. The chapter focuses on three varieties of language activism: projects that involve naming hitherto unnamed injustices, activism that aids in finding language for properly linking unjust actions with their causes and effects, and efforts to reject linguistic forms that legitimize injustice.

The complex connections between justice and narrative imagination are explored in chapter 6. The chapter begins by reflecting on the nature of narrative and the role of imagination in enabling us to construct, as well as to interpret, particular narratives. Given the role of socially and politically consequential narratives, making space for justice sometimes demands *narrative activism* that takes two main forms. First, it often demands what I call emancipatory narrative activism, like that undertaken by authors of antebellum slave narratives in the American South. But second, it sometimes requires concerted efforts to correct accounts of history that may veil, suppress, or actively deny important details about the facts and faces of injustice. Chapter 6 also considers the extent to which failure to find shared understandings of a common history can produce what Luvell Anderson has described as "hermeneutical impasses" that limit our ability to identify and respond to injustice.

Finally, the two chapters that make up part 3, "The Importance of Political Hope," examine the nature and sources of hope as a basis of political stability, but also as a means of sustaining those who participate in, and support the projects of, constructive social movements seeking justice. Chapter 7 begins by considering the political importance of our affective responses— which I divide into ordinary emotions, volitional dispositions, and affective orientations. The chapter then analyzes sociologist Arlie Hochschild's concept of the "deep story," articulated in her book *Strangers in Their Own Land*, as a means of understanding the role of affective responses in recent political conflicts. The chapter also explores and defends Spinoza's understanding of the essential interrelatedness of hope and fear but argues that there is a way of generating a constructive political hope with the potential to overcome the expected—but not inevitable—political dominance of collective fear over collective hope. I argue that some destructive collective action—the kind that shapes many backlash or countermovements of recent years—rests on a simulacrum of hope rather than on politically constructive hope. The discussion concludes with reflections on Nelson Mandela's effort in 1990 to save South Africa from civil war, as a powerful example of constructive political hope.

Chapter 8 concludes the book by arguing that the most defensible social movements seek a sustainable balance among three projects: a future-oriented politics of broadly shared social progress, a historically sensitive politics that may involve specific backward-looking claims for reparations, and a politics of reconciliation and possible redemption. The chapter stresses the importance of exemplars like Martin Luther King, Jr., Vaclav Havel, and Nelson Mandela, who embody political values that can be sustained only by an expansive, socially constructive political hope. I end by arguing that sustaining collective hope depends on cultivating and displaying the democratic virtue of civic grace, by which I mean a readiness to extend good will to fellow citizens whom we may never meet face to face, and even to many of our most determined political opponents.

I

UNDERSTANDING
SOCIAL MOVEMENTS

1

WHAT IS A SOCIAL MOVEMENT?

Walker, there is no road
The road is made by walking.

—Antonio Machado

1.1 SOCIAL MOVEMENTS AND THE SOCIAL THEORY OF "THE CROWD"

This book argues that social movements can be vital sources of moral enlightenment and advances in collective rationality, and that they often make space for constructive social transformation, in ways that ought to shape theorizing about justice as well as practical efforts to promote justice in the world. This claim will provoke multifaceted resistance, perhaps most notably due to widespread association of "the crowd" with fundamental irrationality and destructiveness. Plato's attack on Athenian democracy in book 8 of the *Republic* suggests the importance of this association in the history of political philosophy. Later claims about the dangers of the crowd focused on collective action *outside* of normal political channels, particularly the excesses of the French Revolution's "Reign of Terror," which in turn provoked anxious responses to the waves of political movements that occurred in nineteenth-century Europe and America.[1] Because the social movements discussed here also occur outside of conventional political institutions, some readers will presume that they ought, on the whole, to be feared—and possibly even suppressed—as intrinsically subject to destructive and irrational impulses and forces.

Gustave Le Bon's analysis in *The Crowd: A Study of the Popular Mind* (1895) is by far the best-known effort to find grounds for fear and mistrust of extra-institutional collective action. As the historian J. S. McClelland notes, Le Bon begins by assuming that essentially *every* social group is a crowd.[2] He then argues that once we understand their collective psychology, we will acknowledge that crowds "are only powerful for destruction": "In consequence of the purely destructive nature of their power crowds act like those microbes which hasten the dissolution of enfeebled or dead bodies. When the structure of a civilization is rotten, it is always the masses that bring about its downfall. It is at such a juncture that their chief mission is plainly visible."[3] On this view, mass politics could never be a source of collective rationality or the engine of constructive social change, because crowds are fundamentally impulsive, incapable of sophisticated reflection, and too readily influenced by authoritarian leaders. Le Bon did allow that crowds can sometimes display "lofty" virtues, and often "to a degree rarely attained by the wisest philosophers."[4] But he insisted that when they display virtues, they do so "unconsciously," and thus the tendency to virtue is always subject to being overwhelmed by the tendency to collective immorality and "crime."

For much of the twentieth century, theoretical reflection on the nature and value of social movements echoed Le Bon's mistrust. Moreover, for many mid-twentieth-century thinkers, not even India's examples of Gandhian *satyagraha* (mainly in the 1930s), could override the impressions produced by the rise of Nazism in Germany and Austria, and of fascism in Spain and Italy. The ruthless and murderous character of those movements, encouraged by demagogues who embraced violence as a first resort, helped to reinforce fears that, ultimately, collective action outside of institutionalized political life would always lead to wanton destruction and mass despair.[5] Yet by the end of the twentieth century, many social theorists and political philosophers had come to a vastly different conclusion. In particular, they came to assume that social movements can often be defensible examples of what Charles Tilly called "contentious politics"—and, indeed, that they are sometimes catalysts for strengthening democratic institutions and processes, and even for producing democracy where it had not existed before.[6]

What happened to change the general tenor of the debate about social movements? Many social theorists explain the change as a crucial consequence of the "classic" phase of the American Civil Rights Movement, which began with the Montgomery bus boycott in 1955 and concluded with the Voting Rights Act in 1965. It has been argued, and with good reason, that as many social elites came to appreciate the motivations, methods, and goals of participants in the Civil Rights Movement, it became increasingly difficult to assume that collective political action that is extra-institutional must inevitably be irrational and socially destructive.[7] To be sure, by the end of the movement's classic phase, even its sympathetic critics urged, in the words of Bayard Rustin, that it was time to move "from protest to politics."[8] These critics believed that with the passage of the Voting Rights Act, the marches, sit-ins, and mass boycotts of the classic phase had lost their value for the African American freedom struggle, and that the time had come to seek conventional forms of political power. Yet, among its many accomplishments, the classic phase of the movement succeeded in showing that large groups of ordinary people, protesting injustice outside of "standard" political channels, could be morally enlightened, collectively rational, and socially constructive. Martin Luther King, Jr., helpfully observed that during the Montgomery bus boycott the philosophy of nonviolence was disseminated in meetings where "physicians, teachers and lawyers sat or stood beside domestic workers and unskilled laborers," and that "the Ph.D.'s and the no 'D's' were bound together in a common venture."[9]

King also believed that a successful emancipatory movement must be grounded in "a philosophy that wins and holds the people's allegiance." He was convinced that the philosophy of nonviolence provided that grounding and that it was as critical to the movement's cohesiveness as its commitment to the freedom struggle itself.[10] This is why we cannot understand the power of the movement to supplant Le Bon's suspicions about "the crowd" unless we can appreciate how deeply rooted the movement really was in the philosophy of nonviolence. King's distinctive version of the philosophy of nonviolence was an amalgam of three important traditions: (1) the philosophical legacy of the Platonic Socrates; (2) Gandhi's understanding of the constructive political possibilities of noncooperation; and (3) Christian commitments to human dignity and equality, and to the virtues of faith, hope, and agape (disinterested love). The movement's participants were deeply committed to this amalgamation of ideas, values, and principles, and the consistent expression of that commitment helped to quell fears that there might be a necessary connection between collective action and violence. By countering Le Bon's suspicions that the lofty virtues of the crowd always give way to immorality and crime, the movement made it possible for theorists and ordinary citizens alike to take social movements more seriously as collectively *rational* forms of political action.

Another significant outcome of the movement's success, like that of Gandhian satyagraha before it, was to generate provocative questions about the relationship between violence and power. Gandhi and King always maintained that nonviolence was the most powerful force available to humankind. Their confidence influenced the work of other twentieth-century movements, including the methods and goals of the Farm Workers Movement: Cesar Chavez and Dolores Huerta (the movement's best-known leaders) modeled many of their efforts on values and principles defended by Gandhi and King. In the late 1960s Hannah Arendt reiterated the distinction between violence and power and emphasized the dangers of ignoring it. In "On Violence," she argued:

> To substitute violence for power can bring victory, but its price is very high; for it is not only paid by the vanquished, it is also paid by the victor in his own power. . . . It has often been said that impotence breeds violence, and psychologically this is quite true. . . . Politically speaking, the point is that loss of power becomes a temptation to substitute violence for power—in 1968 during the Democratic convention in Chicago we could watch this process on television—and that violence itself results in impotence.[11]

More recently, the work of social theorists such as Erica Chenoweth and Maria Stephan has echoed this stance, urging that, on the whole, nonviolence is collectively more rational for social movements than violence could ever be.[12] The philosopher Gene Sharp even based both his theory and his practical advice to real social movements on the idea that nonviolence is the most effective strategy for moving "from dictatorship to democracy."[13] Serious debate about the power of nonviolence in politics thus continues to shape discussion of twenty-first-century social movements. This shows how fully the nonviolence of the Civil Rights Movement helped to transform the valuation of social movements in general.

Of course, when a social movement has a long history, and comparatively large membership, the strategies and tactics that define it will be complex. Some analysts believe, for instance, that at some point in their evolution nearly all social movements can be divided into "moderate" and "radical" factions. They urge, further, that even when the moderate faction becomes the dominant presence in a movement, the continued existence of more radical factions can have "radical flank effects" that can take either negative or positive forms, depending on how the factions interact with each other and with wider publics.[14] If we think of the Civil Rights Movement as the moderate faction of a larger, historically extended African American freedom struggle, we may well need to ask how much of the success of the classic phase of Civil Rights Movement depended on the efforts of agents outside of the movement to support and encourage the movement's "moderates."[15] That is, the political and cultural success of the Civil Rights Movement might be traced, at least in part, to "third-party" support for moderation, as a positive radical flank effect. Yet, whatever we make of these considerations about radical flank effects, the Civil Rights Movement's commitment to nonviolence—a commitment that did not waver, even when participants were met with violence from racist countermovements—was clearly an important element of the processes that changed the theoretical, as well as the everyday, valuation of collective action.

Part of the argument of this book is, of course, that changes in the theoretical valuing of social movements have not had appropriate impact in philosophy. Even as the twenty-first century unfolds, there is still more attention paid to social movements by sociologists, social psychologists, and political scientists than by social and political philosophers. As I argue in the introduction, this largely reflects the dominance of the Platonic conception of the "philosopher king" in discussions about the requirements of justice. Yet despite this dearth of philosophical attention to social movements, *Making Space for Justice* is not the first contribution to social and political philosophy to take social movements seriously. Two of the most important examples of serious philosophical attention to the value of social movements can be found in the work of John Rawls and Iris Young.

Rawls's account of civil disobedience continues to stimulate important debates about the role of social movements in a democracy, about whether social movements must be nonviolent to be justifiable, and about what social movements can teach us about political obligation.[16] Some of the most important philosophical treatments of social movements have thus emerged as part of the effort to assess the merits of Rawls's view. But I am defending a view of *the value* of social movements to which Rawls would not—and could not—have consented: the idea that social movements can sometimes be sources of inquiry that might inform, and possibly even transform, theoretical reflection about justice itself. Rawls defends the view that social movements engaged in civil disobedience can be necessary to the realization of justice in the situation of "partial compliance" with the demands of justice in the nonideal realm. But Rawls does not seem to assume that social movements can tell us anything about justice itself that philosophy would otherwise not appreciate.

This becomes especially clear in Rawls's later work, which developed his conception of political liberalism and the account of public reason associated with that conception. On Rawls's account of public reason, the principles guiding even fully justified social movements could rightly shape public discourse under one condition only: that their participants could plausibly promise that those principles could eventually be "translated" into terms acceptable to public reason. Yet progressive social movements have consistently revealed serious moral and epistemic deficiencies in many of the basic concepts and principles shaping the public reason of the societies they have confronted.[17] For example, the women's movement showed that unwanted sexual advances at work are not an unavoidable cost of allowing women in the public sphere but a morally and legally unacceptable form of employment discrimination. Analogously, the Civil Rights Movement showed that Jim Crow laws did not, and could not, create "separate but equal" institutions and that the institutions that were created were morally unconscionable and constitutionally indefensible. But it was only by fundamentally transforming the *content* (and sometimes the boundaries) of public reason, in ways explored more fully in part 2, that any of these efforts could move us closer to genuine social justice.

In this context, it must be stressed that Martin Luther King was deeply skeptical of the power of discursive reason *alone* to produce the kind of transformations that could really remedy American racial injustice.[18] King sometimes argued, for instance, that only the "purifying power of faith"—primarily in the form of Christian agape—could challenge what he viewed as he "distortions and rationalizations" of reason.[19] By this, he did not mean that one had to be a professing Christian to be an effective agent of social justice. King famously insisted that the Christian notion of agape was implicit in Gandhi's doctrine of satyagraha, and since Gandhi had been deeply affected by his reading of Tolstoy's book *The Kingdom of God Is Within You: Christianity Not as a Mystic Religion but as a New Theory of Life*, there is every reason to believe that King was correct.[20] Still further, though King always argued that unearned suffering could have redemptive value for the sufferer, he also recognized—I believe reluctantly—that the sacrifices required by nonviolent direct action during the movement were, at least in part, a means of enlarging "perceptual space" for justice. King famously observed that "every step towards the goal of justice requires sacrifice, suffering and struggle; the tireless exertions and passionate concern of dedicated individuals."[21] He understood that images of nonviolent protesters being attacked with billy clubs, set upon by police dogs, and struck down by high-pressure water hoses would eventually make it difficult for America's "white moderates" to affect ignorance of, or avert their glance from, the grave wrongs of racial segregation.[22] More generally, King accepted the power of suffering and personal sacrifice to dislodge the prejudices and unreflective habits of belief that limit our ability to see the world and our place in it in a novel way. He accepted, that is, the power of suffering and sacrifice to do the kind of work that might make space for justice in contexts where discursive reason proved ineffective.

Reflecting on recent history, the power of suffering and sacrifice to make space for justice was clearly at work following release of the video depicting the police killing of Minneapolis citizen George Floyd in May 2020. The response to that video was immediate and widespread, sparking national and global multiracial protests affirming that "Black Lives Matter." Even people who reported being unable, or unwilling, to watch the video in its entirety nonetheless reported being profoundly affected by descriptions of the events depicted in it. Still further, national surveys showed that in one two-week period after the release of the video, support for the Black Lives Matter Movement grew almost as much as it had in the preceding two years.[23] The broader significance of these developments might seem to support one observer's response to the harrowing experience of women who filed the first class-action sexual harassment lawsuit, in *Jenson v. Eveleth Taconite Co.*, 130 F.3d 1287 (8th Cir. 1997): "The nature of social change is that we make martyrs out of pioneers. We have yet to figure out how to make social change without sacrificing people along the way."[24] I will argue in part 2 that we can sometimes lessen the need for reliance on actual suffering to make space for justice by appealing to the creative powers of imagination, especially the power of art. Yet the larger point is worth reiterating: King was clearly right to deny that we can rely on the power of discursive reason *alone* to remedy serious injustice.

A similar concern about the limitations of discursive rational argument in the contexts of certain kinds of political discussion and debate was a compelling aspect of Iris Young's political thought, for instance, in *Inclusion and Democracy*. Young's sense of the limitations of discursive argument was, at least in part, a product of her reflections on the activities of late twentieth-century social movements. But this was just one important way in which Young's work took social movements seriously. In *Justice and the Politics of Difference*, Young drew directly on lessons gleaned from progressive social movements to strengthen her challenge to the "distributive justice paradigm": the idea, defended by Rawls and others, that an adequate conception of social justice can be captured by the idea of a fair distribution of the benefits and burdens of social cooperation.[25] As I argue more fully in chapter 3, Young's account rightly centers on the very different idea that injustice refers to various kind of "disabling constraints" on choice and action, and that achieving justice demands identifying and then eliminating the most important such constraints.

But Young too quickly dismisses the possibility that what animates most progressive social movements, even those movements she properly understands to be engaged in seeking emancipation through a "politics of difference," might be the same ideal of "universal citizenship" that drove nineteenth-century abolitionism and the mid-twentieth-century Civil Rights Movement.[26] I will show that, for the most part, even the most "radical" progressive social movements have sought equal recognition and respect for the human dignity of their members and equal compassionate concern for their members' vulnerability to pain and suffering. This search for equal concern and respect is the defining goal of nearly all of the most influential social movements, and it expresses their commitment to the ideal of universal citizenship.

1.2 THE CONTENTIOUS POLITICS OF SOCIAL MOVEMENTS

I have argued that irrationality, impulsiveness, and susceptibility to violence are not essential features of social movements, and that the groups involved in many social movements are therefore not the essentially dangerous crowds presumed in Le Bon's analysis, or in the views of social theorists influenced by his work. But what are the *actual* characteristics of social movements, and how might those characteristics inform the movements' capacities to contribute to collective rationality, engage in constructive moral inquiry, and make space for constructive social change? My reply begins with a simple definition. A social movement is a sustained, organized endeavor in extra-institutional "contentious politics" through which a group either (a) asserts an unaddressed need; (b) demands attention to an insufficiently acknowledged interest; or (c) seeks respect for the dignity or worth of some marginalized or excluded group or project, with the goal of changing relevant institutions, policies, and practices. This definition draws on what is now received wisdom in social theory, especially the concept of "contentious politics" developed by sociologist Charles Tilly, and gradually refined by Tilly and various coauthors.[27] In a recent contribution to the discussion, Tilly, Castañeda, and Wood acknowledge that the label "contentious politics" might apply to a broad spectrum of activities, including riots and uprisings, and even rebellions and revolutions. Yet they insist that the activities of social movements constitute a distinct category of contentious politics because they involve organized, collective, yet noninstitutional activities that in some way appeal to governments to help address their dissatisfaction with the political status quo.[28] On my account, we must also distinguish progressive or constructive social movements, which seek to promote justice by expanding the circle of people and beings to whom justice applies, from "backlash-" or "countermovements," which generally seek to contract the circle.[29] But for the sake of simplicity, I use the phrase "social movements" mainly as a synonym for "progressive social movements," except where the adjective "progressive" is critical to prevent confusion.

Understanding the work that social movements do demands careful analysis of the concept of contentious politics, since we can reasonably wonder what kinds of projects make a group's political activity "contentious." On one influential account—I will call it the narrow view—social movements always involve the "collective making of claims that, if realized, would conflict with someone else's interests."[30] At first glance, this account looks unproblematic. But the narrow view is inadequate in three important respects: (1) it ignores the diversity and variety of claims that social movements make by assuming that they always assert interests; (2) it underestimates the complexity of social movement activity that does involve interests; and (3) it obscures critical differences between asserting an interest and making a declaration of moral standing and value. We can understand the contentious politics of social movements only by briefly considering each of these ways in which the narrow view goes wrong.

I have urged that the narrow view's first deficiency is its failure to appreciate the variety of claims that social movements make. Of course, some social movements mainly, or even exclusively, assert interests. The United Farm Workers Movement, for example, was principally an effort to advance unacknowledged interests. But other social movements mainly assert unaddressed *needs* that may or may not be linked with some being's interests. Still others principally declare *moral entitlements* (usually rights) *or moral standing and value* (such as dignity or intrinsic worth), sometimes on behalf of entities that do not have interests. Consider that environmental movements can assert claims of need on behalf of rainforests, oceans, and even the environment in a general sense, even though neither rainforests nor oceans nor the environment have interests. In another example, social movements sometimes make claims about what is needed to preserve endangered cultures or endangered languages, or they may even focus on the intrinsic importance or worth of preserving the culture or language, sometimes independently of the interests of particular people in participating in the culture or speaking the language. In all such cases, the movements' goals are something like getting other people to attend to the flourishing, or even just the continued existence, of some entity or phenomenon that cannot assert interests.

Some critics may want to argue that rainforests, oceans, cultures, and languages do have interests.[31] But I contend that they *cannot* have interests, because saying that some good is "in x's interest" is not simply saying that it is likely to benefit x, or to promote x's well-being, or even to support x's continued existence. It is also saying that the good is something that x *could* "*take an interest in*." That is, there must be "a point of view" from which the potential recipient could want the good in question or (more substantively) find the good worth having and even worth making a commitment to pursue.[32] But rainforests, languages, and cultures cannot have commitments. Of course, people who engage in political action to protect such phenomena can certainly have commitments, and they can therefore count as members of "interest groups." Yet when an environmentalist is engaged in a political disagreement with someone who does not acknowledge the claims of the environment, the disagreement is not a conflict of interests. It is a conflict between a claim that we ought to recognize the special value of the environment and the convictions of those who believe they have an interest in rejecting that claim.

It is important to emphasize that, in this regard, social movements regarding animals are quite different from movements promoting the environment or promoting language diversity or cultural survival. This is because nonhuman animals can and do have interests that should carry weight in our moral and political deliberations and actions. Of course, defenders of animal rights will argue that the very existence of animals also gives them moral standing and worth that should shape political deliberation and action. This is why social movements that focus on animals often ask us to act on both the special moral claims that animals can make on us and the important interests that animals can have.

Regrettably, it can be difficult to make compelling arguments on behalf of phenomena like the environment that are not capable of having interests—that is, on behalf of entities that are incapable of having a point of view. This is because the effectiveness of some claims that social movements make depends, at least in part, on their capacity to appeal to sympathetic imagination—just as Adam Smith suggests in *The Theory of Moral Sentiments*.[33] But clearly we cannot sympathize with the inanimate phenomena that (mostly) constitute the environment. This is why many in the environmental movement now try to supplement discursive argument about the importance of preserving the environment with appeals to science fiction about climate change—or "cli-fi."[34] Cli-fi imaginatively depicts the dire consequences of climate change and vividly presents the environment as something thus worth caring about and preserving. Whether in literature, in live theater, or on film, climate-focused science fiction draws on the powers of epistemic imagination and narrative imagination to change our sense of meaning and value. When we appeal to science fiction for this purpose, we implicitly acknowledge the distinction between asserting the value of protecting some entity and declaring that that entity might somehow have "an interest" in being preserved.

The second problem with the narrow view of social movements is that it rests on a simplistic understanding of political conflicts of interest. For even when social movements are plausibly understood to be promoting group interests, any conflicts of interests they generate usually unfold quite differently from, and get resolved by processes mostly distinct from, conflicts of interest in ordinary institutionalized politics. To begin with, in ordinary political life, conflicts of interests are resolved through processes that have a clear beginning, middle, and end—with the "end" usually occurring at the ballot box and possibly, eventually, in a legislative outcome. But the interest politics associated with social movements often look profoundly different from this conventional model. This is because, for social movements, the path from formation and articulation of interests to attainment of desirable political outcomes is not officially marked out in advance. The epigraph from the poet Antonio Machado that begins this chapter is thus especially apt: in the context of social movements, "the road is made by walking." Further, while the success of social movements is often appropriately measured by legislative outcomes, such outcomes will be out of reach unless a movement can generate serious attention for its interests. There are often no established channels for this, and social movements must then rely on strikes, boycotts, marches, and even fasting to get public attention for their interests, generate public concern, and reshape political debate.

Conventional conflicts of interest in politics get settled mainly through elections and legislation (although in societies with judicial review, a supportive ruling from the highest competent court may be needed to undermine challenges to controversial legislation and even to defend a contested electoral victory, as in the U.S. presidential election of 2020). Moreover, elections are resolved by achieving what theorists of organizational behavior call "domination": a victory of one disputing party (or of a group of disputing parties) over all the others. Of course, in some contexts—even in the processes leading up to decisive elections—conflicts of interest may be resolved by one of two other additional methods. As Mary Parker Follett famously observed in her essay on "Constructive Conflict," in addition to *domination*, conflicts of interest can sometimes be resolved by *compromise* (in which all contending parties get *some* of what they want while also giving something else up) or by *integrative consensus* (in which neither party has to sacrifice because the parties find a solution in which all their main desires and interests are satisfied). Follett plausibly considers integrative consensus to be the best result because, whenever it is available, it best "stabilizes" the conflicts it addresses.[35] But integrative consensus is extremely difficult to achieve in many ordinary political contexts, where compromise is often the second-best resolution, overall. While compromise may be available in the political negotiations that precede decisive elections, and often in the negotiations that take place in legislative assemblies before a bill is decisively signed into law, institutionalized political life provides ordinary *voters* with few opportunities to seek compromise.[36]

Participants in (progressive) social movements are often quite open to compromise. Indeed, the spirit of compromise played a prominent role at pivotal moments in the Civil Rights Movement, as we learn from King's recounting, in "A Letter from Birmingham Jail," of the conversations he had with Birmingham's business leaders in the hope of getting them to remove humiliating racial signs from city stores. But King's disappointment at their failure to compromise confirms that social movements can encounter enormous difficulty achieving any compromises they propose. All too often, those who oppose their cause will consider compromise only after the movement wins some preliminary "battles" by domination.

The history of the United Farm Workers Movement provides a noteworthy example of this difficulty. The Delano grape strike and its associated national boycott of table grapes required years of strenuous effort and sacrifice (from 1965 to 1970) to get growers to negotiate contracts that would provide the workers with better pay and more humane working conditions. It then took another five years for passage of the California Agricultural

Labor Relations Act of 1975, which, for the first time, established a legal right to collective bargaining for farmworkers in California.[37] This arduous ten-year process exemplifies the thorny paths that social movements must tread: their opponents usually agree to negotiate compromise only grudgingly, and only after hard-won economic and cultural victories. The process helps to confirm the claim that the process of resolving conflicts of interest generated by social movements bears little resemblance to the generally predictable, linear, and temporally defined processes that shape conventional interest politics. The narrow view fails to appreciate that interest group politics is not monolithic. There is a profound difference between ordinary, institutional contentious politics and the contentious politics that define social movements.

The third main deficiency of the narrow view is in some ways the most significant, for the failure to recognize the differences between asserting an interest and making a declaration of moral standing and value can have serious consequences for the quality of political discourse and the health of the public square. It may initially be difficult to accept that there is, in fact, a distinction between assertions of interest and declarations of moral standing and value. This difficulty may reflect the fact that when social movements seek robust respect for the dignity of some marginalized or excluded group, they often expect that obtaining that respect will affect their members' ability to pursue their interests in the future. These movements may also realize that some of the pursuits could, over time, generate real conflicts with even the most morally defensible interests of others. Still further, some movements that start out focused principally on securing respect for dignity or moral standing become more complex over time, directly taking up the pursuit of group interests (especially socioeconomic interests) that may have been thwarted by the denial of respect. But the fact remains that seeking proper respect for one's dignity as a person—that is, seeking respect for one's moral value (and perhaps one's related moral and related legal entitlements)—is not the same thing as pursuing an interest in obtaining some benefit or material good.

The tendency to ignore this distinction has distorted political discourse regarding the goals of many important social movements. In one familiar example, a fundamental goal of the "second wave" of the women's movement was (at least initially) to reject the idea that women are essentially sexual objects, and to insist that women are just as deserving of the rights and privileges of citizenship as men. But the demand to be acknowledged and respected as equal citizens is not an assertion of an interest of any kind. Therefore it does not express any interest that must conflict with the *morally defensible* interests of others. Of course, people who assert an interest in the preservation of patriarchy are right to suspect that the triumph of the women's movement's demand for respect would, over time, prove detrimental to their self-declared interest in patriarchy. But a fundamental aim of the women's movement has been to show that the interest in patriarchy is not a morally defensible interest but one rooted in prejudice and discriminatory attitudes that should not be allowed to protect institutions that deny women equal and genuine respect.

In another example, Native Americans have sought to be viewed and treated as fully human beings, not as mascots or as the sources of nicknames and ritualistic cheers for popular sports teams. Their criticisms of these practices clearly involve demands of respect for human dignity. But such demands are not assertions of interests, and certainly not the assertion of any interest that must conflict with the morally defensible interests of others. People who believe that they have an interest in the persistence of belittling images of Native Americans may suspect that the disappearance of those images from prominent cultural spaces will prove detrimental to the interest they believe that they have in demeaning others. But there is no morally defensible interest in demeaning others. The claim that one has such an interest should not be allowed to protect institutions that deny or discount the claims of Native Americans to equal and genuine respect.

In perhaps the most politically charged example of confusion between interest claims and declarations of moral standing and value, many people fail to understand what is at stake when African Americans—and indeed, people of African descent around the globe—contend that Black Lives Matter. All too often, discussions of the phrase "Black Lives Matter" deteriorate into a series of counterclaims such as "White Lives Matter" or "Blue Lives Matter" or even "All Lives Matter." Those counterclaims would be reasonable responses if the original declaration had been meant to threaten the well-being of anyone else, or to ignore, discount, or deny that those other people also have dignity and value. But the phrase "Black Lives Matter" is simply a declaration of unacknowledged moral standing—that is, a claim about the reach of human dignity. It declares that black people are fully human beings, not exotic curiosities, and not permanent possibilities of danger who somehow "deserve" to be hunted and subdued like wild game. This declaration does not assert an interest that could conflict with the morally defensible interests of others, because it is not a claim about interests at all. Of course, most people who have participated in the Black Lives Matter Movement would support changes in political institutions and policies, and socioeconomic circumstances that would very likely affect their interests. But the immediate conflict between those who contend "Black Lives Matter" and those who are offended by this contention is a conflict between the declaration that Black people have equal moral value and the convictions of those who wrongly believe that they could have a morally defensible interest in ignoring, discounting, or denying the moral value being declared.

It must be stressed that familiar counterclaims to the phrase "Black Lives Matter" sometimes reflect an intent to *explicitly* discount or deny the moral value of Black lives. Indeed, what the Black Lives Matter Movement has sought to do—though this aim is misrepresented and distorted in certain public forums—is to show that this intent, along with the institutions and policies that give it social power, remains all too widespread. Still further, in an analogy to the two previous cases, some people believe that they have an overriding interest in preserving institutions and practices that protect racial inequality and the unearned racial privilege that so often accompanies it. But to reiterate a central point: this is not a morally defensible interest. Of course, the readiness to think otherwise can be explained. It may reflect unwillingness to relinquish racial privilege, for instance, or express grave fears about what acknowledging unearned privilege might really mean. As Linda Alcoff and others have suggested, the anticipation of predicted demographic changes, in which the non-Hispanic white population may become a minority in the United States before the end of the twenty-first century, may be exacerbating fears of what it could mean to have to relinquish white political dominance.[38] Chapter 2 will argue that these fears have been dangerously exacerbated by appeals to racial resentment and by racial scapegoating relied on by purveyors of xenophobic populism.[39]

But, more important, to explain a response is not to justify it. Whatever the sources of the fear and the broader lack of reflection that influence some people's reactions to the phrase "Black Lives Matter," the phrase remains a simple declaration of human dignity. It is a declaration that people of African descent are fully human and fully entitled to be treated as such. Moreover, there is no reason to fear the realization of generalized respect for everyone's moral value, as though it were a "zero-sum" project that must pit one group's defensible interests against the defensible interests of other groups. When grounded in morally defensible institutions, equal respect for moral value is never a zero-sum good.[40]

1.3 CONTENTIOUS POLITICS AND THE OBLIGATIONS OF CITIZENSHIP

The previous section explored the objects of "contention" that shape the activities of social movements and reflected on the ways in which the complex relations between those objects have shaped the work of several social movements. This section will show why we are justified in describing what social movements do as "politics," and that some of the most important collective politics of social movements focus on the concept of citizenship— the obligations of citizenship as well as its boundaries. Following James Jasper in *The Art of Moral Protest*, I will describe these social movements as "citizenship movements."[41] I will also argue that the classic phase of the Civil Rights Movement is a paradigm case of a citizenship movement, convincingly showing that collective action can constitute political action, illuminating the connection between nonviolence and political power, and helping to articulate the obligations of citizenship.

In a provocative challenge to the interpretation offered here, the political scientist Herbert Storing once argued that the Civil Rights Movement was, in fact, the *opposite* of a citizenship movement, and that it failed even to qualify as a form of political action. The argument appears in Storing's essay "The Case Against Civil Disobedience," completed shortly before the assassination of Martin Luther King, Jr. Storing asserted (if somewhat apologetically) that civil disobedience is "an unsuccessful attempt to combine, on the level of principle, revolution and conventional political action. The fundamental choice lies, as Malcolm X often said, between bullets and ballots. . . . Civil disobedience is the resort—always a theoretically and practically weak resort—of the subject of law, exercised because the subject cannot or will not take up the rights and duties of the citizen."[42] Storing's claim that the movement did not count as politics because it did not involve "the ballot" is easily refuted. Most social theorists plausibly agree that the collective activities that we now call "social movements" can be treated as political action simply because governments "of one sort or another" somehow "figure in" that action—often because the movements are seeking some action *on the part* of government in response to its concerns.[43] The Civil Rights Movement was clearly seeking at least some governmental remedies. One of the reasons we can talk about the successes of the movement—however limited—is that its efforts were instrumental in producing two substantial pieces of federal legislation: the Civil Rights Act of 1964 and the Voting Rights Act of 1965.

Of course, as the experience of the Farm Workers Movement shows, the processes through which social movements achieve political outcomes often look quite different from the processes defined by conventional political institutions. In fact, in addition to the strike and the national grape boycott, Cesar Chavez felt the need in 1968 to engage in a twenty-five-day period of fasting that attracted the attention of national leaders like King and Robert F. Kennedy (not long before they were assassinated, months apart).[44] Storing is thus right to argue that the movement's civil disobedience does not qualify as "conventional political action." But he is strangely silent about the fact that, before the Voting Rights Act, Jim Crow regulations in the South effectively denied African Americans genuine access to the ballot box, as well as to conventional political channels in general. Passage of the Voting Rights Act of 1965 was both a remarkable political victory and a necessary condition of any large-scale effort to pursue more conventional political action.

Refuting Storing's claim that the movement was not an exercise in citizenship requires a different tack. But, perhaps unexpectedly, the most compelling counterargument will not appeal to Rawls's account of civil disobedience. To be sure, Rawls convincingly argues that, in a "reasonably just" constitutional democracy, civil disobedience can be justified when it both satisfies certain reasonable constraints and can be shown to help promote justice and encourage political stability. But Rawls never purports to show that justifiable civil disobedience can be a *substantive expression of citizenship*. Equally important, as David Lyons has objected, Rawls never considered that establishing some instance of collective action as justified in a "reasonably just" society might be quite a different project from showing what kinds of collective action are justified in a context of serious and systematic injustice.[45] An effective challenge to Storing's claim that the real choice was between "bullets and ballots" cannot ignore the fact that civil rights protesters confronted deeply entrenched, systematic injustice that too often prevented them from *choosing* to exercise the power of the ballot. I must also address King's conviction that turning to "bullets" would undermine any hope of achieving reconciliation between the formerly oppressed and their former oppressors in a morally reconstituted community, as well as the possibility of furthering the moral redemption of at least some former oppressors.[46]

Candice Delmas's compelling discussion of resistance in *A Duty to Resist: When Disobedience Should Be Uncivil* also fails to provide a substantive account of the obligations of citizenship. Delmas convincingly argues that careful analysis of all major accounts of the source of political obligation reveals that resistance to injustice is our political obligation.[47]. Yet *political* obligation rests on a vertical relationship between the subject of law and the state as the source and enforcer of law. In contrast, the obligations of citizenship arise from our embeddedness in horizontal relations of membership in a particular political community. Among the citizenship obligations most important to contemporary liberal democracies are obligations to endure civic sacrifice, to promote civic trust, to support the spirit of compromise, and of course to show appropriate respect for the dignity of fellow citizens.[48]

To be sure, in any society, the obligations of citizenship also include a prima facie obligation to obey the law of the state. But one of the most important lessons of King's philosophy of nonviolence is that the prima facie obligation to obey the law can be overridden by other obligations, in particular by the obligation to resist injustice. This means that the obligations of citizenship must follow the path *of conscientious citizenship*, which for King demanded conformity to three interconnected principles:

1. Noncooperation with evil is as much a moral obligation as cooperation with good.
2. Injustice anywhere threatens justice everywhere.
3. Nonviolence (in response to injustice) is an imperative, conformity to which is necessary to achieve a beloved community.[49]

As King wrote in "The Birth of a New Nation," upon his return in 1957 from celebrating Ghanaian independence, "the aftermath of nonviolence" is a "beloved" community, by which he meant a community that allows and encourages redemption and reconciliation, rather than the perpetuation of hatred and bitterness.[50] Delmas offers a powerful challenge to the legacy of nonviolence left by Gandhi, King, Chavez, and Huerta that shapes many influential claims that justified disobedience is always "civil." But she offers no grounds for understanding whether "uncivil" disobedience could ever be a direct obligation of conscientious citizenship.

For King, the conscientious citizen should seek to meet the obligations of justice in a way that, whenever possible, respects the demands of ongoing membership in a political community. This means that conscientious citizens must leave cultural and political space for two processes: first, for the *redemption* of at least some perpetrators of injustice (along with some who passively allowed injustice to continue), and second, for the possibility that victims of injustice might achieve *reconciliation* with at least some who perpetrated and passively accepted injustice. It is far from clear whether and how *uncivil* disobedience can ever meet this standard, which is one important reason that King advocated the methods of nonviolence. I stress that, on my interpretation, King never defended an exceptionless pacifism. In particular, he seems to have accepted—however reluctantly—that the violence of war might sometimes be a morally regrettable, but necessary, last resort to combat injustice. This stance may help explain why he never openly condemned either the American Civil War or the Allied struggle against the Axis powers in World War II. Of course, King was a forceful critic of the Vietnam War, most comprehensively in his Riverside Church speech, "A Time to Break Silence" (1967). But his condemnation of the Vietnam War was based on his considered conviction that the American course in Vietnam was "dishonorable and unjust."[51]

In contrast to the accounts defended by Rawls and Delmas, Ronald Dworkin's treatment of civil disobedience offers an extremely compelling explanation of the connection between civil disobedience and the idea of citizenship.[52] Ironically, Dworkin's account was initially a response to certain kinds of protest against the war in Vietnam. In an essay provocatively titled "On Not Prosecuting Disobedience" (1968), Dworkin directly addresses the connection between "reasonable dissent" and the obligations of citizenship in a constitutional democracy. He begins by arguing that, particularly (though not only) in American constitutional democracy, dissenters can sometimes have reasonable doubts about the legal validity of an existing statute, where "reasonable doubt" is doubt shaped by serious questions about whether that statute conforms to that society's "conventional political morality." Dworkin then contends that when the validity of a law can be reasonably questioned, three main options are available to the thoughtful citizen. First, one can obey the problematic law and use the conventional political process to try to change the law. Second, one can follow one's own judgment, and perhaps disobey, until an "authoritative statement" of the law is handed down through judicial review. The third option is to follow one's own judgment and perhaps disobey, even if the "highest competent court" has handed down a "contrary decision," since we have historical evidence that even "the highest competent court" sometimes reverses itself when it realizes it has relied on a mistaken interpretation of the law of the land. Dworkin cites the Supreme Court's reversal of its decision in *Minersville School District v. Gobitis* (1940), in which Jehovah's Witnesses were required to salute the flag in school over their religious objections, through its decision in favor of the students' religious freedom in *West Virginia State Board of Education v. Barnett* (1943).

Dworkin contends that the third option (following one's own judgment, and perhaps disobeying since highest competent courts sometimes reverse themselves) is frequently the most defensible stance. This is because, on his view, the proper development of constitutional law frequently *depends* on reasonable disobedience and dissent by ordinary citizens. He urges that it is especially important to act in ways that acknowledge that dependence when we have good reasons to be concerned about the possibility of judicial mistakes—which may appear even in decisions of the highest competent court. Reasonable dissent and disobedience serve two important functions in such contexts. First, they communicate the existence, and sometimes the regrettable consequences for real people, of important cases of uncertainty in the law. In this regard, though Dworkin does not cite this example, it is instructive to consider the regrettable consequences of the Supreme Court ruling against racial equality in *Plessy v. Ferguson* (1895). According to Dworkin's theory, those who refused to be satisfied with the decision in *Plessy*, from those who formed the 1905 Niagara Movement to those who argued against school segregation in conjunction with *Brown v. Board of Education* (1954), were performing an important communicative function in a society that too often affected ignorance of the wrongs of racial injustice and too easily averted its glance from its effects.[53] But Dworkin identifies a second important role for reasonable dissent and disobedience in a constitutional democracy. Properly conducted, he contends, reasonable dissent and disobedience provide social and cultural arenas in which a society can test out different understandings—that is, different interpretations—of the law. Reasonable dissent and disobedience thereby function as "experiments" with the power to aid a society—especially its judges—in unfolding the real content of its fundamental laws. Such experiments have the greatest value, on this account, when they seek to test a doubtful law against the conventional political morality of the society that contains the law.

These two functions—communicating the existence of significant mistakes in current law and experimenting with interpretations that might improve the law—thus provide the basis for a compelling challenge to Storing's attack. Relying on Dworkin's quite plausible criteria, we can see how the Civil Rights Movement amounts to a paradigmatic exercise in conscientious citizenship.[54] First, it effectively communicated to fellow citizens and government officials alike just how problematic any lingering support for Jim Crow really was—on the terms of America's explicit political morality. It was equally effective in communicating just how far the legal machinery of Jim Crow had taken America from the requirements of the Reconstruction amendments that were nearly a century old at the time of the protests. Of course, some aspects of Rawls's account focus our attention on the communicative function of justified civil disobedience. But Dworkin offers a second, crucial criterion of conscientious dissent: the condition that it must count as a serious effort to test out new interpretations of the law. In my view, the contentious politics of the Civil Rights Movement was a remarkably powerful *national* experiment in legal interpretation that constructively aided in unfolding the real content of American law. Understood in these terms, it is hard to understand how any social movement has ever done more to show what it really means to "take on the rights and duties of citizenship." The path that King followed from the start of the Montgomery bus boycott in 1955 until his assassination in 1968, and the path that he believed we are *all* obligated to follow, was clearly the path of conscientious citizenship.

Of course, focusing on civil disobedience and dissent to the exclusion of electoral politics would likely have proven insufficient to pursue the socioeconomic goals, and concerns about the Vietnam War, that came to preoccupy King not long before his death. Yet the conscientious citizenship exercised in the classic phase of Civil Rights Movement has justifiably been an inspiration for social movements around the globe seeking to draw on the power of nonviolence to make space for justice.[55]

1.4 COMPLEXITY AND THE CAPACITY FOR COLLECTIVE MORAL INQUIRY

At various points in this chapter, I have noted how complex social movements are, even when they might be defined by their focus on a single group's interests, a single unaddressed need, or the dignity and moral value of the members of a single social group. I conclude this chapter with a brief discussion of five main forms of complexity in social movements with regard to (a) historical boundaries and temporality; (b) "membership" boundaries; (c) the boundaries of any movement's defining tactical methods and strategic goals; (d) the nature and degree of a movement's dependence on efforts and actions of people not actively engaged in the movement's contentious politics; and finally, (e) the role of moral visionaries and innovative leaders in the development and evolution of the movement.

Complexity with regard to historical boundaries and "temporality" is, perhaps not unexpectedly, a central feature of many social movements. An important topic of debate in the history of abolition, for instance, is when "the abolition movement" really began. The American wing of the movement is often treated as beginning in earnest during the early nineteenth century. But in a groundbreaking discussion, historian Manisha Sinha argues, in *The Slave's Cause: A History of Abolition* (2016), that the substantive origins of American abolitionism can be found in antislavery thought and action of the eighteenth century, including the writings of eighteenth-century Quakers and antislavery African writers living in Europe, but also in the abolitionism of African American freedom petitioners, whose efforts to petition for freedom are sometimes viewed as an effort to turn the Revolutionary War into a war against slavery.[56] As I suggested earlier, a similar historical complexity confronts historians of the Civil Rights Movement: Should we define the movement with reference to its "classic phase" and understand it as a discrete historical entity that lasted from 1955 to 1965? Or is it better understood as one phase of a historically extended freedom struggle that began in earnest with the Niagara Movement of 1905 to fight racial segregation and disenfranchisement?

The complexities associated with the boundaries of any movement's membership can prove just as vexing as those regarding its historical arc. One source of difficulty is that even when we can identify an organizational structure that claims authority to define a movement's methods and goals, there will not necessarily be a one-to-one correspondence between those who are part of that organizational structure (whether as leaders or as rank-and-file members) and those who actively participate in the political activities arranged and encouraged by that structure. Again and again, in the histories of labor movements, the women's movement, the Civil Rights Movement, and in recent experience of the Black Lives Matter Movement, we can find a divergence between active membership in the organizations that create and shape a movement and active participation in that movement's contentious politics. It might seem obvious, for instance, that the members of a Mennonite family who participated in a Black Lives Matter protest in Minneapolis did not do so as members of the Black Lives Matter Movement but as sympathetic third parties. But if that family showed up to protests day after day, would the boundary between member and sympathetic third party be quite so obvious?

The challenge of definitively identifying the membership of a social movement ultimately generates the third important complexity regarding social movements: the difficulty of definitively identifying the tactical methods and strategic goals of a social movement. This is primarily because of the widespread phenomenon of radical flank effects. Debates about—and within—the feminist movement, for instance, have always been rooted in this phenomenon. We need only remember lively disagreements about the value of the activism of British suffragists like Emmeline Pankhurst, whose Women's Social and Political Union (WSPU) encouraged its members to engage in various kinds of uncivil disobedience. More recently, we can recall heated debates about the merits of theoretical work by feminists like Catherine MacKinnon and Andrea Dworkin, who challenged the idea that regulations governing freedom of speech ought to protect the production and dissemination of pornography.

But the two forms of complexity that matter most for the purposes of this argument are the complex ways in which a social movement can depend on efforts and actions of those not actively engaged in its contentious politics, and the role that moral visionaries and innovative leaders sometimes play in the development and the potential success of a social movement. These two forms of complexity turn out to be critical to creating the conditions in which a social movement can enhance collective rationality, encourage moral enlightenment, and support genuinely constructive transformation. This is because the pursuit of constructive social change is a fundamentally *collective* project. A successful social movement unfolds over time as a complex amalgam of communities of concern and action characterized by a division of socially constructive labor.

The labor to be coordinated may well include the work of artists, historians, philosophers, social theorists, and religious thinkers—many of whom do not, and sometimes could not, actually participate in the political struggles of the movements they help to create and encourage. This is the labor that usually finds its way into what Michael Walzer might call the "social criticism" driving the movement. But as Walzer and King would both remind us, the work of social movements also comprises the physical labor, material sacrifice, and political struggle of various social groups. Thus ordinary women who have worked outside the home, often despite terrible obstacles meant to deter them, have helped to promote the women's movement's goal of gender equality. People who protested chattel slavery, and who endured coercion and violence from countermovements seeking to protect white supremacy, helped to further the cause of racial equality. Coal miners, factory workers, and agricultural workers seeking humane working conditions and reasonable compensation helped to shape the movement for fair labor practices. The uprising of patrons and neighbors of the Stonewall Inn in Greenwich Village in 1969 served as a pivotal moment in the movement for LGBTQ rights. The suffering, sacrifice, and struggles of these communities have clearly been as critical to constructive social change as the intellectual and imaginative labor of those who helped produce the social criticism that defined its goals.

But even as we acknowledge the collective nature of social movements, we must not ignore the roles that moral visionaries and innovative leaders often play in the constructive evolution of those movements. Historians will rightly caution that the "great man" or "great woman" approach to history is no more plausible in reflections on social movements than in reflections on the history of war or economic life. Yet, as I argue in discussing constructive imagination (in part 2) and political hope (in part 3), visionary leaders are sometimes indispensable to furthering the goals of a social movement. A visionary orator can show how to turn occasions of uncertainty, crisis, and fear into opportunities to imagine the possibility of new and better modes of social life. We have powerful confirmation of this fact in the oratory of leaders such as Martin Luther King, Jr., Abraham Lincoln, and Franklin Roosevelt. Still further, the example set by a morally courageous and stalwart leader can convince us to be hopeful about our political future even when we have endured great suffering and great sacrifice. In an echo of the epigraph that begins this chapter, Nelson Mandela's moving account of his *Long Walk to Freedom* (1994) shows us why participants in social movements often look to their leaders to help guide them on the path that the movement must make for itself.[57] Social movements are essentially collective projects, but inspirational leadership is nearly always an important component of those projects.

2

SOCIAL MOVEMENTS AND THE
TASK OF DEMOCRACY

The task of democracy is . . . creation of a freer and more humane
experience in which all share and to which all contribute.

—John Dewey

2.1 SOCIAL JUSTICE AND THE
DEMOCRATIC IDEAL

We have seen that the contentious politics of social movements
can provide invaluable lessons about the moral obligations of
citizenship—most notably, that dissent, protest, and even collective disobedience to law can be fully justifiable expressions of
conscientious citizenship. As Martin Luther King, Jr., understood
it, conscientious citizenship is a commitment to expose and
address injustice wherever it exists, but in a manner consistent
with membership in a community that leaves room for redemption and reconciliation. In this picture, those who participate in
social protest have an obligation to consider the connection
between methods for protesting injustice and the kind of community those methods can help to create.

Yet I have suggested (perhaps controversially) that even for King this element of the obligation was a requirement to treat nonviolence as the first, and principal, resort of social movements, and not as the only available option, even though King most likely believed that only the most extreme circumstances could ever license violence in pursuit of justice. Whatever the merits of this claim as a reading of his views, it raises the difficult broader question of whether citizenship movements in which violence and nonviolence have been deliberately intertwined can count as expressions of conscientious citizenship. But the struggle to end South African Apartheid helps to show why we ought to answer this question in the affirmative. Given the extreme brutality, arbitrary violence, and cruel intransigence of the South African government, the intertwining of violence and nonviolence seems to have been critical to ending Apartheid. Moreover, the awarding of the Nobel Peace Prize jointly to Nelson Mandela and F. W. de Klerk in 1993 seems to have been—at least in part—clear recognition that, even with the complexity of its methods, the struggle to end South African apartheid was an expression of conscientious citizenship. The wisdom of this award was confirmed by Mandela's consistent leadership in laying the groundwork for peaceful reconciliation on the path to a more democratic South Africa.

Whatever their methods, the readiness of the members of most contemporary social movements to endure sacrifice and struggle in pursuit of democracy reflects a broad global consensus that for all of its deficiencies in practice, democracy continues to constitute a desirable ideal.[1] This chapter will consider what social movements can teach us about democratic citizenship: that is, about the habits of mind, social norms, and political values that make democracy possible. This inquiry is a vital component of the effort to understand how social movements make space for justice, because the vast majority of progressive social movements presume that—at least ideally—democracies have the capacity to combine the vigorous protection of individual liberty with a commitment to substantive equality in a manner most conducive to promoting justice. A central claim of this book is that most social movements also involve a second presumption that is rarely made explicit: democracies are best able to vigorously defend liberty and promote substantive equality in a way that really promotes justice when their institutions, policies, and practices are *humane*—that is, when they combine robust respect and compassionate concern for those affected by the exercise of democratic authority and power. Chapter 3 will consider what the humane exercise of authority and power comes to, especially in light of the ever-increasing technological capacity for institutional cruelty and abuses of state monopolies on coercion and violence. The discussion in the current chapter will focus on important elements of democratic citizenship.

I focus on citizenship, rather than on political institutions, in the spirit of John Dewey's view that—especially in times of crisis—democracy can survive only if it is understood as "a personal way of individual life," not as something "institutional and external."[2] In the essay entitled "Creative Democracy: The Task Before Us" (1939), Dewey rejects the notion that democracy is just a "political mechanism" for the aggregation of preferences. A way of life is democratic, he contends, only if it expresses the belief that "the habit of amicable cooperation . . . is a priceless addition to human life." Democratic citizenship thus demands "faith in the possibility of conducting disputes, controversies and conflicts as cooperative undertakings in which both parties learn by giving the other a chance to express itself [*sic*], instead of having one party conquer by forceful suppression of the other—a suppression which is nonetheless . . . violence when it takes place by psychological means of ridicule, abuse, intimidation, instead of by overt imprisonment or in concentration camps."[3]

Faith in this "habit of amicable cooperation" is ultimately a commitment to the morality that makes a way of life democratic. This is because, for Dewey, democracy is a moral ideal of a "freer and more humane" mode of life "in which all share and to which all contribute." Dewey makes a compelling case for the view that the "task of democracy" is to try to create a way of a life governed by these values. This chapter will show that social movements have much to teach us about the first stages of this task: in particular, about how to shape norms of public communication and political deliberation most likely to produce a habit of amicable cooperation, and how to cultivate broader confidence that exercising political agency in pursuit of amicable cooperation can be a "priceless addition" to everyday life.

Many of the movements analyzed in this book involve efforts to reform societies purporting to be (already) democratic. Yet I also presume that movements for democratic reform can be strengthened by appreciating the lessons of revolutionary democratic movements, including those as varied in their methods and strategies as the Arab Spring and the Velvet Revolution in the former Czechoslovakia. All such movements teach us that there are two criteria a society must satisfy if a democracy movement is to achieve its central goals. First, a democracy movement can succeed only where there is a robust civil society, that is, where there are networks of voluntary associations, organizations, and groups that are not controlled by the state. Theorists of political behavior remind us that the associations and groups constituting civil society are potential centers of *power* that can sometimes serve as checks on authoritarian abuses of power but also potential sources of *internal pressure* to make the exercise of state power more democratic.[4] Second, democracy movements can succeed only if authoritarian rulers have not managed to fully corrupt or fully "co-opt" governmental institutions and processes. According to Gene Sharp, it is especially difficult to move "from dictatorship to democracy" when a society's police, bureaucrats, and military forces are at the beck and call of an authoritarian ruler.[5]

The social movements discussed in detail in this chapter have, in fact, operated in societies with relatively robust civil associations, and with government institutions mainly focused on public purposes and goals. This chapter will explore several processes through which, given these conditions, influential social movements have taken on the "task" of democracy. In section 2.2 I argue that social movements are often critical to shaping the political agency and encouraging the political participation of people who initially understand themselves as powerless. Section 2.3 shows that social movements play a critical role in helping to revise norms of public discussion to create space for communicating the interests, needs, and dignity-affirming claims of those who might otherwise be discounted or silenced. The role of social movements in determining the content and boundaries of "public reason" is explored in section 2.4, to show what is involved in shaping criteria for acceptable political deliberation about how to respond to interests, needs, and dignity-affirming claims. Finally, section 2.5 reflects on the means by which democratic social movements can sometimes counter the antidemocratic consequences of xenophobic populism and the politics of "out-group" resentment.

2.2 SHAPING POLITICAL AGENCY

In an influential paper entitled "The Strategy of Protest: Problems of Negro Civic Action" (1961), the political scientist James Q. Wilson attempted to understand the Civil Rights Movement up to that point. He framed the movement as an expression of "the problem of the powerless." He then argued that it was driven by people seeking entry to processes of political bargaining with no stable political resources to exchange, who ended up relying on "negative inducements" such as economic boycotts and negative publicity. Wilson was understandably pessimistic about the merits of civil rights protest, thus framed, as a long-term strategy.[6]

In an effort to refine this approach, Michael Lipsky argued, in "Protest as a Political Resource" (1968), that not every "inducement" adopted by the Civil Rights Movement should be understood as "negative." Indeed, he urged that some of the movement's inducements were not only positive but inherently valuable, particularly those aspects of the movement that were meant to appeal to the "better angels" of white liberals. Lipsky may have been thinking, for example, of the inspiring rhetoric of King's speech at the March on Washington in 1963. Yet Lipsky continued to doubt the long-term value of protest as a political resource. The problem, he claimed, was that protest leaders needed to satisfy too many constituencies with potentially irreconcilable concerns: the protesters themselves; members of the media who were needed to "maximize public exposure" of the protests; the people on whom the movement depended to express outrage at the conditions being protested; and the politicians and social elites with the power to create policies that might change those conditions. He concluded that, given these challenges, Saul Alinsky's analysis in *Reveille for Radicals* was on "the soundest ground" for characterizing protest as mainly a means of "building organization" rather than a "stable" resource that could be offered for exchange in a process of political bargaining.[7]

Yet building organization was certainly not what King understood to be "the true meaning of the struggle": a meaning he found in the emergence of a new self-understanding on the part of many African Americans. King argued, in his book *Stride Toward Freedom* (1958), that the "true meaning of the Montgomery Story"—and ultimately the true meaning of the movement's entire first phase—was revealed in the development of African Americans' consciousness of being "an equal element in a larger social compound" and in their "new determination to struggle and sacrifice" in pursuit of equal citizenship. That determination, King urged, was evidence that "there was a new Negro in the South, with a new sense of dignity and destiny" that enabled a new appreciation of the African American capacity for political agency and the possibility of genuine political efficacy. For King, the movement's protests were not just about building organization but about constructing new grounds for African Americans' self-esteem and self-respect as political agents. On this view, even when protest cannot be converted into a resource for political bargaining, it may still have value in light of its potential to produce important goods that are internal to participation in the movements which rely on it. What King described as the stirring of "dignity and destiny" in the African American community is just such an internal good.

Two decades later, in his influential essay on "The Power of the Powerless" (1978), Vaclav Havel offered a similar picture of the internal goods that can emerge through participation in social movements. The essay described the awakening of "suppressed identity and dignity" associated with resisting the oppressive "post-totalitarian" regime that ruled the Soviet bloc. Havel's essay was originally meant for publication in a volume that would contain several essays on freedom and power authored by activists from Poland and Czechoslovakia. When Havel was arrested in 1979, the decision was made to publish his essay separately, and its resulting impact on the self-understandings of participants in Eastern European democracy movements was profound.[8] Solidarity activist Zbygniew Bujak, who was later elected to serve in Poland's Parliament, explains the nature and scope of the essay's influence:

> This essay reached us in the Ursus factory in 1979 at a point when we felt we were at the end of the road. . . . Why were we doing this? Why were we taking such risks? Not seeing any immediate and tangible results, we began to doubt the purposefulness of what we were doing. . . . Then came the essay by Havel. Reading it gave us the theoretical underpinnings for our activity. It maintained our spirits; we did not give up, and a year later—in August 1980—it became clear that the party apparatus and the factory management were afraid of us. We mattered. . . . When I look at the victories of Solidarity, and of Charter 77, I see in them an astonishing fulfillment of the prophecies and knowledge contained in Havel's essay.[9]

Given the extraordinary things that can happen when formerly "powerless" people become able to acknowledge and assert their agency in the realm of politics, it is worth considering how they can do so, despite being subject to authoritarian oppression or to constraining discrimination on the basis of such characteristics as race, gender, or sexual orientation.

The path to dignity and destiny for participants in the Civil Rights Movement is especially well documented. These accounts reveal that, for the most part, acknowledging and strengthening political agency depended on the existence of a robust civil sphere. Nongovernmental associations and coalitions—both secular and religious—served as sites for reflection and deliberation about movement goals, for debates about the methods and tactics for achieving the goals, and for developing the organizations that would plan political action and train participants in the movement's preferred methods.[10] One of the most important of these organizations was the Highlander Folk School (later known as the Highlander Research and Education Center), cofounded by a former student of Reinhold Niebuhr named Myles Horton.[11] Just four months after taking one of Highlander's workshops on civil rights activism, Rosa Parks sparked the Montgomery Bus Boycott by refusing to relinquish her seat on the bus.[12] But the shaping of the movement's activist leaders did not always occur in the United States. The Reverend James Lawson developed deep insight into the principles of Gandhian satyagraha at Hislop College in Nagpur, India, where he served four years as a campus minister and teacher. Lawson eventually led some of the most effective workshops for prospective protesters hoping to learn how to meet hate-fueled violence with the demanding discipline of nonviolent protest.[13]

Yet developing political agency in the context of oppression and discrimination is not just about learning to do things differently. As social movements teach us, it also requires coming to see oneself and one's circumstances in a new light. Havel argued that for a citizen of an Eastern European country oppressed by the power of the Soviet bloc, developing a true estimate of oneself as a political agent was a matter of rejecting false narratives about the nature and aims of the regime as well as about the regime's claims to have genuine concern for those who were subject to it. This observation echoes the claim, defended by many philosophers and literary scholars, that agency and narrative are intertwined. In *After Virtue*, for instance, Alasdair MacIntyre helpfully observes that "I can only answer the question '*what am I to do?*' if I can answer the prior question, of what story or stories do I find myself a part?"[14] But, as Havel understood, if I am to reclaim an identity and dignity that have been actively suppressed—whether by an authoritarian regime or by the weight of internal discrimination and exclusion—I must also be ready and willing to ask whether the stories of which I find myself a part are true.

The task of questioning the narratives in which one is embedded is never easy. But it is especially complex when one is the member of a group targeted by systematic internal discrimination. The complexity of this task has two main sources. The first stems from the fact that narratives of inferiority and superiority are always intertwined. Of course, we can usually provide an independent account of some social narrative that stigmatizes, demeans, or degrades some group, and that usually also purports to explain and justify social consequences of that narrative by reference to supposedly "natural" or "essential" characteristics or deficiencies. Furthermore, we can independently articulate the related narrative that marks out privileged social statuses and roles for those who are not targets of discrimination. But there is always an important sense in which these vastly different kinds of narratives are conceptually and culturally interdependent. As King famously observed in "Letter from a Birmingham Jail," segregation and discrimination do not merely tend to produce a false sense of inferiority for many who are targets of discrimination, they also tend to produce a false sense of superiority in those who are not. This means that questioning the narrative suppression of identity and dignity in a society that systematically discriminates against some group(s) requires questioning the truth of two quite different, though intertwining, false narratives.

But, as King also recognized, anyone trying to question these narratives will confront a second challenge: considered together, the narratives express and then produce a false asymmetry between those whom the narratives purport to represent. King captures the essence of this asymmetry by appealing to the thought of Martin Buber, rightly insisting that segregation and discrimination serve to substitute an "I- it" relationship for an "I-thou" relationship that relegates the targets of segregation and discrimination to the status of things. The precise manner in which this asymmetry is expressed will depend on the different ways in which targeted groups can be narratively misrepresented. To take just the most familiar cases, narrative asymmetry is embodied in the sexual objectification of women, the pathologizing of gays and lesbians, and the dehumanization of African Americans. But in all of these examples, narrative asymmetry always works to relegate some persons to the status of things.

So how is it possible to replace objectifying narratives with narratives that help a targeted group reclaim their identity and dignity (as in Havel's account) and develop a sense of "destiny" as political agency (as in King's account)? It is important that social movements working to constructively assert their dignity and destiny do not always take the same path. The African American project of narratively asserting dignity and destiny might be thought to begin with emergence of the North American slave narratives (some of which were published in England beginning in the eighteenth century). Indeed, historian Manisha Sinha argues that slave narratives became "the movement literature of abolition" in the nineteenth century.[15] But the African American path toward dignity and destiny took many complex turns over the course of the nineteenth and twentieth centuries and in some respects is still unfolding. In a second example, the "consciousness-raising" sessions from which a great deal of second-wave feminism emerged were critical to the narrative self-assertion of the women's movement. As Nancy Hirschmann writes, these sessions typically sought to replace "the articulation of experience through patriarchal language" with a new, "specifically feminist vocabulary."[16] In a third important instance, in the earliest days of what was initially called the Gay Liberation Movement, the founding of organizations like the Mattachine Society (1950) and the Daughters of Bilitis (1955) served to provide conceptual, as well as physical, space for constructing narratives that actively rejected the homophobic and pathologizing attitudes and assumptions of the dominant culture. The efforts of these organizations provide especially compelling evidence of the connection between collectively constructing new narratives and collectively cultivating political agency. In one of the most striking examples, in 1965 (four years before Stonewall) the Mattachine Society's cofounders led public protests against the Cold War persecution of gays and lesbians who had been purged from government jobs due to their sexual orientation.[17] One of the protest leaders was Frank Kameny, who, after being fired from his position as a government astronomer, went on to become one of the most influential leaders of the national movement for gay and lesbian equality.

2.3 RESHAPING NORMS OF PUBLIC DISCUSSION

But the path to more inclusive democracies cannot be marked out solely by changes in the self-understandings of those seeking social inclusion and greater efficacy in the political process. Groups who have been subject to discrimination and exclusion need to move, first, from the transformation of narratives to the formation of politically efficacious communities of concern and action. But they must also find ways to produce broader public acknowledgment of the moral weight and political importance of their interests, needs, and dignity-affirming claims—most obviously through public discussion and debate. Hence norms of political discussion that limit or deny this opportunity altogether are obstacles to genuine democratic reform. Iris Young vigorously—and compellingly—defended this claim in her work on what she called "inclusive political communication." Regrettably, as she argued in *Inclusion and Democracy* (2002), in both the theory and the practice of contemporary democracy, norms governing political communication are simply too narrow to allow for truly inclusive democratic discussion and debate.[18]

The political philosophy of deliberative democracy—in various versions defended by thinkers such as John Rawls, Jurgen Habermas, and Amy Gutmann and Dennis Thompson—is the primary target of Young's criticisms of democratic theory. Most influential accounts of deliberative democracy, Young objects, wrongly "restrict their conception of proper political communication to arguments, the making of assertions and proposals and providing reasons for them they claim ought to be acceptable to others."[19] Young never denies that reasoned argument is a critical element of the kind of public discussion most likely to produce wise deliberation and good decisions. Her point is, rather, that discursive argument is just *one* critical element of democratic political communication, and that an inclusive democracy should make room for forms of communication that do not privilege discursive argument and "dispassionate" reason-giving. Young helpfully identifies three forms of communication that, in her view, are wrongly excluded by the deliberative democracy view: (a) "public acknowledgment," (b) rhetoric, and (c) narrative. Reflection on the work of social movements can help us understand why these forms of communication matter to the task of democracy, as well as why norms of democratic communication ought to be expanded to include them.

It is useful to begin by considering the political value of what Young calls public acknowledgment. Perhaps surprisingly, social movements often resist Young's basic assumption that what is mostly at issue here are discrete instances or moments in which participants in democratic discussion should take the opportunity to "recognize" others with rituals of respectful and welcoming "greeting." To be sure, respectful ritual greetings have social value. As Young suggests, drawing on Emmanuel Levinas, the right kind of greeting affirms that one is "open" to the other in a way that is not mediated by any "content" referring to the world *outside* of the speaker.[20] Moreover, anyone who has ever been ignored in a meeting, or passed over in a classroom discussion, can understand how deflating and even demoralizing it can be to realize that the relevant audience is not open to one's presence in this rich and respectful way. The effects of not being acknowledged can be especially unsettling if there is reason to believe that one has been ignored on the basis of class, age, race, gender, or some other potentially invidious basis.

But deeper reflection on what social movements can teach us shows two other kinds of public acknowledgment are far more significant in political contexts. First, there is a special kind of acknowledgment displayed when an audience shows itself willing to listen to, and seriously consider the implications of, political proposals that come from groups who are underrepresented in conventional political forums, even if the proposals initially sound outlandish. Consider proposals to "defund the police," or to provide reparations for slavery and racial discrimination, or to require school curricula to teach a fuller account of the history of chattel slavery in America. Even if a community ends up rejecting such proposals or considering only the most minimal steps toward the goals they propose, seriously contemplating and discussing the possibilities inherent in the fully formed proposals is a way of expressing respect for those who put them forward. It is also a way of acknowledging, as Mill might say, that no one is infallible, which also expresses respect for those with whom one disagrees.[21] But, perhaps most important, taking a seemingly outlandish proposal seriously can be understood as respectfully accepting an "invitation" to produce the best possible version of the opposing position. Public discussion and political deliberation ought to challenge us in ways that encourage deep reflection on our values and purposes. Summarily dismissing ideas and proposals that are seriously entertained by others—even if we find them outlandish—is often a sign of smugness and self-righteousness and seems incompatible with defensible norms of political communication in a democracy. Consider, for instance, what it means when a U.S. senator pronounces that American elementary schools don't need to change the way they teach students about chattel slavery, because slavery was really "just a necessary evil."[22]

Social movements have sometimes been invaluable vehicles for public articulation of the kinds of provocative proposals discussed here. That they are provocative of course does not mean that they are right. But when a provocative proposal is dismissed just because it urges established democracies to contemplate radical reform, and not because there might be reasonable considerations to resist that reform, the politically powerful classes display a failure to appreciate the importance of public acknowledgment. In helping to put such proposals on the political agenda for serious discussion, social movements constructively challenge the generally indefensible narrowness of norms of political discussion.

We can understand the second critical failure of appropriate democratic public acknowledgment only by reflecting on persistently dismissive *patterns* of response to repeated instances of serious discrimination, oppression, and harm. One such pattern emerges in the history of democratic discussion of sexual assault. Even after decades of feminist jurisprudence and massive protests by activist elements of the women's movement, it is still possible to encounter painfully dismissive failures of the legal system to publicly acknowledge the seriousness of sexual assault. Consistently failing to treat sexual assault as a serious harm, or assuming that only some *kinds* of sexual assault are serious enough to merit punishment, is a serious and democratically deficient failure of public acknowledgment.

Another problematic pattern of dismissively responding to discriminatory harm is revealed by the frequency with which police unions, prosecutors, and juries effectively excuse citizen vigilantism and police misuse of force when the victims happen to be African American. There are certainly some occasions on which the police abuse of force is publicly acknowledged as too egregious to defend. Many have described the police killing of George Floyd in just these terms. But all too often public acknowledgment of an indefensible wrong is quickly followed by public insistence that the wrong in question is just an "exception": an instance of "outlier" or "rogue" bad behavior that reveals nothing significant about the institutions, policies, and practices that frame the case in question. It is in such moments that constraining (and ultimately cruel) norms of democratic communication do the greatest harm: effectively denying respect and concern to those African Americans who simply seek to have their interests, needs, and dignity-affirming claims taken seriously. If serious public discussion of systematic discrimination is "off the table," this marks a fundamental failure to support norms of inclusive public discussion. Social movements have come to play an increasingly important role in forcing democracies to confront the cruelty and disrespect inherent in such narrow norms. The extensive social protests that emerged in response to George Floyd's death are a critical reminder that social movements can be influential in challenging cruelly narrow norms of democratic political communication.

In Young's account, narrative is a second important form of political communication that is too often excluded in the theory and practice of contemporary democracy. The importance of transformative narrative in articulating a group's suppressed dignity and destiny has been discussed earlier and will be developed further in chapter 6. Here, I consider how a social movement's use of narrative can serve as a significant challenge to narrow norms of political communication. One of the most important recent developments in this regard is the emergence of what is sometimes called "digital activism," and perhaps most notably "hashtag activism."

As sociologist Guobin Yang expresses it, hashtag activism is what unfolds "when large numbers of postings appear on social media under a common hash-tagged word, phrase or sentence with a social or political claim"—such as #BlackLivesMatter, #Me Too, and #ArabSpring.[23] There might seem to be a special kind of naïveté in the idea that posting a comment containing a hashtag could have the power to produce political change in the real world. In particular, critics will object that hashtag activists too easily assume that postings on social media might be appropriate substitutes for painstaking political struggle. But these criticisms mostly miss the mark because hashtag activism is often most important for its capacity to reshape the realm of political communication itself. Many postings are deliberate attempts to introduce a particular personal narrative into to the swirl of discussion in the public square and to thereby connect that narrative to similar narratives of others. Such efforts typically have two main goals: first, to create political solidarity with those who have a similar narrative to share, and second, to try to enhance the political efficacy of those who have struggled with similarly unacknowledged experiences.

Digitally sharing a narrative can thus constitute an immediate, and especially effective, affirmation of individual political agency as well as a contribution to the formation of collective political agency.[24] For instance, when a woman posts a story of sexual harassment or sexual assault marked with the phrase

"#MeToo," she is declaring her participation in a social movement potentially as powerful as many movements that in the
past have relied on communication of their efforts through
newspaper reports, radio announcements, or televised images.
Catherine MacKinnon has recently characterized the #MeToo
Movement as "the world's first mass movement against sexual
abuse," which "took off from the law of sexual harassment,
quickly overtook it, and is shifting cultures everywhere."[25] In
MacKinnon's account this movement is "butterfly politics in
action"—by which she meant what happens when a small and
simple action ends up producing a large, complex political outcome.[26] Whether or not we accept MacKinnon's characterization, it seems clear that the #MeToo Movement has confirmed
the value of Young's account. When social critics claiming to
defend democracy from "decline" question the importance
attached to making personal narratives part of public discussion, or when they dismiss those narratives as "interesting anecdotes" without the rationally compelling force of genuine data,
they risk silencing some of the most important forms of political communication with which a democracy can be asked to
contend.

Yet we must still be cautious about proclaiming the virtues of
digitally mediated social movements that depend on the internet, especially when they seek to produce dramatic social and
political transformations in an entire society. Some digitally
mediated campaigns have indeed provided powerful reasons to
be hopeful about what such movements can accomplish. Manuel Castells provides convincing evidence of their power, in discussing the social movements and political upheavals of the Arab
Spring that began with Tunisia's "revolution for liberty and dignity." In his view, the combination of communication via digital
social networks and the large public gatherings that they could

regularly facilitate created a "hybrid public space" of autonomous communication that was (initially) largely beyond the control of those in power.[27] Moreover, according to the Freedom House 2020 study of "global freedom statuses," Tunisia's democratic transition—which began with the ouster in 2011 of a long-time autocrat—continues, despite persistent economic and social challenges.[28] But scholars such as Safwan Masri have argued that because of its distinctive and relatively "liberal" and open culture, of all the twenty-two Arab League countries, Tunisia was uniquely positioned for a transition to democracy.[29] Still further, as Zeynep Tufecki argues in *Twitter and Teargas: The Power and Fragility of Networked Protest*, while the internet may facilitate the growth of social movements in autocratic societies, it may also enable the movements' participants to bypass too much of the preliminary work that allows social movements to succeed in the longer term. Participants may not fully understand the oppositional challenges they must overcome if they are to succeed, and they are unlikely to have built what Tufecki describes as the "formal or informal organizational and other collective capacities" that could prepare them to overcome those challenges.[30] It may even be that having a narrative of how that capacity-building has unfolded makes an important contribution to democratic communication, as an affirmation of the capacity of movement narratives to shape collective political agency for the longer term. This is surely why Martin Luther King believed it so critical to quickly record the "The Montgomery Story" in works such as *Stride Toward Freedom* and to make sure that this story was widely disseminated in African American churches and communities.[31]

As the third important form of democratic communication, Iris Young defends "affirmative uses" of political rhetoric. Since Plato, Young notes, Western philosophical thought has wrongly focused on the uses of rhetoric to distort facts and to thereby manipulate political agents in ways that undermine their capacity for careful deliberation and decision. Though Young does not explicitly suggest how one might respond to this tradition, the fact that a method of communication can be misused should not obscure the political value of its *proper* uses. If potential for misuse were the standard for excluding a mode of communication from public discussion, we would have to ban all human speech and writing. More important, as Young contends, rhetoric is often the most effective means of getting an important issue on the agenda for political discussion and deliberation, and for moving people to act on the outcome of a politically important decision.[32]

Part 3 of this book will more fully develop the case for the political value of rhetoric. At this juncture, it is simply worth emphasizing two of the most politically constructive features of appropriate political rhetoric: First, at dire moments in the history of many democracies, socially constructive rhetoric has shown us how to calm even the most powerful and potentially disabling fear. Second, the right kind of rhetoric has proven at other times to be a source of inspiration and political hope in contexts where ordinary discursive argument falls flat and proves ineffective. When it succeeds in this aim, we may discover opportunities for social and political renewal even in extreme crises. We can find seminal examples of this kind of rhetoric in Lincoln's Gettysburg Address, Franklin Delano Roosevelt's first inaugural speech, and King's "I Have a Dream" declaration from the March on Washington. In fact, these orators offer numerous examples to help make the case in favor of norms of political communication that allow us to celebrate the affirmative uses of political rhetoric.

2.4 EXPANDING THE BOUNDARIES
OF PUBLIC REASON

Even if is reasonable for a society to move toward less confining norms governing everyday political discussion, might it still be important to limit the kinds of considerations that count as appropriate grounds for legislation regarding basic rights and duties, or for reshaping fundamental political institutions? Influential theorists of deliberative democracy have argued for such limits. Rawls did not initially align his views with the work of theorists expressly adopting the label "deliberative democracy," but over time he came to see the important connections between deliberative democracy and his conception of political liberalism.[33] His account of the requirements of public reason is an especially helpful presentation of the kinds of constraints on democratic deliberation that Young thinks we ought to reject. As Rawls argues in the expanded edition of *Political Liberalism*, when public reason-giving is meant to shape deliberation about "constitutional essentials" and questions of basic justice (that is, about basic rights and duties), it should appeal only to public "political values" and not to considerations dependent on "private" commitments such as religious beliefs or comprehensive moral conceptions.[34]

It is important to understand the presuppositions of Rawls's stance. To begin with, what Rawls means by "reason" in this context is "a way of putting one's ends in an order of priority and making decisions accordingly." The decisions that result from this ordering of priorities will identify *reasons to act*. Second, echoing Kant's account in "What Is Enlightenment?," Rawls contends that there is a fundamental distinction between public and private reasons, which he explains by reference to three linked criteria: *the source, the focus,* and *the content* of the reason. A reason is public for Rawls when its source is the "reason of the public" (that is, the reason of "citizens as such"), its focus is the good of the public constrained by considerations of fundamental justice, and its content is determined by society's (political) conception of justice. The exercise of coercive power is democratically legitimate, Rawls insists, only when it can be shown to rest on reasons that are public in all three senses. Appreciating the connection between Rawls's conception of public reason and his account of political legitimacy is thus critical: public reason is ultimately "the reason of equal citizens who, as a collective body, exercise final and coercive power over one another in enacting laws and in amending their constitution."[35]

As his view evolved, Rawls came to allow that there could be cases in which what would normally count as private reasons (say religious convictions, or deliverances of one's moral conscience) could be legitimate contributions to democratic debate about basic rights and duties and "constitutional essentials." But they could be legitimate only "provided that in due course public reasons . . . are presented sufficient to support" any conclusions that the considerations from religion or moral conscience were introduced to support.[36] Rawls was fully aware of historical examples, perhaps especially in the abolitionist movement and the Civil Rights Movement, when claims about basic rights and constitutional essentials that were initially justified by appeals to religious and moral convictions served as catalysts for political reforms to address serious injustice. The "in due course" provision is therefore Rawls's way of making public reason more inclusive.

But is his inclusive conception of public reason really inclusive enough? Several of Rawls's characterizations of public reason should give us pause. In particular, they raise questions about whether a convincing case for abolition, or for the end of Jim Crow segregation, could ever have been made from "inside" the public reason of the day. If political deliberation is to appeal (only) to the "reason of equal citizens" who exercise political power "as a collective body," will there be conceptual space for attributing legitimacy to the claims of those who are *excluded* from the exercise of conventional political power and who are simply not accepted as equal citizens? Rawls believed that nineteenth-century struggles to end slavery and twentieth-century struggles to end Jim Crow segregation needed to achieve public consensus on a *reinterpretation* of the "constitutional essentials"—which, no doubt, included the question of who counted as citizen in the first place. On that, he was clearly right. But what it ultimately took to achieve the appropriate reinterpretation in each of these struggles was a fundamental extension of the boundaries of public reason and a profound transformation of the content of public reason. This is because it was necessary to make room for *new kinds and new sources* of legitimate public claims. This demanded, first, a fundamental redefinition of "citizen." Moreover, we should think of this redefinition as requiring two stages: (a) a stage involving recognition, through the Reconstruction amendments, of every former slave as a full legal person, not three-fifths of a person, and (b) a stage involving more gradual rejection of the post-Reconstruction recrudescence of white supremacy with the Civil Rights Act of 1964 and the Voting Rights Act of 1965. But second, extending the bounds of public reason also demanded conceptual and cultural reconstitution of the "collective body" of equal citizens. In the American idiom, this required reframing the very idea of "we the people." Some readers will insist (with good reason) that neither the American redefinition of "citizen" nor the reconstitution of the American "collective body" has been complete, or at least they will insist that it has not been sufficient to produce robust liberty and genuine substantive equality for African Americans. But such objections notwithstanding, the path traveled from chattel slave to not-yet-fully equal citizen has been marked out by a remarkably forceful liberatory movement, which fundamentally challenged the bounds, as well as the content, of public reason.

Reflecting on the broader, historically extended African American struggle of which the Civil Rights Movement is a part, it seems clear that its phases proved effective (when they were) only because, in addition to discursive argument and dispassionate reason-giving, they turned to the power of narrative and the affirmative uses of rhetoric to deepen understanding of the injustices being challenged. In the nineteenth century, slave narratives were supplemented by fictional narratives, most notably Harriet Beecher Stowe's *Uncle Tom's Cabin*. The rhetoric and activism of white abolitionists were enriched by the rhetoric of activism of former slaves such as Frederick Douglass and Harriet Tubman. Moreover, when abolitionists like Douglass insisted that former slaves ought to join the Union forces in the Civil War, he appealed to the idea that the readiness to sacrifice for the union would be perceived as powerful evidence (for those inclined to look) of their worthiness to be recognized as equal citizens. Each of these efforts—powerful narratives, affirmative rhetoric, and moral example—drew on deliberative resources that did not resemble "ordinary" discursive reason-giving and argument. But if Iris Young is right, an inclusive democracy will stand ready to expand the norms of political discussion and deliberation to make room for such efforts.

Of course, as Young acknowledges, whenever a society displays its openness to enlarged norms of political discussion and deliberation, there is always the chance that it will seem to be licensing modes of communication that could result in attempts at large-scale manipulation and deceit.[37] This tendency will be exacerbated by the proliferation of essentially unregulated forums for political communication—such as many of the forums created by the emergence of the internet and the growth of social media. The combined effect could be quite dangerous for any democracy since it could lead to the deterioration, and even the destruction, of a robust public forum for *constructive* discussion and debate. Hence, for all that is democratically quite valuable about the development of social media, we must still find ways to encourage the responsible exercise of free speech. Here, the criteria of responsible exercise include concern for the truth, for civility in the manner in which we seek to communicate the truth, and mutual respect for the right of others to disagree. Otherwise, new modes of communication combined with less restrictive norms on communication will contribute to the "deconsolidation" of established democracies and to instability in emerging democracies seeking to resist return to authoritarian rule.

One of the great ironies of contemporary life is that even as the idea of democratic government continues to appeal to citizens across the globe, the internal health of many democracies seems to be in peril.[38] The most familiar signs of democratic decline are typically characterized as evidence of deconsolidation. As described by political theorists Robert Foa and Yascha Mounk, the deconsolidation of established democracies has involved three main processes. First, there has been a decline in citizen trust in democratic institutions, political parties, and political elites, as well as a decrease in citizen engagement in political life. Second, disaffection with contemporary democracies has often been linked with (and sometimes strengthened by) distress at economic stagnation and declines in living standards seemingly due to globalization and the increasing automation of work. Third, democratic deconsolidation has been accelerated by the forces of xenophobic, antidemocratic populism seeking to exploit citizen mistrust and economic uncertainty. Those forces further endanger democracy with the charge that political elites have manipulated democratic institutions to further global projects that impoverish "ordinary" people and to promote the interests of allegedly "undeserving others," a category typically claimed to consist of immigrants and domestic minorities. Ironically, these allegations about undeserving others are sometimes strengthened by complaints from liberalism's self-described sympathetic critics. The political scientist Mark Lilla, for example, charges that by supporting the "identity politics" that seem to have emerged out of many social movements, liberalism has "slipped into a kind of moral panic about racial, gender and sexual identity" that has "prevented it from becoming a unifying force capable of governing."[39] Such criticism implies that the growth and success of social movements claiming to seek reform of democracy have ultimately contributed to the breakdown of democracy.

2.5 THE PRECARIOUS FUTURE OF DEMOCRATIC CITIZENSHIP

In his provocative and prescient book *Achieving Our Country* (1998), Richard Rorty challenged his readers to consider what it might mean if the democratic breakdown posited by such criticisms were actually to occur. Although some aspects of Rorty's discussion focus principally on possible developments in American democratic life, developments that many believe actually came to pass with the presidential election in 2016, some of the book's most important observations resonate in many national contexts. One of Rorty's most prescient observations was that, at some point in the contemporary world, a certain portion of the electorate would decide that democracy had failed them and that they would then look around "for a strongman to vote for— someone willing to assure them that, once he is elected, the smug bureaucrats, tricky lawyers, overpaid bond salesmen and postmodernist professors will no longer be calling the shots. . . . Once such a strongman takes office, nobody can predict what will happen."[40]Interestingly, Rorty's reluctance to venture predictions did not prevent him from offering one especially troubling conjecture: the thought that the social, economic, and political gains made by many domestic minorities and women would mostly be "wiped out" as the resentments that some in the electorate have felt "about having their manners dictated to them by college graduates" finds an outlet. What Rorty seems to posit is a process by which, at the start, one or more socially regressive movements begin as a backlash against social changes that are seen either as involving gains made by formerly oppressed at "the expense" of social groups fighting to remain socially and politically dominant or as challenging social and cultural values that they have taken to be central to their collective identity. Aided by the construction of xenophobic narratives serving to pit those who think they have lost out in a zero-sum game against the perceived winners—socially progressive movements—what begins as isolated incidents of regressive backlash can become a politically powerful expression of xenophobic populism.

Unlike other critics of what some describe as the "moral panic" emerging out of socially progressive movements, Rorty never concludes that taking the social dangers of resentment seriously ought to lead anyone to deny, or give up on, the democratic value of protest.[41] Rorty was especially adamant that universities should not stop being open to challenging institutional cruelty, arbitrary use of state power, and various other forms of serious injustice. Yet he does not directly address the question of what kinds of protest might yield robust responses to injustice without undermining the democratic ideal that Dewey defended: that freer and more humane way of life "in which all share and to which all contribute." But Rorty does offer two suggestions of special interest in this context. First, he argues for the importance of protest that can be compatible with the patriotism and national pride that he thought many "ordinary" citizens value—but he offers a conception of patriotism that has less to do with American exceptionalism than with the nation's capacity to "take control of its destiny and make itself a better place."[42] It must be stressed that he offered this as a conception of national pride that even a vehement critic of American racism like James Baldwin could accept. Indeed, the title of Rorty's book— *Achieving Our Country*—is adapted from the final paragraph of Baldwin's book, *The Fire Next Time*. In the conclusion to *The Fire Next Time*, Baldwin urges that "we the black and the white, deeply need each other here if we are really to become a nation."[43]

Rorty's second important suggestion about constructive social protest in fact draws directly on Baldwin's view. He urges that defining a shared national identity must be viewed as a critical democratic project and should be a rooted in an understanding of the political value of hope. Rorty does not conceive of this project as a matter of producing a narrative that is true: "Stories about what a nation has been and should try to be are not attempts at accurate representation. . . . The argument . . . about which episodes in our history we should pride ourselves on will never be a contest between a true and false account of our country's history and its identity. It is better described as an argument about which hopes to allow and which to forego."[44] This reference to the political hope was another echo of some of the core commitments of Baldwin's view. Baldwin, of course, was no Pollyanna: in an interview with German writer Fritz Raddatz in 1978, he remarked that as an "American Negro writer . . . *I live* a hope despite my knowing better."[45] But despite "knowing better," Baldwin remained committed to the importance of political hope.

One characteristic of Baldwin's thought that was especially compelling to Rorty—and that has special relevance to democratic social movements—was Baldwin's capacity to combine stern indignation at the moral failures of American racism with unrelenting hope for America's moral renewal. This feature of Baldwin's thought reflects a commitment to what many commentators label "the Black Jeremiad," a form of political discourse that has deep roots in African American social thought and shaped so much of the African American emancipatory project from its origins. It may seem that there is something paradoxical—perhaps even irrational—in the idea that one can genuinely combine anger and hope in the pursuit of social justice. But, as Baldwin and Rorty both understood, when social protest loses the capacity to live with this tension between moral indignation and political hope, it may well lose its ability to communicate the importance of its projects to those who do not already share its commitments. We know that social movements driven by despair can sometimes produce dramatic political transformations. Some of the forces that have driven twenty-first-century xenophobic populism seek to produce anxiety and fear—especially fear of various demonized "others"—through images of a future of degradation and despair. But as King understood, revolutions born of despair "cannot long be sustained by despair."[46] Indeed, revolutions born purely of despair are often the first to deteriorate into mass destruction and chaos.

But what should democratic social movements look like once we understand the destructive powers of resentment, so vividly depicted in Rorty's account? Here both the successes and the shortcomings of contemporary social movements have much to teach us. First of all, there is a critical difference between the politically constructive expression of righteous indignation and the politically destructive self-righteousness that some people try to substitute in its place. For instance, when the quest for social justice becomes a vehicle for the relentless policing of micro aggressions, for chastising people who have allegedly failed to "check their privilege," or for suggesting that one is permanently tainted by benefiting from a system shaped by discrimination and oppression, there is little room left for the possibility of moral repair and even moral reconciliation. Hannah Arendt argued for the political relevance of a notion of forgiveness as a means of "releasing" people from the "predicament of irreversibility." Some kinds of self-righteous politics simply leave insufficient room for this kind of forgiveness. To be sure, not everything is forgivable, and (leaving religious convictions aside) there may be no morally preordained schedule on which what is forgivable must in fact be forgiven. But the politics of self-righteousness tends to characterize every kind of injustice as the source of a politically irreversible predicament.

What the politics of self-righteousness is also likely to do is, first, to blind its proponents to the undeserved suffering of some people who, though they have not experienced the kinds of injustice they protest, have endured a kind of hardship that is often difficult to distinguish from injustice. One of the virtues of Judith Shklar's argument in *The Faces of Injustice* (1991) is that she challenges our confidence that once we can call something "misfortune" rather than "injustice," we have thereby been absolved of any responsibility to try to do something about it. But second, the politics of self-righteousness can also make it difficult to consider the possibility of political cooperation between (conventional) victims of serious injustice and (potentially controversial) subjects of serious misfortune. At the end of the classic phase of the Civil Rights Movement, King came to believe that it was important to explore the possibility of cross-racial collaborations and political mobilization to enhance socioeconomic well-being.

The opening of the twenty-first century has brought widespread disappearance of work and the rise of unprecedented inequality to create new hardships for people from a broader range of racial and ethnic groups than King could probably have imagined. But participants in democratic social movements often understand better than anyone else what it means to identify and address problems of social and economic inequality in ways that do not stigmatize those subjected to it. They may therefore have a lot to teach the social elites who have for too long ignored the hardships confronting members of the "majority" who have lost out in the face of globalization and automation. Social movements interested in the genuine task of democracy may thus have something to teach us about how to collectively resist the forces of xenophobia and authoritarianism that seek to turn economic hardship and despair into a politics of resentment and hate. Part 3, on the power of political hope, will consider what these unexpected social collaborations might look like and what they might be able to accomplish.

3

SOCIAL MOVEMENTS
AND THE MORAL LIFE

Not everything that is faced can be changed, but nothing can be changed until it is faced.

—James Baldwin

3.1 SOCIAL MOVEMENTS AS ENGAGED MORAL INQUIRY

Progressive social movements offer valuable lessons about some of the habits of mind, social, norms and political values that form the critical foundation of democratic cooperation. This chapter shows that such movements are just as important for their capacity to deepen understanding of the morality that makes democracy possible. The moral reflection produced by social movements is engaged moral inquiry: moral insights that emerge from the painstaking struggles of their participants, initially as "situated" knowledge that is deeply enmeshed in ordinary life and political practice. These insights may be articulated in a movement's policy proposals and manifestos, in reflective essays and autobiographies written by movement participants, or in documentary and journalistic accounts produced by external observers.

Social movements also produce organic intellectuals, in Gramsci's sense, and their work often plays a critical role in generating understanding of a movement's commitments and contributions. Yet the work of such thinkers is rarely "abstract" theory, since it almost always continues to bear evidence of engagement with practice. When we read Gandhi, King, MacKinnon, or Havel, for instance, it is clear that their thought originates in political struggle and that it is often intended to illuminate that struggle, although these origins seldom limit the broader reach of their reflections.

The engaged moral inquiry that social movements produce reminds us that the community of moral inquirers extends, in principle, to include any human being—or any group of human beings—capable of reflection, and especially self-reflection. As William James argued in "The Philosopher and the Moral Life," "We all help to determine the content of ethical philosophy so far as we contribute to the [human] race's moral life. In other words, there can be no final truth in ethics any more than in physics, until the last man has had his experience and said his say."[1] Following James, a fundamental presupposition of this account is thus that everyday moral argument and philosophical moral inquiry are species of the same genus.

This account also presumes that moral argument and inquiry are always interpretive projects. This is why, throughout the history of moral and political thought, influential philosophers have insisted that they are not introducing new moral ideas but systematically reformulating, or rationally reconstructing, central elements of ordinary moral consciousness to reveal its unstated regulative commitments.[2] Jeremy Bentham insisted, for instance, that the principle of utility is deeply rooted in the "natural constitution of the human frame."[3] Immanuel Kant even asked: "Who would want to introduce a new principle of morality

SOCIAL MOVEMENTS AND THE MORAL LIFE ❧ 81

and, as it were, be its inventor as though the world had hitherto been ignorant of what duty is or had been thoroughly wrong about it?"[4] Of course, the interpretive projects that shape the engaged moral inquiry of social movements do not aim to systematize or rationally reconstruct general moral knowledge and belief—nor should they. Indeed, the moral insights generated by social movements are sometimes most valuable for their capacity to show where ordinary moral consciousness falls short.

The interpretive character of moral inquiry is a function of what the philosopher Mark Platts calls the "semantic depth" of moral concepts. These concepts are "semantically deep," Platts contends, because they pick out features of the world that are "of indefinite complexity in ways that transcend our practical understanding." This means that no single interpretation of a moral concept can adequately capture its semantic depth.[5] It also means that no single historical era, no one cultural understanding, and not even any single philosophical theory or tradition can capture what C. D. Broad called "the whole truth" about moral concepts.[6] Still further, the complexity of moral concepts is often compounded by the variety of circumstances in which we must interpret those concepts. Thus an account of justice that would be appropriate for a small traditional society without private property would look quite different from an account that is appropriate for a large contemporary liberal democracy.

Yet a "minimal" or "thin" account of a moral concept can sometimes yield a useful general picture of what morality requires in a particular domain. As some ancient theorists urged, it is helpful to know that in every society, justice concerns that sphere of moral life in which we must try to ensure that people get their "due."[7] Admittedly, such a minimal account may raise the question: How do we determine what people are due? Reflecting on the demands of liberal democracies, for instance, one might seek to adapt the Rawlsian idea that social justice requires a fair distribution of the benefits and burdens of democratic cooperation. But, as we learn from *A Theory of Justice*, the task of explicating "justice as fairness" demands still more interpretation. As John Rawls understood the task, it required interpretations of further concepts such as equality, reciprocity, and fraternity, and arguments to show that those interpretations capture defensible elements of "our considered convictions" about justice.

These observations about the interpretive character of moral inquiry raise two questions of vital importance. First, is there any reason to value thin accounts of moral concepts, if only thick accounts produce the interpretations needed to justify substantive outcomes in particular social contexts? The best answer to this question—perhaps surprisingly—is a resounding "yes." Consider Michael Walzer's analysis of a demonstration during the Velvet Revolution in Prague in 1989:

> These citizens of Prague were not marching in defense of utilitarian equality or John Rawls's difference principle or any philosophical theory of desert or merit or entitlement. Undoubtedly, they would have argued, if pressed, for different distributive programs; they would have described a just society in different ways; . . . What they meant by the "justice" inscribed on their signs, however, was simple enough: an end to arbitrary arrests, equal and impartial law enforcement, the abolition of the privileges and prerogatives of the party elite—common, garden variety justice.[8]

This example shows that appeals to "common, garden variety justice" can connect us in morally substantive ways to the suffering and hardship of those who have been subject to injustice. In some contexts, such appeals can even be catalysts for fairly robust responses to injustice. For instance, employing the simple phrase "no justice, no peace," hundreds of thousands of protesters across the globe have condemned police use of excessive force against African Americans and other marginalized groups within the United States, as well as in other multiracial societies. There are thus good reasons to take seriously a minimal conception of moral concepts like justice.

But second, can any "mere" interpretation of an existing moral concept be sufficient to promote moral progress? Might we perhaps need to discover, or even invent, new moral concepts either to enable moral condemnation of practices that our forebears failed to condemn or to keep pace with moral challenges emerging in domains such as gene science and artificial intelligence? The best answers to these questions must return to the assumption with which this project began: social movements matter to moral and political thought because moral progress in social practices never involves—and, in fact, never requires— "paradigm-shattering" advances in moral knowledge. Moral progress depends *primarily* on the engaged social criticism and political struggles bound up with social movements.

Some thinkers will resist this claim. For instance, in asking "Is Virtue Possible?," Michael Slote argues that ancient Greeks mounted no widespread criticism of slavery mainly because they lacked the moral tools to do so.[9] According to Slote, with the emergence of utilitarianism and Kantianism, philosophy produced "new moral ideas" that made it possible to condemn slavery as morally wrong. Yet we know that in the *Politics*, Aristotle felt compelled to challenge the stance of unnamed opponents of slavery; we also know that his opponents did not have access to modern moral philosophy to ground their challenge. It is certainly true that ancient Greeks did not, as a whole, subject the institution of slavery to substantive moral scrutiny. But there is no reason to attribute this failure to anything other than their willingness to "*affect ignorance*," in Aquinas's phrase, of the injustices of slavery.[10]

It has sometimes been argued that social movements generate progress by creating "abnormal moral contexts" *themselves*, making advances in moral knowledge "faster than they can be disseminated or assimilated" by the rest of us. Cheshire Calhoun contends that feminist thought has been an especially rich source of revolutionary moral ideas.[11] But not even the most uncompromising feminist jurisprudence and political theory defended by Catharine MacKinnon can qualify as paradigm-shattering in Calhoun's sense. To be sure, MacKinnon claims to be unveiling a concealed reality that even liberal feminists failed to see: the fact that the subjection of women is not the product of "mere sexism" but of systematic male dominance. Yet the values by reference to which MacKinnon criticizes the *effects* of male dominance are not morally revolutionary at all but surprisingly familiar. Feminism, she maintains, is "a tacit belief that women are human beings in truth" if "not in social reality."[12] Equally familiar are the values that MacKinnon relies on to determine when a society really treats women as human beings. If women had substantive equality, she urges, they would have "a chance at productive lives of reasonable physical security, self-expression, individuation, and minimal respect and dignity."[13] These values are not so different from the values defended more than a century earlier by John Stuart Mill in *On Liberty* and *The Subjection of Women*.

MacKinnon's work has certainly shattered paradigms in legal theory. MacKinnon was an influential early proponent of the idea that sexual harassment is a legally prohibited form of sex discrimination. She made the theoretical argument for this stance in *Sexual Harassment of Working Women* (1979). She also served as cocounsel on the first sexual harassment case argued before the U.S. Supreme Court, *Meritor Savings Bank v. Vinson* (1986), in which the justices ruled unanimously that sexual harassment is sex discrimination. Justice Ruth Bader Ginsburg rightly described MacKinnon's work on sexual harassment as "a revelation": the beginning of a field in the law that did not exist before.[14] MacKinnon has also been a pioneer in the international law of human rights, defending the claim that mass rape and sexual violence against women in war are human rights violations that ought to be criminally prosecuted and that can ground civil lawsuits against the perpetrators.[15] But the emergence of sexual harassment law and the extension of human rights law to address sexual violence have enriched our understanding of the demands of the concept of justice. It is true that some of Mac-Kinnon's claims about the conditions for women's equality call for a radical rethinking of what is "natural" in the realm of human sexuality. In her political theory and jurisprudence, however, as well as in her practice of the law, MacKinnon has been articulating a new and deeper interpretation of the concept of justice on which women get their "due" only when they have substantive social equality.

The principal problem with the claim that progress demands paradigm-shattering moral ideas is that it simply is not possible to *produce* such ideas. Whatever may be true about conceptual revolutions in enabling scientific progress, we cannot recognize a new insight as moral (in the most general sense), or as a revision of an existing moral concept, unless we can fairly quickly assimilate the relevant insight into our already existing complex of moral beliefs and judgments.[16] Moreover, in cross-cultural and transhistorical moral disagreement, we cannot even recognize that the disagreement is about morality unless there is substantial agreement between the conflicting positions on the "thin" content of moral concepts that are critical to the discussion. When moral disagreement is closer to home (in space and in time), we can appreciate something as a new moral insight only when we can recognize it as an interpretation that proposes to deepen understanding of an existing moral concept. Most important, a new moral insight about how to interpret an existing moral concept cannot count as a paradigm-shattering moral idea, even when that interpretation requires us to revise fundamental assumptions about to whom, or to what, the concept applies.[17]

Since the mid-nineteenth century, social movements have served to deepen understanding of the concept of social justice and to better illuminate its role as an element of the morality that makes democracy possible. When their insights expose deficiencies in familiar understandings of justice, they may challenge considered moral convictions held by theorists and ordinary people alike. The rest of this chapter explores three such insights: (1) we have a duty not to look away from serious injustice; (2) social injustice occurs when a society fails, in some significant way, to show humane regard for persons; and (3) the facts that are relevant to recognizing injustice cannot be fully understood until they are properly framed. That is, we have a duty that is both moral and epistemic to try to get "the story" right.

3.2 THE DUTY NOT TO LOOK AWAY

In August 1955, while visiting extended family in a small Mississippi town, an African American teenager named Emmett Till was abducted at gunpoint and lynched—brutally tortured and murdered—a few days after a local white woman falsely charged that he had grabbed her and whistled at her in a grocery store.[18] After much resistance, local officials returned

Emmett's body to his family in Chicago. But they did so with the expectation that his body would be placed in a closed casket to avoid provoking outrage at the brutality of his killers. Emmett's mother, Mamie Till Mobley, not only insisted on an open casket, she ensured that her son's body would be photographed by the press and then invited the larger community to the viewing with the exhortation: "Let the world see what I have seen." It is estimated that over four days, at least fifty thousand people answered Mobley's call.[19] In so doing, they acknowledged one of the most important moral insights defended by progressive social movements: we have a fundamental moral duty not to look away from injustice. As James Baldwin expresses it, one must face "as much of the truth as one can bear" because "nothing can be changed until it is faced."[20]

This insight has been central to the African American freedom struggle, from the earliest antilynching efforts of the NAACP all the way through the Civil Rights Movement's reliance on the media to document violence against nonviolent protestors. Moreover, the notion that there is a moral requirement to face injustice informs the work of many other social movements, including the international human rights movement, which exhorts us not to ignore the realities of genocide, ethnic cleansing, and the horrors of war, as well as the LGBTQ movement, which challenges us to acknowledge the brutality and cruel violence to which members of their communities have too often been subjected. Still further, the quest for environmental justice has recently required us to acknowledge how often poor, working-class, and minority communities become what Steve Lerner calls "sacrifice zones," expected to bear the risks and endure the sacrifices of industrial capitalism despite reaping relatively few of the benefits.[21]

Conventional moral and political thinkers have seldom considered the possibility that we have a duty to face injustice, and not simply to acknowledge that injustice exists—or may exist—in our midst. There are some noteworthy exceptions. In *The Faces of Injustice*, for instance, Judith Shklar argues that we cannot understand injustice unless our account genuinely includes "the victim's version."[22] This conviction is also a presupposition of Iris Young's argument, in *Justice and the Politics of Difference*, that we have a duty to confront the "faces of oppression" and to take seriously the claims of movements struggling to end that oppression.[23] Young incorrectly presumes, as I noted at the end of chapter 1, that these movements have rejected—and, in her view, should reject—the enlightenment ideal of common democratic citizenship. Yet Young rightly insists that these movements' perspectives on the injustices they face, and their beliefs about what would be required to remedy those injustices, should be central to political debate about substantive and sustainable remedies.

In the medieval world, Aquinas acknowledged the moral deficiencies of *affected ignorance,* that phenomenon of choosing not to know what one can and should know, and his discussion is an implicit recognition of a duty to face injustice.[24] Aquinas does not provide many details, but it is clear that affected ignorance is a remarkably complex phenomenon that comes in many varieties and can operate at different "levels" of the human psyche. Some of the most important forms of affected ignorance are (a) denying the existence of injustice, (b) deliberately mischaracterizing the phenomena that constitute injustice, and (c) moral temporizing—in the sense, here, of yielding to dominant beliefs and attitudes of the current era to justify being silent about the existence of serious injustice. Moral temporizing has been the defining characteristic of the U.S. government's approach to lynching: even after 120 years, efforts to make lynching a federal crime have still not succeeded as of this writing.[25]

In the contemporary world, the existence of photography and film has expanded the range of circumstances to which the duty to face serious injustice can apply. But having the capacity to regard suffering from a distance, mediated by a camera and by the sensibilities of a photographer, creates certain substantive moral risks. One set of risks is connected with what can be called "viewer responsibility" with regard to the depiction of grave harm. In particular, what is the viewer's responsibility when the injustice being depicted is rooted in systematic targeting of socially marginalized, stigmatized, or demonized groups? Photographically documenting brutality against such groups and then circulating the images for broader consumption can be exploited to solidify social support for such brutality by suggesting that its targets "deserve" their suffering. Critics have plausibly wondered whether viewing American lynching photography, for example, might implicate the viewer in *ongoing* rituals of marginalization, demonization, and objectification that continue to shape contemporary life. Moreover, as MacKinnon famously suggested, analogous questions arise in regard to certain kinds of pornography, when it represents violence or can be determined to involve the overriding of consent.[26]

The question of viewer responsibility can arise even with photography intended to awaken a sympathetic response to suffering. The problem is especially acute when the suffering is ongoing—as when we first encounter photographs of an ongoing war. In such contexts, we may need to ask how to distinguish viewing from voyeurism, especially if we do nothing to intervene after viewing the suffering. More broadly, we must ask whether obsessively contemplating atrocity—or depictions of atrocity—may sometimes reveal a prurient interest. As Susan Sontag suggests in *Regarding the Pain of Others*, the need to ask such a question did not begin with the development of photography. Indeed, it may be an element of Plato's concern, in *Republic* 4, with the failure of one of Socrates's interlocutors to suppress a desire to view corpses left by the public executioner.[27] But what if some photographic images effectively "demand" that we find a way for moral outrage to crowd out morally dubious responses? Several iconic photographs taken during the war in Vietnam might be thought to have such a morally compelling aspect.[28] Even as some critics objected that photojournalism during that war was simply anti-American propaganda, many observers believed that several photographs of that era served as morally necessary means of forcing Americans to confront and condemn the injustices of the war.

A quite different moral danger is associated with the possibility that images sometimes take a morally damaging toll on the viewer. One kind of damaging effect can result when an image has too intense an impact on a viewer. Thus, in *On Photography*, Sontag describes a moment, viewing Holocaust photographs in a bookstore, when she realized that "some limit had been reached" and that perhaps she had seen too much.[29] In a similar vein, *New York Times* columnist Brent Staples publicly objected that a controversial exhibition of American lynching photography simply posed too great a risk of traumatizing the African American viewer.[30] A second, quite different, effect results when images have too little impact on a viewer. In this context, historian Carolyn J. Dean wonders whether repeated viewing of photographs of Nazi brutality during the Holocaust threatens to reveal the "fragility of empathy." This possibility raises, in turn, concern that a kind of "compassion fatigue" may lead people to systematically turn away from images of brutality, resulting in the morally dangerous "normalization" of brutality.[31]

Yet, as the art critic John Berger suggests in *Ways of Seeing*, seeing is never simply a matter of "mechanically reacting to stimuli."[32] That is, there is really no such thing as "naïve seeing." We learn *how* to see—how to look at the world—by reference to various conventions regarding what it is important to look *at* and to look *for*, and concerning what we should presume to be true about who and what we look at.[33] This suggests that we can learn to see differently; that we can learn to look at the world, and the people we encounter in it, in a new way. Art often functions as a vehicle for encouraging us to develop new ways of seeing and to avoid the kinds of responses likely to lead to compassion fatigue.

Social movements can also assist us in developing and cultivating new ways of seeing. According to literary scholar Courtney Baker, Mamie Till Mobley came to understand the capacity of social movements to encourage new ways of seeing, and this recognition shaped her decisions regarding the display of her son's body. What Mobley recognized, Baker contends, is that there is a way of looking "in which the onlooker's ethics are addressed by the spectacle of others' embodied suffering."[34] Baker describes this way of looking as "humane insight'" to distinguish it from what, in the spirit of Jacques Lacan, is often called "the gaze":

> Whereas the gaze ignores or denies the humanity of the person being looked at, humane insight seeks knowledge about the humanity of that person. It is an ethics-based look that imagines the body that is seen to merit the protections due to all human bodies. Humane insight describes a decision to identify the body being looked at as a human body, a gesture that is integral to the formation of our social interactions. It is a look that turns a

benevolent eye, recognizes violations of human dignity, and bestows or articulates the desire for actual protection.[35]

Baker's account of "humane insight" certainly enhances our understanding of a pivotal episode in the African American freedom struggle. But it also deepens our grasp of the moral truth that transcends that episode: the insight that we can *decide* to look for the humanity of others even when we confront or contemplate injustice that seeks to dehumanize them.

But what does it mean to look for the humanity of others when we encounter them as targets of brutal injustice? Social movements have shown that, in such contexts, if we are *really* looking for the humanity of others we cannot focus solely on their capacity for autonomous agency. If we are to achieve humane insight into their suffering, we must also confront the material reality of their embodiment, and especially their capacity for suffering and pain. Regrettably, as Baker notes, when a body has been terribly disfigured by human brutality, humane insight must sometimes begin simply by trying to identify the body being looked at as a *human* body. In her autobiography, *Death of Innocence: The Story of the Hate Crime That Changed America*, Mamie Till Mobley reports that she struggled with this task even though she knew that completing the task was essential to gaining humane insight in that terrible context.[36]

Admittedly, respect for the autonomy of persons is almost always a critical element of what is involved in achieving humane insight. The failure to acknowledge and respect Emmett's autonomy was one of the most important moral failures of the Mississippi jury that acquitted Emmett Till's killers. The acquittal was a denial that Emmett had a right to live free from undue coercion and unwarranted violent interference. The jury's verdict ultimately sanctioned the killers' plan (confirmed by brazen boasting after the acquittal) to make an example of that "Chicago boy," in order to intimidate other African Americans who might have hoped to challenge the racial restrictions of the Jim Crow South.[37]

Yet giving moral *priority* to respect for autonomy—as some moral views require—can distance us from the reality of human embodiment. Compassionate concern for the other and, most basically, for the other's vulnerability to suffering and pain is sometimes an essential component of any effort to seek humane insight. As Jonathan Glover argues in *Humanity: A Moral History of the 20th Century*, respect for "moral standing" and compassionate concern for human suffering are *together* the "human responses" most likely to serve as moral constraints on cruelty, brutality, and moral disregard.[38] But lack of compassionate concern is often the more immediate source of great cruelty and brutality. There are terrifying catalogs of such brutality in Glover's book, as well as in David Livingstone Smith's volume, *Less than Human: Why We Demean, Enslave and Exterminate Others*.[39] In recent experience, the brutality that extinguished the life of George Floyd provides a vivid illustration of what can happen when compassionate concern fails to constrain violence against another. To use the weight of one's own body to extinguish the life of another human body, as though the use of deadly force might be appropriate "punishment" for allegedly circulating counterfeit money, is not just a failure of respect for agency but a profound failure of compassionate concern for another human being's vulnerability to suffering.

In a provocative essay on "Black Radical Kantianism," Charles Mills is properly critical of contemporary political philosophy for its failure to provide theoretical resources that show us how to constructively transform societies in which such brutality could be tolerated and even encouraged.[40] Somewhat surprisingly, despite his earlier criticisms of Kantian views, Mills began to believe that we might find such resources from within a Kantian view—reshaped, of course, to focus on demands to remedy racial injustice. Yet Mills's hope is unlikely to be realized. A Kantian moral view must always privilege respect for the rights of autonomous agents and can neither articulate the morally fundamental demands of compassionate concern nor help us learn how to meet those demands. Some critics may claim that Kant was correct to presume that there cannot be a moral demand to develop and act on compassionate concern. But there is growing evidence from neuroscience research, and ordinary human experience, that this stance may simply be incorrect. There is compelling evidence that people have extraordinary control over their emotional responses to the world and that compassion can be developed and refined.[41] There is even evidence that criminally violent psychopaths, whose upbringing failed to fully develop the human responses (and the brain functions) on which compassion depends, can be trained to feel—and not simply to feign—at least some compassion for suffering and pain.[42]

But even apart from concerns about the limits of a Kantian moral stance, there are reasons to doubt whether *any* conventional moral philosophy contains the resources to frame and help resolve the most urgent problems of compassionate concern—even the ethics of care, as well as those varieties of utilitarianism that focus on the capacity to suffer pain. The difficulties that confront conventional moral philosophy are a function of two important facts about the patterns of social meaning that usually underwrite the worst kinds of brutality and cruelty toward human beings. First, surprisingly durable patterns of social meaning serve to construct some groups of people as not *worthy* of compassionate concern—alleging, for instance, that they are permanent possibilities of danger, or untrustworthy invaders, or agents of "infestation." Second, these constructions are so durable because they contain both cognitive and quasi-cognitive phenomena—including unusually recalcitrant forms of fear and distrust—that are particularly resistant to the discursive argument and reason-giving on which philosophy typically relies. This is why philosophers as varied as Plato and Wittgenstein are right to insist that we must sometimes try to *show* what might be wrong with a way of understanding or perceiving the world, when attempts to *say* what is wrong by means of discursive argument prove insufficient. But showing people how to look at other human beings with humane insight has rarely been philosophy's strength. Recognizing these limitations, thinkers such as John Dewey and W. E. B. Du Bois have maintained that art is an indispensable element in any effort to break down barriers that divide human beings, and possibly altering socially constructed meanings that demonize and dehumanize socially marginalized groups.[43] Moreover, in the current age of photo editing and deceptive video editing, art may once again become a powerful tool of social transformation.

In an arresting example of the power of art to provoke humane insight, Kerry James Marshall's triptych *Heirlooms and Accessories* (2002) challenges the viewer to reflect on the troubling implications of a double lynching that occurred in Indiana in 1930. Each of the three panels reproduces an original photograph of the events but fades most of the image in order to foreground the face of one of three women in the crowd—with each highlighted face representing a different generation.[44] The women are foregrounded as *accessories* to two brutal murders. But, as Marshall contends, each woman's expression also reveals the shocking indifference with which the women viewed the spectacle of brutality, along with their disregard for the rule of law and their expectations that they would be immune from prosecution despite their willing participation in public torture and killing.[45] In framing the faces as representatives of different generations, Marshall also invites us to reflect on the legacy of lynching photography as *heirlooms* of racial hate and socially sanctioned brutality.

Marshall's work thus provides important evidence that we can sometimes satisfy the demand to face injustice without direct confrontation with injustice. Indeed, we may meet the demand through engagement with certain kinds of nonfiction, poetry, or fictional narrative, through documentary photography and film, through the music of social protest, and certainly through visual art. Yet these considerations should not obscure the moral wisdom embodied in the choices and actions of Emmett Till's mother and of those who shared the terrible but morally necessary burden of directly viewing her son's body.

3.3: SOCIAL JUSTICE AS HUMANE REGARD FOR PERSONS

The insight that we have a moral duty to face injustice and that, when we do, we must look for the humanity of the *subject* of injustice is inextricably linked with a second, more foundational, insight that social injustice is a failure of humane regard for persons. Framed more hopefully, what progressive social movements have consistently shown is that social justice is fundamentally humane regard for persons. This means that a society gives people their due when its basic institutions and defining practices combine respect for the human capacity for agency with compassionate concern for human vulnerability to pain and suffering. MacKinnon's insistence that women are human beings in truth if not in social reality, and King's insistence that segregation and discrimination wrongly substitute an "I-it" relationship for an "I-thou" relationship, serve as powerful reminders of how central the demand for humane regard has been to many of the most important social movements in history.

Humane regard generates social justice when it is embodied in the legal, political, economic, and social institutions and practices that help to define a particular way of life. This means that humane regard is not the kind of good that can be "distributed" as a benefit of social cooperation. Thinkers such as Iris Young and Axel Honneth have thus rightly challenged the idea that we can provide an adequate account of social justice by relying on what Young called the "distributive justice paradigm."[46] To be sure, some account of distributive justice may be an indispensable guide to an important dimension of social justice. In particular, such an account may be crucial for providing a defensible vision of what a society must do to display humane regard for its citizens through institutions that generate and preserve such goods as political rights and privileges and opportunities for education and employment, and that distribute income and wealth. But the wisdom of social movements confirms that distributive justice is only part of the comprehensive phenomenon of social justice.

Further, when we consider the semantic depth, and the consequent complexity, of the concept of justice, it becomes clear that no single principle, nor any one finite set of principles, can be an adequate guide to designing institutions to meet the demands of justice. This is why few social movements (if any) have ever been committed to the idea that we can promote a just society by means of some algorithmic decision procedure for determining what justice requires. But what are the overall demands of justice? If progressive social movements are right, as

I think they are, social justice is achieved when people are able to constructively exercise their capacity for choice and action without unwarranted interference, coercion, or violence, and when they are also able to live a life that is relatively free from unnecessary pain and suffering. Social movements thus presume what Young labeled an "enabling conception of justice."[47] Young goes on to defend this way of thinking about justice, arguing quite plausibly that such a conception helps us understand that *injustice* refers to certain kinds of "disabling constraints" that are created and sustained by a society's fundamental institutions and practices.

On Young's analysis, since the late 1960s progressive movements have focused on two broad categories of disabling constraints. There is, first, *domination*, defined as what occurs when institutional conditions "inhibit or prevent people from participating in determining their actions or the conditions of their actions."[48] Young makes a compelling case for the idea that domination is a critical source of injustice, and that social movements have rightly understood it as such. Less convincing is Young's claim that all the other important disabling constraints that social movements plausibly challenge are varieties of a single phenomenon of *oppression*, defined as "structural phenomena that immobilize or diminish a group."[49] Young does argue that there are five main kinds of oppression: "exploitation, marginalization, powerlessness, cultural imperialism and violence." But even in social movements where concepts such as oppression and exploitation are appropriate elements of the vocabulary needed to describe their efforts, we find more nuanced conceptions of the constraints that embody failures of humane regard and thus constitute social injustice.

Five kinds of disabling constraints have been challenged by progressive social movements: (1) domination (in Young's sense); (2) persistent threats to physical security and safety; (3) environmental degradation; (4) poverty and the economic insecurity affecting many who may not qualify as poor; and (5) limited access to material and often cultural conditions of human flourishing. Over time, efforts to make space for justice by eliminating these disabling constraints have had two main consequences. First, rather than articulating a single principle of justice, or a single finite set of principles of justice, social movements have shown that five basic categories of *values*— each category associated with the conditions for eliminating a major disabling constraint—ought to shape a society seeking to establish and preserve humane regard. Second, social movements have helped to reshape at least some important institutions and practices in accordance with those values and thus to show what it might mean to realize justice in particular domains. What social movements have to teach us about the concept of justice, and how to realize its demands, is thus very far removed from most of the debates that have shaped analytic political philosophy since the mid-1970s, which has been dominated by a search for the right principles for distributing (mostly) material goods. It will be helpful to explore the several categories of values that social movements have articulated as the core commitments of social justice.

We can begin by considering the cluster of values that embody a commitment to prevent domination, looking first at values that prevent the arbitrary exercise of coercive political power and the unwarranted use of state violence. Here, it helps to recall Walzer's informal survey of the basic commitments of the Velvet Revolution, as well as the lessons of the civil rights era and the movement for international human rights. These movements confirm, most fundamentally, that institutions and practices are just when they can be preserved with minimal reliance on the arbitrary use of power, minimal dependence on officially sanctioned violence, an absolute prohibition on state-sanctioned cruelty and brutality, and a commitment to accountability in the administration of law. Of course, many social movements have presumed that a democracy provides the most reliable political context for preventing domination, and the conditions on the legitimate exercise of political power within democracies are much more demanding. Two of the most important democratic values critical to preventing domination are a commitment to inclusive deliberation and decision-making in shaping the content of law (discussed at length in chapter 2) and to transparency in the operation of basic legal and political institutions.

But a commitment to accountability in administering the law as a way of preventing domination is often considered the sine qua non of any society—democratic or not—that purports to care about social justice.[50] This is because ensuring accountability before the law is a critical means of preventing unwarranted state violence and the arbitrary use of state power. A commitment to accountability helps to ensure that laws apply to government officials as well as private citizens, and to political and socioeconomic elites as well as to those who are less powerful and less materially well off. As Judith Shklar argued, accountability matters because injustice

> does not appear only on those rare occasions when a political order wholly collapses. It does not stand outside the gate of even the best of known states. Most injustices occur continuously within the framework of an established polity with an operative system of law, in normal times. Often it is the very people who are supposed to prevent injustice who, in their official capacity commit the greatest acts of injustice, without much protest of the citizenry.[51]

This passage actually identifies two distinct, but equally important, ways in which a society might fail to preserve the accountability necessary for justice. One kind of failure of accountability occurs when there is a persistent tendency, "within the framework of an established polity," to let certain groups go unpunished for legal violations with respect to which other groups are treated very harshly. In an example of harsh treatment, in some U.S. jurisdictions, if a person of modest means gets caught attempting to circulate a counterfeit bill, or writing a few bad checks, the consequences could destroy any hope for a normal life. As Michelle Alexander has shown, such ramifications may include an involvement with the criminal justice system—that complex "system of carceral control"—from which it is often difficult to ever break free.[52] By contrast, in the aftermath of the financial crisis of 2008, only one Wall Street executive went to jail for fraud, specifically for concealing hundreds of millions in losses in his employer's mortgage-backed securities portfolio.[53] Other investment bankers who did far worse were never even prosecuted, even where it could be shown that their actions were directly connected with producing one of the most devastating foreclosure crises in American history. It is difficult not to construe such a class-based contrast in treatment as a failure of humane regard: that is, as a failure to respect the value of accountability in the interest of social justice.

The second kind of failure implicit in Shklar's overview is the failure to hold a system's *officials* accountable for clear and overt wrongdoing. This is the kind of injustice decried by the protesters who participated in Czechoslovakia's Velvet Revolution. Opposition to this kind of injustice has also been a driving force of the activism that has challenged police brutality in the United States. Shklar might have added that the unjust consequences of this kind of accountability failure are compounded when officials are complicit in the crimes of private citizens. Marshall's *Heirlooms and Accessories* is a vivid reminder that this kind of complicity undergirded the practice of lynching in America, whereby representatives of "the law" consistently granted private citizens impunity for grave forms of criminal brutality.

But a third, equally important, kind of failure of accountability is not addressed in Shklar's observation: the failure to hold people accountable for a violation of law when those harmed by that violation are socially stigmatized and marginalized, and deemed "unworthy" of any effort to prosecute the violation. In the contemporary social world, this phenomenon is all too common in cases involving police who use excessive force against some populations, and by all accounts frequent failure to hold such police accountable seems to be a problem in several ethnically and racially diverse liberal democracies—including the United Kingdom and France as well as the United States.[54] The failure to prosecute sends an especially destructive message in legal systems (perhaps especially the United States) where a prosecutor undertakes prosecution on behalf of "the people." In such a context, the failure to prosecute is a way of saying not just that the victim is "unworthy" but that the victim is not even a full member of the community.

A commitment to holding people accountable for violations of law, regardless of who might have been harmed by the violation, is an equally important component of the values that acknowledge the importance of humane regard for physical safety and security. But this cluster of values must embody a commitment to physical security in several additional ways. To begin with, a just society must have a robust set of laws that function, in H. L. A. Hart's phrase, as primary rules of obligation to govern the daily conduct of ordinary citizens. It must also have what Hart calls secondary rules of adjudication that provide reliable methods for determining when violations of the primary rules occur and for ensuring that the administration of punishments for such violations is transparent, is timely, and respects substantive equality before the law. When a society's legal institutions fail to embody these values, the society fails to show humane regard for persons. Feminists like MacKinnon who exposed the failure of many legal systems to prosecute crimes of sexual violence against women have revealed one kind of failure of humane regard in this domain. Social movements and organizations that object that substantive equality before the law cannot be achieved in a system that allows mass incarceration, and racial disparities in sentencing practices, identify yet another failure of humane regard in this sphere of social life.

The safety and integrity of our physical environments constitute the third cluster of social commitments expressing humane regard. This cluster of values must build on accountability, inclusive deliberation, and institutional transparency. But there are very distinctive values in this cluster: in particular, commitment to the equitable spreading of the risks of social cooperation, and to equality of access to mechanisms for correction of, and compensation for, undeserved harm.[55] The growth of the environmental movement, and especially the movement for environmental justice, has helped to show why such values are important. One way in which a society displays humane regard for its members is by protecting access to a physical environment that will not severely endanger the human capacity for agency or subject anyone to undue suffering and pain. Framed more positively, the quality of the environment has a deep and comprehensive impact on the most basic elements of the quality of life. Of course, this insight was certainly articulated before the mid-twentieth century; Thoreau's *Walden Pond* (1854) is rightly recognized as a pivotal document in the environmental movement. But it is Rachel Carson's *Silent Spring* (1962), vividly describing the damage done by toxic chemicals used in commercial pesticides, that is most often credited with creating the modern environmental movement. Testifying before the U.S. Congress a year after the publication of *Silent Spring*, Carson argued: "Our heedless and destructive acts enter into the vast cycles of the earth and in time return to bring hazard to ourselves."[56] Environmental justice is now a central component of social justice because too often the hazards wrought by "heedless and destructive acts" have a disparate effect on communities inhabited by people who are stigmatized and marginalized in ways that make it all too easy to flout the values demanded by humane regard.

The water crisis that publicly unfolded in Flint, Michigan, in 2014 provides a vivid recent example. As environmental sociologist Paul Mohai describes the crisis, it owes it origins primarily to a failure to respect deliberative inclusivity. The crisis began in April 2013, when an official appointed by the governor of Michigan as an unelected "emergency manager" (presiding as part of a state-enforced receivership) approved a cost-cutting switch of Flint's water supply from the Detroit water system to a new, but at that point unconstructed, pipeline. It was also decided that as an interim, and additional cost-cutting, measure during construction of the pipeline, Flint's water would be supplied by the Flint River—long known for its poor water quality. Still further, the Michigan Department of Environmental Quality somehow failed to require that the Flint Water Treatment Plant meet federal corrosion control standards. But this was just the beginning of a large-scale failure to ensure the equitable spreading of the risks of social cooperation—a failure that is a common feature of circumstances that produce environmental injustice.

When the change to Flint River water took place in April 2014, it led to the corrosion of water service lines and lead-based plumbing throughout the city. The result was widespread lead poisoning and what is now acknowledged to be one of the most severe and deadly outbreaks of Legionnaire's Disease in American history. In early 2015 the Flint City Council voted 7 to 1 to return to the Detroit water system, but the emergency manager at the time overruled the vote on financial grounds. As the crisis unfolded, residents were also confronted by repeated failures of institutional transparency, as well as continued exclusion from decision-making about their own fates. Officials initially refused to acknowledge the scope of the Legionnaire's outbreak, and some even insisted that residents were hyperbolic and unreliable in their claims about the levels of lead, and other contaminants, in the city's water.[57] Further, until reaching a $600 million settlement with the state of Michigan (in August 2020), affected residents had been consistently denied access to mechanisms for corrective and compensatory justice.

Some have heralded the settlement with the state of Michigan as a remarkable victory for the grassroots activists and their local allies who fought for water safety in Flint, although some observers urge that, given the scope of the damages the community suffered, this settlement is only a part of the compensation rightly due to the community. Yet whatever the merits of the settlement, the lingering long-term health effects of the water crisis suggest that the Flint situation was an especially egregious example of government officials failing to ensure the equitable distribution of risk. In fact, Flint can plausibly be seen as a paradigm case of the "sacrifice zone" phenomenon. The activists who fought back against the events and policies that turned the city into a sacrifice zone properly understood them as serious violations of humane regard and thus serious social injustice.

Of course, many would argue—I think rightly—that we cannot understand the circumstances that led to the crisis unless we also acknowledge the relevance of the inequalities of class and race at stake in the case. At 54.3 percent, Flint's African American population was four times greater than the 14.1 percent representation of African Americans in the state of Michigan. Moreover, the poverty rate in Flint was 41.9 percent, three times the state poverty rate of 15.0 percent. These inequalities surely strengthened the tendency of some Michigan officials to look away from, or even to actively deny, the injustices generated by the water crisis.[58]

One of the most difficult questions raised by the Flint crisis is the question of how to assess the relevance, in this context, of the value of accountability. Two years after the crisis became public, Michigan's attorney general announced that criminal charges were being brought against several officials involved in decision-making that led to the crisis. Yet from the start, there was concern that the wrong people (mostly bureaucrats) had been targeted for prosecution, but also that the failures of governance that made the crisis possible were "political failures" best addressed by the political system, not the judicial system.[59] These considerations have not silenced concern that justice demands holding someone criminally accountable for the Flint crisis. Yet that is unlikely to happen, although efforts to obtain criminal convictions may continue.[60]

Even apart from details of the Flint crisis, there remain broader questions about what accountability could really mean in such contexts. The difficulty of answering these questions is compounded by the fact that, according to many social movements, some of the worst forms of social injustice are "structural." But when we confront structural injustice we may be unable to definitively (and uncontroversially) identify individual intentional wrongdoers responsible for the injustice or conclude that any intentional wrongdoers we can identify must be viewed as only part of the total cause of, and any adequate remedies for, the relevant injustices. As Young defines structural injustice, it "occurs as a consequence of many individuals and institutions acting to pursue their particular goals and interests, for the most part within the limits of accepted rules and norms." Structural injustice, she adds, is a kind of moral wrong "distinct from the wrongful action of an individual agent or the repressive policies of a state."[61] Yet few accounts of structural injustice—whether in theoretical contexts or in the work of social movements— carefully consider the question of how to respond when a single event or crisis involves both serious and identifiable individual wrongdoing *and* structural injustice. This question regularly arises in contexts as different as police uses of excessive force against socially marginalized groups and environmental crises like the water quality crisis in Flint. Given how often such events and crises occur, it is critical to have some account of how to strike a proper balance between holding individuals responsible for wrongdoing and addressing the structural forces and processes that create the circumstances in which that wrongdoing can have such damaging effects.

Where injustice is principally (or, if possible, entirely) structural, we may want to adopt some variant of Young's "social connection" model of responsibility for justice on which responsibility "derives from belonging together with others in a system of interdependent processes of cooperation and competition through which we seek benefits and aim to realize project." But for injustices associated with police abuse of force, we may need to consider models of responsibility that allow for something analogous to "joint liability" in tort law. With such a model, intentional wrongdoers can be properly assigned criminal or tort liability (or both), even while society as a whole remains responsible for eliminating the conditions that tolerate or encourage such wrongdoing in ways that produce and sustain systematic social injustice.

3.4 THE LINK BETWEEN EPISTEMIC INJUSTICE AND SOCIAL INJUSTICE

The challenge of adequately resolving tensions among competing conceptions of accountability has always been especially difficult for movements addressing the disabling constraints arising from poverty, economic insecurity, and their resulting limitations on access to conditions of human flourishing. For contemporary social movements, this difficulty has been compounded by globalization and the increasing automation of work, which have intensified inequality, economic insecurity, and poverty. Understanding who is ultimately accountable to remedy economic injustice, which policies and institutions need to be changed, and what values those changes should embody has become a monumental task. The difficulty of the task may help explain the unexpected trajectory of the Occupy Wall Street Movement: after its remarkable success in gaining a global audience for that idea that the enrichment of "the 1 percent" was taking place at the expense of "the 99 percent," Occupy Wall Street never produced a concrete set of movement goals or offered a plausible path by which to pursue those goals in support of economic justice.[62] Still further, even when a particular social movement makes a plausible case that a particular *aspect* of the problem of economic injustice is linked with discrete and identifiable domestic processes in a given liberal democracy—as with social movements focused on access to health care in the United States or the problem of student debt —democratic deconsolidation is endangering the possibility that arguments about economic justice can successfully appeal to a shared sense of the rights, privileges, and obligations of democratic citizenship.

Of course, social movements sometimes experience serious internal disagreements about what constitutes economic justice and about the values that economic institutions, policies, and practices must embody if they are to display humane regard. A particularly momentous rift among participants in the Civil Rights Movement eventually undercut that movement's ability to make a substantive contribution to debates about economic justice. The project began with extraordinary promise, shortly after the passage of the Voting Rights Act in 1965, when several leaders who had organized the March on Washington two years earlier produced a detailed policy document, "The Freedom Budget," that had the goal of ending poverty in America within a decade without any real long-term cost to taxpayers. The document sought to "attack all the major causes" of poverty, including "unemployment and underemployment; substandard pay; inadequate social insurance and welfare payments . . . ; bad housing; deficiencies in health services, education and training; and fiscal and monetary policies which tend to redistribute income regressively."[63] The proposal was the called the "Freedom Budget" because it was based on the presumption that poverty and deprivation "erode human freedom and democracy," just as surely as the denial of the right to vote. The plan was to apply principles that had shaped the classic phase of the Civil Rights Movement to get America to attack economic problems affecting people of all races and ethnicities, and the document initially had broad support from labor leaders, academics, politicians, and influential activists in the African

American freedom struggle. But the coalition that originally supported the proposal broke up, mainly due to the document's claim that the nation could abolish poverty in a decade without addressing the many costs, human as well as economic, of the Vietnam War. Even King eventually distanced himself from this dimension of the document, in his famous Riverside Church speech in April 1967, "A Time to Break Silence."[64]

Yet even when social movements are able to build a robust internal consensus around a set of values to promote economic justice, and a plausible understanding of accountability for justice, they may still confront a serious obstacle. This is because economic institutions and practices comprise one of those domains of social life in which outcomes are fully intertwined with what Miranda Fricker calls the "ethical aspects" of epistemic practices.[65] Fricker has convincingly defended a theory of "epistemic injustice," according to which some people are harmed in their capacity as knowers by the ways in which a society's epistemic practices shape their social identities, as when their testimony is discounted or disbelieved because of stigmatizing conceptions of gender or race, or when they have difficulty characterizing or even recognizing some harm to which they have been subject. But Fricker's account has also helped to show that people can be *morally* harmed by epistemic practices, in several ways. As I argued in previous chapters, this is what happens when socially accepted narratives and concepts purport to justify excluding some groups from the rights and privileges of democratic citizenship, or when they rationalize subjecting marginalized groups to the cruelty and indignities of brutality and violence. The economic consequences of a society's epistemic practices can be just as dire when widely accepted concepts, categories, and narratives construct poverty as primarily an individual moral failing and represent those who are poor as therefore undeserving of any kind of assistance or compassion. In such contexts, it is difficult to make a broadly compelling argument for the idea that the status of people who are poor, or economically insecure, is often the result of economic injustice.

Given the interdependence of socially influential narratives, the narrative of the (allegedly) irresponsible, "undeserving poor" is inextricably bound up with a narrative of the hard-working, deserving economic elites who must constantly fight off predatory efforts to undermine their liberty and transfer their hard-earned wealth to people who are *allegedly* too lazy or untalented to earn greater wealth themselves. In recent years, this narrative has come to be accepted even by some people who are not themselves part of the economic elite and who realistically have little chance of becoming such, but who all too readily assume that if they were ever to become part of the economically elite, they could plausibly come to see those who don't through the narrative lens that constructs them as irresponsible and undeserving. In one of the most jarring recent expressions of how deep the commitment to the narrative of the undeserving poor can be, in a televised political debate that occurred during the 2012 presidential campaign in America, some of this narrative's defenders loudly cheered at the prospect of letting sick people die if they arrive at the hospital without health insurance.[66] To be fair, the debate moderator raised the issue of whether an uninsured person should be allowed to die after a serious accident, possibly (though not certainly) as a rhetorical question. But the moderator asked the question only after then presidential candidate Ron Paul objected, on libertarian grounds, to the idea that "you have to take care of everybody" and insisted that "that's what freedom is all about, taking your own risks."[67]

In a forceful and insightful response to this episode, the largest professional organization of nurses in America—National Nurses United (NNU)—reminded us that if we care about the demands of justice, we have a responsibility to ask whether narratives that purport to make sense of social experience are epistemically defensible and genuinely morally illuminating. Several NNU representatives invited us to challenge the extreme libertarian narrative with an alternative narrative that puts *justice as humane regard* at the center of the story. For instance, according to then-Executive Director RoseAnn Moro, "Most of us, other than the most wealthy, are just one illness away from bankruptcy and lack of health insurance." Moreover, "nurses do not regard lack of wealth or personal misfortune as a handicap or an excuse to withdraw needed and appropriate medical care. Nor should that ever be acceptable in a just and humane society."[68] A companion challenge to Paul's libertarian account might ask whether people who ask us to celebrate their superior self-discipline and individual responsibility could ever succeed were it not for the complex acts of the other people who cooperate—sometimes at great personal sacrifice, and often with little personal reward—to help create and protect a society in which it is possible for people of "superior self-discipline" and a great deal of luck to succeed. One task of social movements interested in economic justice is to challenge us—including the libertarians among us—to sincerely ask which narrative (or set of narratives) is cognitively and perceptually more adequate: the one on which the allegedly superior disciplined individual succeeds *solely* on the basis of individual effort, or the one in which superior discipline and individual responsibility allow one to succeed when one's efforts are fortuitously embedded in a social context—including social cooperation on the part of those who may be socially less well-situated—that allows one to succeed.

But, as I will show in part 2 of this book, challenging narratives that unfairly stigmatize and dispossess some groups is just part of the broader responsibility that progressive social movements must accept, if they hope to successfully address any one (or more) of the five categories of injustice discussed in this chapter. Social movements must be ready to help make space for justice not simply by means of protest and dissent, but by taking on the challenge of making conceptual, perceptual, and motivational space for justice. To do this, social movements must be ready to draw on the constructive powers of imagination in three important endeavors: creating consensus on the claim that there are social conditions in need of redress, motivating the readiness to act on that consensus, and sustaining confidence in the value of acting despite the delays, disappointments, and uncertainty with which human effort and action inevitably must contend.

II

SOCIAL MOVEMENTS AND THE POWER OF COLLECTIVE IMAGINATION

4

TAKING IMAGINATION
SERIOUSLY

You can't depend on your eyes when your imagination is out of focus.

—Mark Twain

4.1 IMAGINING COMMUNITY

A striking feature of many recent social protests has been the vehemence with which some protesters have sought to deface, remove, and even destroy monuments and memorials deemed symbolic expressions of systematic oppression. Campaigns linking social protest with vigorous challenges to public monuments came to worldwide attention with the "Rhodes Must Fall" Movement in 2015, which sought the removal of a statue of Cecil Rhodes that had stood at the entrance to the University of Cape Town in South Africa since 1934. The success of that movement in getting the statue taken down encouraged similar efforts in other places, perhaps most notably in 2016 at Oriel College, Oxford, where students sought the removal of another statue of Rhodes. But in summer 2020 the project of targeting monuments for removal—and sometimes toppling them on the spot—became an astonishingly global phenomenon. Protesters in the United States, the United Kingdom, Belgium, Portugal, France, and Brazil targeted monuments thought to celebrate colonialism, slavery, and white supremacy—dramatically reshaping public spaces as they protested police brutality and demanded racial justice.[1] These protests were vivid examples of a phenomenon I describe as aesthetic activism.

Influential critics have objected to these campaigns as misguided and dangerous attempts to erase the past and deny history, and sometimes even as simple vandalism. But such criticisms miss the mark. The iconoclasm that has driven global campaigns against problematic monuments is a reminder of three critical but frequently overlooked truths: (1) the intertwining of art, memory, and politics is a central feature of political life; (2) the civic art of remembrance (which produces public monuments and memorials) is often the most visible evidence of those connections; and (3) when civic art is informed by narratives that legitimize oppressive systems and regimes, the only way to remake the world is to reject the narratives and the cultural artifacts that symbolically sustain the narratives. Of course, it is far from obvious that unceremoniously toppling the offending monuments is the best way to reimagine the world. But the belief that it might be a necessary prelude to reimagining the world has shaped political resistance and rebellion for centuries. In one of the most famous examples, after hearing a public reading of the Declaration of Independence on July 9, 1776, a crowd of civilians, aided by some of George Washington's soldiers, descended on a park in lower Manhattan to topple a two-ton equestrian statue of King George III.[2]

Contemporary global challenges to the symbolic celebration of colonialism and racism are thus a powerful restatement of a familiar idea: the notion that we cannot remake the world in the pursuit of human freedom and human dignity unless we can first reimagine it. The three chapters in this part of the book explore the implications of this idea. They investigate the circumstances in which it makes sense to draw on the transformative power of imagination and consider the methods through which noteworthy imaginative transformations have occurred in the realm of "political aesthetics" (this chapter), in regard to the language that shapes conceptual space (chapter 5), and in the socially influential narratives that purport to shape collective identities and guide common projects (chapter 6). All three chapters reflect on important general insights that emerge from analyzing empirical examples and review the significance of those insights for future efforts at social transformation.

One of the most fundamental insights underwriting contemporary political iconoclasm is the idea that imagination helps to constitute communities as political entities, and that it plays this role even in large, doctrinally complex modern democracies. Anthropologist Benedict Anderson offers one of the most widely cited defenses of this insight in his influential book *Imagined Communities*. Anderson argues that any political community larger than a village that allows regular, face-to-face contact is always an imagined community: "It is imagined because the members of even the smallest nation will never know most of their fellow-members, meet them, or even hear of them, yet in the minds of each lives the image of their communion."[3] As the political theorist David Miller explains, Anderson does not mean that nations are "wholly spurious inventions," but rather that "they depend for their existence on collective acts of imagining."[4] *Imagined Communities* urges that the emergence of "unified fields of exchange and communication" made possible by the rise of commercial printing (among other things) allowed "rapidly growing numbers of people to think about themselves, and relate to others, in profoundly new ways" as members of communities.[5] This account makes it reasonable to believe that the recent proliferation of increasingly insular modes of communication (worsened by the algorithmic "filter bubbles" shaping online communication) may be contributing to social division and discord by narrowing the scope of political imagination.

Many contemporary political philosophers presume that reason and agreement on rational principles are the most important sources of stability for complex modern democracies. But Anderson rejects this approach, observing that "regardless of the actual inequality and exploitation that may prevail in each, the nation is always conceived as a deep, horizontal comradeship. Ultimately it is this fraternity that makes it possible, over the past two centuries, for so many millions of people . . . willingly to die" in the name of their collective national imaginings.[6] Anderson's appeal to imagination to explain this phenomenon rests on what he seems to consider an "inference to the best explanation," as philosophers of science might describe it. Anderson is implicitly urging that only cohesion around "collective acts of national imagining" could explain the kind of solidarity that makes people willing to endure extreme civic sacrifice, despite their societies' imperfections.

We can appreciate the explanatory power of this inference only when we recognize that Anderson understands the phenomenon in need of explanation—the *explanandum*—quite differently from the standard view that has shaped conventional debates about stability in recent political philosophy. In the standard view, the explanandum is something like "why people obey the law," or "why people take themselves to *have an obligation* to obey the law," or even simply "the origin of political obligation." Given this conception of what is to be explained, it is entirely plausible to try to explain it by appealing to reason and agreement on rational principle.[7] Yet if the explanandum is, instead, "why people will endure great sacrifices even in support of imperfect political arrangements," Anderson is surely right to presume that explanations appealing to reason will be insufficient. More precisely, he is right to assume that the best explanation of a widespread readiness to sacrifice in order to support political life is that political communities depend for their existence on their members' capacity to imagine themselves as part of a "deep horizontal comradeship."

Anderson's conception of the explanandum builds on Ernst Renan's claim, in the essay "What Is a Nation?," that a nation is "a large-scale solidarity" constituted not by race, language, religion, or even community of interests, but primarily by appreciation of shared sacrifice, including sacrifices that citizens have made in the past and those they are prepared to make in the future.[8] As Anderson understands this phenomenon, the sacrifices that citizens make in war are often a focal point of their collective valuing of sacrifice. Moreover, in reflecting on the modern practice of building tombs to "the unknown soldier," Anderson suggests that public *commemoration* of civic sacrifice plays a foundational role in the symbolic expression of those "national imaginings" that constitute a collective identity. This observation helps to show why is it not unreasonable for some social movements to focus critical concern and the energies of public protest in campaigns challenging the meaning and value of certain public monuments and memorials.

Yet, as Danielle Allen powerfully argues in *Talking to Strangers: Anxieties of Citizenship Since Brown v. Board of Education*, even in a smoothly functioning liberal democracy, everyday political life demands continual and substantial sacrifices that are independent of the demands of war.[9] Consider that conforming to the demands of liberal toleration requires us to refrain from interfering with attitudes and pursuits that we may find offensive or even frightening. Moreover, advancing democratic equality may involve contributing to social welfare schemes that benefit people we will never meet—and at least some people whose values and choices we might reject. Still further, respecting the rule of law can mean accepting disheartening imperfections in basic legal institutions and processes. We all know that guilty people sometimes go free, that innocent people are sometimes convicted, and that mass incarceration is decimating many communities and diverting important resources from socially valuable aims. Perhaps most important, when our "side" loses in democratic elections, the stability of democracy depends on a widespread readiness to accept the loss with grace and with continuing regard for the broader value of democratic political institutions. Sustaining robust political commitment in the face of such serious and persistent demands requires a capacity for "self-transcendence" that sometimes involves serious sacrifice.[10] This is why political philosophers like Charles Taylor have followed Anderson in denying that reason alone can explain what constitutes and sustains political communities that make such demands.

Taylor rightly argues that democratic stability requires solidarity rooted in "cohesion around a collective identity."[11] In this view, a democratic order is stable not simply because the vast majority cooperate in obeying the law, or because they agree on the underlying principles to which the law gives expression. Rather, a stable democracy has three principal characteristics: citizens take their individual identities to be partly defined by the collective identity of their political community; they presume that at least some of their "meaning-giving" commitments are rightly shaped by shared values; and they are willing to endure at least some serious sacrifices to preserve their society.

To be sure, the "horizontal comradeship" that Anderson describes can be a morally vexing phenomenon. First, the values around which such comradeship coheres are sometimes profoundly antithetical to dealing justly with those outside the bounds of its fraternity. This can lead to xenophobia, hostility, and even grave inhumanity toward those conceived of as outsiders. The horrible spectacle of migrant families separated at the U.S.–Mexico border in 2018 was an especially egregious example of the narrowness to which a nation's horizontal fraternity can be subject. But second, as Anderson observes, political solidarity may serve to mask, or even effectively deny, the existence of internal injustice and oppression. Throughout recent history, liberal democracies have seemed especially unstable when they prove unable to provide deliberative space for reconstituting the collective identities around which they cohere, in order to render those identities more internally inclusive in the cultural realm and more internally humane in the material realm.

Some contemporary liberal democratic theorists have argued for something akin to what former UK prime minister David Cameron once called a "muscular liberalism" that would simply foreclose the possibility of certain kinds of multiculturalism.[12] But the first step in any project of achieving internal "fraternal openness," as Pope Francis argues in the encyclical *Fratelli Tutti* (2020), is for citizens of contemporary liberal democracies to learn how to noncoercively reconstitute their collective identities in ways that remain "open" and "flexible" enough to accommodate cultural and doctrinal complexity.[13] Such an open identity is possible only if the activity of constituting a democratic people is recognized as an ongoing political project, and if we can accept that genuinely democratic politics is thus always "identity politics."[14] This may also help to explain why so many societies have now become what many call "social movement societies."

Of course, some theorists will continue to object to this linking of identity, solidarity, and stability. In *Political Liberalism*, John Rawls rejects the idea that nations might be "imagined communities" by denying that doctrinally diverse, modern liberal democracies could be genuine communities at all. True political communities, in his view, must be shaped by consensus on "comprehensive conceptions," and he contends that liberal democracies cannot achieve such a consensus without coercion.[15] For Rawls, the problem of democratic stability is ultimately an extension of the problem of *democratic political legitimacy*: the challenge of finding rationally defensible principles that can justify the exercise of political power in a society composed of free and equal citizens. Rawls presumes that if we can articulate a *political conception* of justice, composed of principles that could be affirmed by all "reasonable" comprehensive conceptions held by a given society's members, we can reasonably hope for that society to achieve "overlapping consensus" on those principles. We can then be cautiously optimistic that, over time, the society regulated by the principles will generate its own support. Rawlsian democratic stability thus depends on the emergence of overlapping *rational* consensus on a "political" conception of justice.

But even some of Rawls's sympathetic critics have viewed his optimism as unwarranted. For instance, Samuel Scheffler suggests that it is unrealistic to expect ordinary citizens to be ready to review complex philosophical theories about the difference between "comprehensive moral conceptions" and "purely political conceptions," and to engage in sustained reflection on what it means for justifications to appeal to one kind of conception rather than the other.[16] Yet the difficulty with Rawls's account goes deeper than the theoretical complexity of its presuppositions. The problem is that Rawls still accepts the "standard view" of the challenge to be addressed—that is, he understands stability in terms of people's readiness to see themselves as having an obligation to obey the law. But the really important question is why they are willing to obey the law, despite the fact that obedience demands *persistent sacrifice* in so many ordinary aspects of daily life. To be sure, Rawls always recognized that securing democratic stability was never just a matter of imposing "order," but that it was ultimately a matter of shaping political institutions that can generate their own support. Moreover, in *A Theory of Justice*, Rawls famously coined the phrase "strains of commitment" to characterize the demands of democratic cooperation even in a well-ordered democracy.[17] Still further, he acknowledged in *Political Liberalism* that democratic social cooperation sometimes constrains our ability to promote our deepest meaning-giving commitments. But these observations do not fully address the fact that, for all the advantages that democratic cooperation provides, as citizens of contemporary liberal democracies we are actually required to sacrifice a great deal, and *on a regular basis*, to preserve the communities that ground those advantages.

We know from the American presidential election in 2020, for instance, just how dangerous it can be when any significant number of citizens refuse to accept that their candidate has lost out in a momentous election. We also know how much social upheaval can result if a significant number of citizens react not just with peaceful dissent but with visceral anger and despair when imperfect legal institutions and processes consistently fail to hold law-enforcement officials accountable for abuses of power. The stability of a complex modern democracy is deeply dependent on citizens' willingness to accept their political losses with grace and with good will toward their political opposition and to treat the deficiencies of their legal institutions as occasions to seek reform rather than destruction. This way of framing the problem of democratic stability informs Charles Taylor's assertion that a central element of the "social imaginary" of a stable democracy is a particular kind of *political identity*: one that includes the idea of membership in "an ongoing collective agency" through which each member realizes freedom, whether or not any particular exercise of democratic sovereignty produces an outcome with which every member agrees.[18]

Taylor articulates the conceptual framework underlying this claim in his *Modern Social Imaginaries*. He argues there that a social imaginary is neither "an intellectual scheme" nor a theory, but a complex combination of the principal ways in which a given people "imagine social existence, how they fit together with others, how things go on between themselves and their fellows, the expectations that are normally met, and the deeper normative notions and images that underlie their expectations." A social imaginary is the "common understanding" that makes possible a society's "common practices and a widely shared sense of legitimacy"; and this understanding is an *imaginary* because it is mainly "carried in images, stories and legends."[19] It is that collection of "images, stories and legends" through which the members of a given a society sustain their sense of the collective practices that make up, and ought to make up, their social world. A social imaginary "is both factual and normative" involving a sense "of how things usually go . . . interwoven with an idea of how they ought to go." Though Taylor does not develop the possible connections between his account of the democratic social imaginary and the focus on sacrifice so central to Anderson's view, there is a strong case for the idea that the willingness to sacrifice and the willingness to suppress political resentments when our "side" loses are part of a larger set of civic virtues that make up the civic ethos of a stable democracy. On this view, which I have developed elsewhere, a fully worked out alternative to the Rawlsian view of stability would involve more fully fleshing out the central elements of this civic ethos.[20]

Despite their different emphases, however, there are important, constructive common elements in the views of Anderson and Taylor. Both thinkers convincingly argue that we can understand the nature and sources of democratic stability in any given democracy only by understanding (1) how citizens conceive of their "horizontal" relationships to other citizens, (2) how they see and understand themselves in relation to their community's collective identity, and (3) to what extent they feel solidarity with at least some of the values that shape that identity. Still further, if Taylor and Anderson are right—as I think they are—we cannot understand how to constructively reshape a collective identity to better realize demands of justice in a given society unless we first understand these critical elements of the relevant social imaginary. The success of any social movement in making space for social justice will thus be a function of its capacity to analyze and identify the content of a *particular* social imaginary and then to find ways to revise, reform, and sometimes reconstitute those elements of that imaginary that stand in the way of social change.

4.2 APPRECIATING THE HETEROGENEITY OF IMAGINATION

This approach rests on what I call the "high confidence" view of the power of imagination. The high confidence view presupposes what many consider to be an obvious truth: through the exercise of imagination, human beings can generate ideas, images, stories, and experiences that present constructively unfamiliar possibilities and perspectives and stimulate novel reflection on what is actual and familiar. But the high confidence view makes the further claim that the products of imagination can promote human advancement in almost any area of human concern. This view shapes the work of epistemologists and philosophers of mind who contend that imagination can directly aid in the acquisition of empirical knowledge and in the development of our problem-solving abilities.[21] The high confidence view also informs the claims of moral theorists who urge that reliance on—and appeals to—imagination in the context of moral judgment can deepen moral understanding, strengthen constructive affect, and engage the will.[22] Influential experts in large-scale conflict resolution accept the high confidence view on the basis of empirical evidence, for instance, that societies can sometimes transcend historical patterns of conflict and violence if their members can learn to imagine themselves in constructive "webs of relationships" that include those they once took to be their enemies.[23] Of course, imaginative activities and processes are being used in many different ways, and combinations, in these varied contexts. Succeeding chapters will show how these varied uses can further collective efforts to make space for justice in three important endeavors: (1) creating consensus on the claim that a particular injustice needs redress, (2) motivating readiness to act on that consensus, and (3) sustaining confidence in the value of acting despite delays, disappointments, and uncertainty.

Proponents of the high confidence view thus acknowledge, as Leslie Stevenson expresses it, that imagination is an "extremely flexible notion." Stevenson's own analysis, examining standard dictionary definitions and influential uses of the concept in philosophy and literature, finds twelve different conceptions of imagination at work. Some of these conceptions even seem to be in fundamental tension with one another. Consider, for example, these three conceptions: (1) "the ability to think of something not presently perceived, but spatiotemporally real"; (2) "the ability to think of something that the subject believes to be real, but which is not"; and (3) "the ability to think of things that one conceives of as fictional."[24] Whatever Stevenson thinks we ought to make of the differences and connections between these conceptions, he does not conclude that recognizing the heterogeneity of the standard senses of the word "imagination" requires us to adopt a deflationary stance and to give up talking about imagination altogether. In this, he echoes several other philosophers who acknowledge heterogeneity but continue to rely on particular conceptions of imagination to do important theoretical and practical work. P. F. Strawson famously defends this approach in the conclusion to his essay "Imagination and Perception": "I am not sure that either the question, what we *really* do *mean* by the word ["imagination"], or the question, what we *ought* to mean by it, are quite the right ones to ask in this particular case. What matters is that we should have a just sense of the . . . various and subtle connections, continuities, and affinities, as well as differences, which exist in this area."[25]

There is, however, one remaining worry about the heterogeneity of imagination that any defense of the high confidence view must address—especially in relation to the work of social movements. Amy Kind has shown that the varied mental processes and activities that get characterized as imagining are *remarkably* heterogeneous—so much so that some features of imagination that plausibly play an explanatory role in one context must be entirely excluded from plausible explanations in other contexts.[26] For instance, the activities and processes that help to explain our capacity for certain kinds of hypothetical reasoning—such as the capacity to suppose that there is a round square—seem profoundly different from activities and processes that explain a reader's capacity to imaginatively engage with a work of fiction, or an impressionist's capacity to pretend to be someone else. In the latter cases, we do not seem to need or make any kind of hypothetical "supposition": the impressionist simply tries to "be" and to act like someone else, while the reader is drawn into another way of being and acting by a narrative. If social movements required a single homogeneous mental activity to produce the transformations that make space for justice, the inescapable heterogeneity of imaginative capacities would mean that their projects simply could not get off the ground.

Yet the heterogeneity of imaginative activities and processes cannot undermine the projects of social movements because those projects actually *presuppose* that heterogeneity. First, in the context of social movements, the word "imagination" is understood to be shorthand for a decidedly heterogeneous set of processes and activities that generate ideas, images, stories, and experiences that allow us to consider "the unfamiliar" and to reflect in novel ways on "the familiar." Four main kinds of imagination shape the work of social movements: epistemic, sympathetic, narrative, and aesthetic. Each of these four kinds—or uses—of imagination draws on a complex array of cognitive, affective, and even volitional capacities that can be quite heterogeneous. Second, the most socially progressive phenomena that imagination produces are often the result of complex collaborations involving many different people, over greatly extended periods of time. When a new concept, such as sexual harassment, emerges as a product of epistemic imagination, it draws on the thought, feeling, and experience of sometimes incalculably large groups who have tried to solve the problem of increasing the epistemic adequacy of the language we use to describe the world. More generally, the notion that imagination might *essentially* be a matter of the workings of a single mental activity in an individual mind fails to accommodate the possibility of collective imagination. But third, the imaginative phenomena that "explain" progress toward justice are not mental activities and processes at all, but the phenomena that such activities and processes (individually or collectively) produce. When it is reasonable to attribute social change to "the workings of imagination," what serves as the *explanans* is the products of imagination, not the mental activities and processes that produce them.

Four kinds of imaginative products (generated by different types of imaginative activity) most often figure in plausible explanations of the way in which imagination helps to promote justice: First, *epistemic* imagination is sometimes essential to the production of epistemically adequate concepts—concepts such as sexual harassment, expressive harm, or genocide—that best capture the facts of injustice that are in need of remedy. Second, *sympathetic* imagination can often produce or deepen "humane insight" into the suffering and pain of others. Third, we sometimes make space for justice by appealing to hopeful visions of social life (and sometimes even cautionary tales of dystopia) produced by the *narrative* imagination of novelists, poets, and philosophers. Fourth, constructive social change is sometimes made possible when the *aesthetic* imagination of creative artists produces art and architecture that help to alter a society's "political aesthetics" in a morally expansive way. In short, it is not the heterogeneous activities of epistemic, sympathetic, narrative, or aesthetic imagination that explain (because they help to cause) the possibility of progress toward justice, but the extraordinarily varied products they help us to produce.

4.3 SHARPENING OUR FOCUS
ON THE FACTS

Social movements, I have argued, already embrace the hetero-geneity of imagination and its products. Some critics may still object that encouraging reliance on the products of imagination is a way of denying the importance of the "brute" empirical facts of injustice. Indeed, for some thinkers, the greatest obstacle to social progress is not failure to harness the constructive power of imagination but, instead, tenacious resistance to compelling articulations of the facts of injustice by those with the power to remedy injustice. According to Steven Pinker, we already rely too heavily on imagination: "too many leaders and influencers . . . surrender to the cognitive bias of assessing the world through anecdotes and images rather than data and facts."[27]

I contend, however, that far from constituting "cognitive bias," appeals to the products of imagination are sometimes the only means of countering biases—cognitive and otherwise—that encourage resistance to the facts that constitute remediable injustice. This claim echoes the insight in Mark Twain's observation that "you can't depend on your eyes when your imagination is out of focus."[28] Of course, the resistance that makes it necessary to engage in imaginative "refocusing" has many complex sources. But four sources have proven especially challenging for the constructive projects of social movements: (a) the epistemic inadequacy of many culturally dominant concepts; (b) persistent perceptual biases that distort affect, restrict sympathy, and limit understanding; (c) persistent cognitive biases that incline us to political inertia and sometimes make us fearful and mistrustful of those who challenge that inertia; and (d) the willingness of some influential speakers to manipulate others by offering lies and willful delusions as "alternative facts." But there are clearly identifiable processes and methods by which imagination can address these sources of resistance.

We can start by considering cases in which the epistemic inadequacy of some concept or concepts serves as a powerful obstacle to constructive change. This usually happens when a culturally dominant concept works to disguise, distort, or deny facts that more careful conceptual framing could show call for remedy or redress. Dissenting voices may sometimes challenge the concept's dominance and heighten awareness that it limits understanding. But a robust challenge to an inadequate concept must not simply articulate the concept's limits, it must draw on the resources of imagination to reframe relevant facts in more epistemically defensible, and more morally illuminating, ways. Sometimes that reframing may even demand articulating an entirely new concept. An instructive example is the concept of sexual harassment that first emerged in 1974, during a collective act of brainstorming in a consciousness-raising session at Cornell. That session was part of a broader effort to reject the traditional framing of unwanted sexual advances at work as the unavoidable cost to women of entering allegedly "male realms" of paid employment.[29] Before the existence of the concept of sexual harassment, even targets of unwanted advances struggled for a concise means of expressing the way in which the conduct can undermine equality, violate autonomy, and endanger personal security. With its gradual adoption by the press, the courts, and the broader culture, the concept of sexual harassment gradually helped to transform the social meaning of unwanted sexual advances in employment—and in social life more generally.

The concept of sexual harassment did not simply challenge us to think differently about unwanted advances, but also to reflect more broadly on the connections between gender and social roles, on the moral and legal status of women, on the nature of unwanted sexual objectification, and even on the value of women's testimony regarding their *experience* of such objectification. This last point is critical. Miranda Fricker's work on epistemic injustice reminds us that accepting the legitimacy of a concept like sexual harassment involves taking women's testimony seriously.[30] On my account, imagination played a central role in the process of "conceptual engineering" that made this happen, In fact, framing the concept of sexual harassment ultimately drew on two quite different kinds of imagination. It appealed to the heterogeneous cognitive processes that comprise *epistemic imagination* to find a description that could properly acknowledge the harm done by unwanted advances. But eventually it also engaged the *sympathetic imagination* to help reveal what is wrong about being subjected to such harm.

As a second common source of resistance to the brute facts of injustice, consider that we frequently perceive the world in ways that presuppose poorly substantiated, unreflective, and even harmful habits of belief and expectation. Such habits are most often products of the various biases people may hold regarding race, ethnicity, gender, sexual orientation, class, and disability status. Left unchecked, the resultant beliefs and normative expectations may severely constrict perceptual space, limiting what we can perceive as salient, and often masking the implications, or even the very existence, of facts that, with clearer perception, could be recognized as situations meriting redress. For instance, when racial and ethnic minorities are perceived as essentially threatening, or as dangerous invaders, or as agents of infestation, it becomes easy to deny that subjecting them to certain kinds of coercion or excessive force could constitute injustice. But, as I argued earlier, we can combat the restriction of perceptual space if—along with art critic John Berger—we acknowledge that seeing is rarely a matter of "mechanically react-ing to stimuli."[31] Perhaps especially when we consider the jus-tice or injustice of social, political and economic arrangements, what we see depends on what we take to be important and what we have learned to presume true of the things we look for.[32] Armed with this knowledge, we can turn to imagination to chal-lenge beliefs, inclinations, and presumptions that function as unacceptable constraints on perceptual awareness. John Dewey and W. E. B. Du Bois have shown that art is an especially effec-tive means of mounting these challenges.[33]

It is no simple matter to dislodge perceptual biases involv-ing deep-rooted racial and ethnic stigmatization and to produce or deepen the humane insight that, as we saw in chapter 3, is essential to the realization of social justice. Part of the chal-lenge is that such biases do not simply limit cognition of rele-vant facts; they also interfere with the capacity to appreciate the humanity of stigmatized others and constrain our ability to sympathetically imagine that certain ways of treating them could constitute the sort of harm that merits concern and redress. Addressing the damage done by such bias requires extensive imaginative efforts involving a broad range of essentially collab-orative imaginative projects carried out over extended peri-ods of time. In these contexts, socially transformative projects must have a particular focus on affirming the humanity of the stigmatized other and encouraging sympathetic concern for important details of their experience. As we might expect, art has often played a pivotal role in these efforts, from Harriet Beecher Stowe's antislavery novel *Uncle Tom's Cabin* to Picasso's antiwar painting *Guernica* and Billie Holiday's powerful protest of lynching in the song *Strange Fruit*.[34] It is especially important for the members of marginalized and stigmatized communities to produce visual art, literature, music, and dance that gives

voice to their own understanding and experience of the humanity that the larger culture has tried to deny.

The third important source of resistance to facts of injustice
is the persistent cognitive biases, such as confirmation bias and
politically motivated reasoning, that incline us to political inertia and tend to make us fearful and mistrustful of anyone who
somehow challenges that inertia (whether directly or indirectly).
These biases can be especially challenging when the tendency to
political inertia is reinforced by a potent "status quo bias" that
encourages resistance to changes involving significant loss, or by
adaptive preferences that can make those with little to lose from
social change unexpectedly (and quite irrationally) hostile to that
change. These phenomena have played a distressing role in the
twenty-first-century resurgence of the racism and xenophobic
populism that have damaged many contemporary liberal democracies. Still further, when influential voices not only deny relevant facts but also seek to undermine trust in those who claim
authority to articulate them, simply restating the facts will not
yield a compelling case for social change. This is why, for example,
many climate change activists have turned to the literary genre
known as "cli-fi"—science fiction addressing the nature, sources,
and implications of climate change—to help create motivational space for constructive responses to climate change.[35] Creating that space involves convincingly portraying the scope and
urgency of the problem, the value of human intervention, and
the importance of mobilizing the political will to intervene.

The fourth, and final, source of resistance to facts where
imagination might be a critical antidote is the epistemic stance
that sometimes develops in response to the deliberate presentation, by socially influential speakers, of lies and willful delusions as "alternative facts." People who come to believe such lies
and delusions can become especially resistant to new ideas if

their acceptance of relevant beliefs is partly a function of epistemically unreliable standards of assessment. They may be driven
to accept and retain false beliefs because of cognitive biases such
as confirmation bias and politically motivated reasoning, and
their refusal to scrutinize those beliefs may reflect a dogged
determination to protect themselves from cognitive disso-
nance. Their epistemic stance will be especially intractable if is
also shaped by racial or class-based affinities and antipathies.

Yet we must hold on to the hope that responsible and transparent appeals to products of the imagination can reach *some*
recalcitrant believers who have been manipulated by—and failed
to question—skillful lies and willful delusions. The first step is
to provide relevant subjects with socially and politically "low-
stakes" opportunities to entertain considerations that they have
come to believe untrue or impossible. Low-stakes opportunities might involve reading engaging works of fiction, viewing
compelling films, or encountering striking visual imagery in
painting or sculpture that present them with ideas, images, and
stories to challenge the untruths they have come to believe.
Such imaginative engagement may prompt recalcitrant believers to seriously entertain possibilities they have come to discount, such as the idea that most people who are poor may not
deserve their lot in life, or that people who don't look or sound
like them are still deserving of humane regard. It may then be
possible, as a second step, to engage them in "higher-stakes"
projects like "difficult conversations" in which disputing parties
learn to respect each other as human beings, rather than merely
as dangerous opponents to be devalued and defeated.[36] As a
third step, we might eventually be able to involve recalcitrant
believers in the "deliberative citizen assemblies" on which
some theorists of deliberative democracy rely to reinvigorate
divided democracies for the longer term.[37] But any involvement

of "experts" in these assemblies must be accompanied by the acknowledgment that even experts can sometimes be wrong, and that ordinary citizens are often the source of local knowledge that experts lack. Recalcitrant believers are more likely to respect others when they feel respected themselves.

4.4 TAKING SYMBOLIC EXPRESSION SERIOUSLY

But while imagination sometimes advances the cause of constructive social movements by helping to sharpen our focus on the facts of injustice, imagination has sometimes been used to disguise or deny injustice, or even to provide spurious legitimacy to institutions and practices that actually preserve injustice. This is another critical insight of the global iconoclasm that emerged with such vehemence during the summer of 2020. This chapter will conclude (in section 4.5) by discussing a fact that the campaign to topple monuments sometimes overlooks: that the civic art of remembrance sometimes renders the past in ways that constructively shape the present. But any account of how imagination constitutes political communities must acknowledge that it sometimes does so by symbolically sustaining narratives that legitimize oppressive regimes by suppressing, and even by denying, some people's agency, dignity, and even their very humanity. This is the distressing truth that connects the aesthetic activism of the "Rhodes Must Fall" and Black Lives Matter protests to French revolutionaries' rejection of the art of the ancien régime, the destruction of Nazi art and architecture following the fall of the Third Reich, and the removal of Communist era monuments following the Eastern European revolutions of 1989 and the fall of the Soviet Union in 1991.

Confederate monuments and memorials provide especially instructive examples of the ways in which the civic art of remembrance can be used to support oppressive and dehumanizing narratives. Indeed, as historian David Blight observes in *Race and Reunion: The Civil War in National Memory*, the cult of the "Lost Cause" of the Confederacy has left an "enduring burden" in America's national memory.[38] That burden is a function, in part, of the cult's mythologizing narrative that from 1866 to 1915 unfolded to falsify Civil War history, deny the evils of slavery, and defend the oppressive and violent excesses of white supremacy as critical to postwar "reconciliation."[39] As then New Orleans mayor Mitch Landrieu wrote in defending the New Orleans City Council's decision to take down the last of the city's confederate monuments, the statues could not plausibly be understood as "innocent remembrance of a benign history." Rather, they were symbols of the Confederacy's efforts to "deny the humanity" of African Americans and of the death, enslavement, and terror the Confederacy sought to preserve. Landrieu compellingly argues that because the statues were "erected purposefully" to "send a strong message about who was still in charge in the post–Civil War South, they were as much a part of the terrorism for which the confederacy stood as burning a cross on someone's lawn."[40]

But the burden of the Lost Cause narrative is rooted in a second important fact: for a large portion of the twentieth century, monuments, memorials, and other symbols informed by the narrative became inextricably bound up with institutions, practices, and actions intended not only to stigmatize and demean African Americans, but also to intimidate anyone attempting to challenge the social, political, and economic implications of white supremacy. This claim is supported by extensive research conducted by the Southern Poverty Law Center in an effort to understand the nature and origins of the thousands of symbols of the Confederacy in thirty-one states and the District of Columbia. That research shows that two distinct historical periods produced the vast majority of Confederate monuments, memorials, and symbols. The first period lasted from about 1900 to 1924 as an accompaniment to Jim Crow segregation and the southern disenfranchisement of African Americans; the second period began in the early 1950s and lasted through the mid-1960s, as a segregationist backlash against the Civil Rights Movement.[41]

Some commentators contest this entanglement between the Lost Cause narrative and Confederate monuments and symbols. But if these objects and symbols are genuinely and intrinsically benign, why have they so predictably served as focal points for the violent expression of racial hatred? Just three months after Landrieu's' speech in defense of his city's removal of its last Confederate statues, an August 2017 gathering of white supremacists and neo-Nazis erupted in hate-filled violence in response to a decision by the City Council of Charlottesville, Virginia, to take down their city's statue of Robert E. Lee. Indeed, that episode was a terrifying echo of the 2015 murder of nine black churchgoers in Charleston, South Carolina, which led the then governor of South Carolina, Nikki Haley, to confirm the racist symbolism of the Confederate flag.

Three important lessons can be gleaned from these terrifying events in Charleston and Charlottesville. The first is that if we hope to understand the expressive content of some symbol, social institution, or practice, we must begin by placing it in the context of what I call the "total expressive situation." This claim adapts an idea from J. L. Austin, who insisted that we can fully understand what a *linguistic utterance* might "do" only when we consider the "the total speech act"—by which he meant "the total situation in which the utterance is issued." The concept of the "total expressive situation" makes an analogous point about various symbolic and cultural phenomena and processes. Moreover, the total expressive situation of Confederate monuments and symbols is not exhausted by the Lost Cause narrative. It also includes all the contemporary evidence that many contemporary agents continue to view those monuments and symbols as symbolic expressions of white supremacy.

Of course, the significance of the art and artifacts of public commemoration is always a matter for interpretation. Moreover, as Marcel Duchamp once claimed, "the creative act is not performed by the artist alone," since in the process of interpretation, the spectator "adds his contribution to the creative act." Duchamp's claim has special relevance to projects of remembrance in democracies, where commemorative projects are usually commissioned by committees whose members disagree about the projects' goals, and created for communities of spectators who may disagree about whether the finished product meets those goals. The democratic art of remembrance is always entangled in the political controversies that proceed it, and in the interpretive controversies to which it gives rise. But in the case of Confederate monuments and symbols, the overwhelming weight of interpretations clearly and forcefully reiterates the legacy of post–Civil War Black Codes (of 1865–1866), which legally excluded black people from many of the activities of basic citizenship, but especially the post-Reconstruction legacy of Jim Crow segregation and the white supremacist violence meant to enforce its dictates. Taken together, this legacy and the intentions and actions that draw on it render Confederate monuments and symbols "conventional expressions" of white supremacist ideology in Austin's sense of "conventional."

The second lesson to emerge from reflecting on events in Charlottesville and Charleston is that the expressive harm constituted by the legacy of the Confederacy is a function of that legacy's (ongoing) connections to the expressive content of systematic discrimination and exclusion. Drawing on Landrieu's analysis, I urge that this expressive content is best understood as a matter of stigmatizing and intimidating the targets of discrimination. It is certainly true that physical violence (in a variety of forms) is often a critical element of the material reality of systems of discrimination. But the focus here is on what we can call the *expressive* harm that can be constituted by the social meanings associated with systematic practices of discrimination and exclusion, and with the ways in which imagination has helped to constitute the social meanings through the civic art of remembrance that seeks to commemorate the Lost Cause of the Confederacy.

Finally, contemplating the events at Charlottesville and Charleston yields a third critical insight: the harmful expressive content of systematic discrimination can have a life that extends well beyond the demise of any formal legal structures that may have actively licensed discrimination. In this way, that expressive content can continue to constitute what legal scholars Robin Lenhardt and Bennett Capers have described as "citizenship harm," in which the state treats any individual members of significant social groups as inferior, or as though they were nonparticipants in the collective life of the community.[42] When federal, state, or local governments continue to display Confederate monuments and symbols in places of public honor, they are preserving them in ways that "perform" citizenship harm—in a manner analogous to "performative utterances" of citizenship harm—or at least echo the citizenship harm that is done by discrimination itself. Unsympathetic critics sometimes complain that objections to Confederate monuments simply reflect the preoccupations of an overly sensitive contemporary culture that encourages people to react to expression that (simply) offends them with all the resilience of "snowflakes." But protesters who challenge the public display of the monuments in places of public honor are challenging us to acknowledge that they are informed by, and expressively inseparable from, a stigmatizing and demeaning narrative. As Chimamanda Ngozi Adichie has urged, stories matter when they are used to empower and humanize their subjects, but also when they are used "to dispossess and to malign" and to "try to break the dignity of a people."[43]

To be sure, we cannot remedy the material realities of social injustice simply by transforming, removing, or destroying a statue—or any other physical structure. But no social movement challenges a society's *symbolic* commitments to injustice because they believe that doing so will immediately and directly result in a more just world. Indeed, despite its somewhat misleading name, even the "Rhodes Must Fall" Movement was never interested in simply removing a statue. In fact, the resistance to the continuing presence of Rhodes's statue was always part of an attempt to protest lingering effects of colonialism and white supremacy in South Africa's higher education system.

Still further, it is sometimes possible to transform the expressive meaning of some artifact, symbol, act, institution, or practice. Indeed, as Duchamp might have insisted, what spectators add to a particular artifact by virtue of their reinterpretations may over time prove quite different from, or even entirely antithetical to, the values and social meanings intended by its initial creators. This is how Nelson Mandela's election to the South African presidency allowed for the transformation of Robben Island prison into part of a national museum (and a World Heritage site) that many South Africans view as a symbol of "the triumph of the human spirit over adversity." But there are good reasons to doubt that Confederate monuments and symbols can be transformed in this way until their true expressive content is openly acknowledged and scrutinized and public veneration of the statues is rejected. It would require a massive denial of historical fact, or a highly improbable evolution in the social meaning of Confederate monuments and symbols, to recast those monuments and symbols as something other than expressions of white supremacy. If and when the statues that have been removed are relocated to museums, it will be important to preserve the truth about their meaning as part of the exhibits.

Some critics may object that removing and relocating even morally irredeemable monuments might encourage us to forget—or sometimes to deny—parts of our history that we have epistemic and moral obligations to remember. But there is an important distinction between remembering something and commemorating it. To commemorate is to remember either as a way of paying respect and according honor to some person or some achievement, or as a means of giving appropriately solemn attention to great suffering and loss. Simple remembrance, in contrast, can be achieved by documentation alone. For instance, the Nazi Documentation Center in Munich, dedicated in 2015, preserves the memory of Munich's role in the rise of Nazism without celebrating it, and without honoring those who designed and participated in it. Still further, in a different kind of project, Budapest's "Memento Park," created in 1992, is an effort to preserve several monuments and statues from the Communist era in Hungary without celebrating that era's totalitarian, antidemocratic values. Regrettably, the American approach to Confederate monuments and symbols has unfolded in a haphazard fashion that has discouraged analogous efforts at systematic management. Because of continual intimidation and threats of violence in some communities, removals sometimes occurred in the dark of night, often with little advance reflection about where to house the displaced monuments and how to display them. In other contexts, as in summer 2020, some removals—and occasionally outright destruction—occurred with little advance reflection on whether the statues and structures being targeted were appropriate objects of disapproval.

4.5 RECLAIMING THE CONSTRUCTIVE POWER OF "COLLECTIVE IMAGININGS"

I have argued that protestors who object to Confederate monuments and symbols are justified in believing that America cannot achieve substantive racial justice until American social imagination is freed from the "dead hand" of the Confederacy. Yet during the 2020 protests some highly publicized attempts to *act* on that belief went dangerously awry. Some protestors seemed to assume that any nineteenth-century monument depicting Americans in uniform might be a Confederate monument. Others adopted an unreflective strategy of "remove-and-destroy-first" and attend to reasonable objections later. But many simply failed to consider that even when we cast off the Confederacy's dead hand, there will still be good reasons to create and preserve public projects of remembrance. They failed to see, that is, that monuments and memorials still matter. Aesthetic activism that refuses to acknowledge that monuments and memorials can sometimes have constructive value is a positive detriment to the cause of justice.

Three categories of constructive civic art are especially important: (1) projects that promote solidarity around an inclusive collective identity; (2) projects that seek to imaginatively reshape an exclusive identity; and (3) projects that encourage a respectful, nonexploitative horizontal comradeship by celebrating the "better angels of our nature." The Boston Memorial to Robert Shaw and the 54th Regiment is a remarkable example of the first category: civic art of remembrance that encourages inclusive solidarity. I will show that protestors who vandalized the memorial in June 2020 wrongly failed to recognize this.[44] The Emancipation Memorial in Washington, D.C., is a historically significant example of the second category, since it was an effort by former slaves—many of whom were Civil War veterans—to imaginatively reshape a collective identity that excluded them. The project was funded almost entirely by *their donations*, and, as such, it is a powerful expression of political self-assertion in the cultural domain. Yet, reviving familiar criticisms of the memorial's representation of the emancipated slave depicted in the tableau, some 2020 protesters sought to have the memorial taken down. I'll show that Frederick Douglass was right to argue that, given its origins, we should try to improve the memorial, not remove or destroy it.[45] Finally, I'll show that protesters in Madison, Wisconsin, wrongly destroyed a statue of a local man named Hans Christian Heg, who had been an active opponent of slavery and eventually became Wisconsin's highest-ranking Union Army officer killed in the Civil War. Some protestors (curiously) objected that the statue failed to acknowledge the struggles of Madison's contemporary Black residents. But I will argue that the statue was, in fact, a worthy effort to celebrate the "better angels of our nature," and that even the most morally serious civic art can be only a *catalyst* for action to address injustice, not a *substitute* for human endeavor.

My defense of these projects presumes the truth of John Dewey's view that art can sometimes break through "barriers that divide human beings," even when those barriers seem to be "impermeable in ordinary association."[46] Building on Dewey's understanding of the links between art and democracy, I hold

that public art—and in particular, civic art of remembrance—
can promote democracy by enriching perception and deepening
understanding in ways that discursive argument cannot. In the
spirit of Iris Young's political thought, as discussed at length in
chapters 2 and 3, it is also important to acknowledge the role that
civic art of remembrance can play in properly shaping the public sphere. As Young rightly argues, an *inclusive* democracy
will make room in the public sphere for modes of communication that do not privilege discursive argument. My contention is that the civic art of remembrance is sometimes a critical
addition to the democratic public sphere.

The concept "civic art of remembrance" must be understood
broadly. It includes material expressions of collective memory
such as monuments, memorials, commemorative museums,
battlefields, and certain civic landscapes. Yet it also includes
oratory, written rhetoric, and poetry, as well as instances of the
performing arts—especially music—that are meant to express
some dimension of a society's collective memory. Thus, while the
Lincoln Memorial on the Mall in Washington, D.C., is an
example of the civic art of remembrance, so is the concert by con-
tralto Marian Anderson that was held on the grounds of the
memorial in 1939. So too is Lincoln's Gettysburg Address, which
so brilliantly relies on metaphors of national rebirth to show that
the commemoration of sacrifice might at the same time be a
forward-looking call to imagine a more fully democratic future.

Civic art can play a constructive role in shaping the democratic
public sphere because it is sometimes able to communicate values such as equality, respect for human dignity, and concern for
human vulnerability, even when it is difficult to produce a discursive argument that convinces people that these values matter. In fact, civic art can sometimes do what discursive argument *cannot*, because it can help to expand perceptual space in

ways that enhance the capacity for recognizing commonality—
and even "deep" comradeship—with those initially construed as
outsiders. Nowhere is such an expansion of perceptual space
more evident than in Augustus Saint-Gaudens's Memorial to
Robert Gould Shaw and the 54th Regiment. The memorial's
capacity to expand perceptual space is mainly a function of the
many ways in which Saint-Gaudens resisted aesthetic and cultural conventions of the time. Consider, first, the singularity of
its subject matter. The memorial commemorates the July 1863
battle of Fort Wagner, South Carolina, in which the Union Army
suffered a crushing defeat. The battle was deemed worthy of
commemoration, despite the defeat, because the Black soldiers
of the 54th Regiment who fought at Fort Wagner were among
the first of nearly 180,00 African Americans to volunteer for service in the Union Army. The regiment set an example that many
believe helped turn the tide in favor of the Union's cause. Their
story is vividly told in the movie *Glory* (1989).

Yet it is equally important that Saint-Gaudens placed the figure of Colonel Shaw in the midst of the figures of the regiment's
soldiers, rather than depicting him riding in front of the soldiers
or even riding alone, as more conventional Civil War memorials
might have done. As art historian Kirk Savage notes, that decision produced a distinctive synthesis of the "great officer monument" and the "common soldier monument" that is one of only
three nineteenth-century monuments to depict Black soldiers in
military service.[47] It is also the only one to depict Black soldiers
in military uniforms. These facts help us appreciate the force of
William James's observation, in his oration at the memorial's
dedication, that in depicting courageous Black soldiers fighting
beside courageous white soldiers, the monument was a "noble
work of bronze" that captured the "true meaning" of the Civil
War.[48]

Still further, the care with which Saint-Gaudens sculpted the faces and physiques of the regiment's Black soldiers was clearly distinctive for its time. Contemplating the dignity and determination on the faces of these soldiers in the memorial is not so different from considering Diego Velasquez's painting of his Black assistant Juan de Pareja from 1650. In each case, the artist seems to have recognized the humanity of his subjects, in spite of the ways in which the conventions of the day sought to deny it. Regrettably, the artists themselves were sometimes the worst offenders when they were not creating art: de Pareja was Velasquez's slave, and Saint-Gaudens's notes are full of the racial epithets he used to describe the men he hired to pose for the figures of the Black soldiers.

The memorial suffered an extended period of neglect, most likely because it was dedicated a year after the Supreme Court decision in 1896 in *Plessy v. Ferguson*, which historian C. Vann Woodward correctly called America's "national decision against equality." Moreover, the memorial did not resist all the racist conventions of the nineteenth century. In particular, while the names of all the white officers who died at Fort Wagner were originally listed on the base of the monument, the Black soldiers who died were originally described as "the black rank and file." The committee that oversaw the memorial's restoration in 1980 decided to have the recoverable names of the Black soldiers inscribed on its base. Critics objected that this would unwisely obscure the truth about nineteenth-century race relations. But whatever the cost in historical accuracy, inscribing the names enhanced the memorial's capacity to depict commonality, and the possibility of deep comradeship, between the white political majority and the freed Black soldiers initially cast as outsiders. The restoration thus confirmed the truth of Marcel Duchamp's claim that "the creative act is not performed by the artist alone," since in the process of interpretation the spectator "adds his contribution to the creative act." It seems likely that what spectators added to the memorial helped it eventually become the first stop on Boston's Black Heritage Trail.

As we reflect on the fate of the Emancipation Memorial, erected in 1876 in Washington, D.C., it must be stressed that what spectators "add" to a commemorative project can sometimes result in the work's expressing collective imaginings, memories, and values that are profoundly different from what the original artist intended. For instance, the Lincoln Memorial was dedicated in 1922 as a symbolic expression of a reconciliation between North and South that accepted Jim Crow segregation. Yet many now consider it to be a powerful symbol of efforts to promote racial equality.[49] After the Daughters of the American Revolution denied Marian Anderson permission to sing in Constitution Hall in 1939, Anderson's concert at the Lincoln Memorial—drawing seventy-five thousand people and a large national audience for the radio broadcast—helped to begin the transformation. In another example discussed earlier in this chapter, Nelson Mandela's rise to the South African presidency in 1994 allowed for the transformation of Robben Island prison (where he had been confined for eighteen years) into part of a commemorative national museum now described as a symbol of the triumph of the human spirit over adversity. In each case, what later audiences added, through their interpretations, helped to transform exclusionary and racially divisive public art and architecture into projects of remembrance affirming racially inclusive, and more genuinely democratic, collective identities.

With such examples in mind, we must therefore allow that it is possible to constructively transform the Emancipation Memorial—even despite its demeaning depiction of a kneeling black man, naked from the waist up, being granted freedom by the towering figure of Abraham Lincoln. In a recently discovered letter to the editor of the *National Republican* newspaper, written shortly after the dedication of the memorial in 1876, Frederick Douglass helpfully acknowledged this possibility. He began by observing that the monument's demeaning image did not "tell the whole truth" about the African American freedom struggle. He then urged that there is room in the surrounding park for another monument that could depict African Americans in a dignified way: not "like a four-footed animal," but "on his feet like a man."[50]

In summer 2020 historian David Blight reiterated this idea in an op-ed article, imploring the monument's critics to "consider the people who created it and what it meant for their lives in a century not our own." Blight then proposed creating a commission to seek contemporary artists who might represent the freedom struggle in a fuller and more informative way. He reminded us that Douglass would be an important part of the story—not least because of his extraordinary oration at the memorial's dedication, in which he refused to overlook the morally murky character of Lincoln's attitudes toward African Americans. Of course, not every monument or memorial can be constructively transformed. But people who care about justice—and not self-righteous insistence on contemporary moral superiority—have a duty to try to transform the memorial. The failure to do so implicitly denies its status as a critical *artifact* of the African American freedom struggle.

In the letter in which he asserts that the Emancipation Memorial fails to tell the whole truth, Douglass also speculates that "perhaps no one monument could be made to tell the whole truth of any subject which it might be designed to illustrate."[51] This observation is particularly apt when we reflect on the fate of the Hans Christian Heg statue in Madison, Wisconsin, which protestors attacked on the (curious) grounds that the statue did not portray the reality of contemporary Black life. To put the challenge of understanding the real significance of the Heg statue in the proper perspective, we should remember that the Martin Luther King, Jr. Memorial in Washington, D.C., was opened to the public in 2011, nine years before the deaths of African Americans such as Breonna Taylor, George Floyd—and of so many others struck down in the ongoing wave of police violence and brutality. If we must judge the worth of monuments and memorials by the standards of the protestors who destroyed the Heg statue, not only should we tear down the current King Memorial, but we also shouldn't try to erect a new one until it has become impossible, or at least unlikely, for anti-Black police violence to happen again. I suspect that we would have to wait an exceptionally long time to complete the project. Equally important, civic projects such as the Heg statue and the King Memorial are much-needed symbolic expressions of the values to which a genuine democracy and its citizens ought to aspire. Such public projects of remembrance perform their proper "service" when they provoke reflection and discussion about how to realize those values in practice, and hopefully inspire human beings to act on those values in constructive ways.

Of course, the civic art of remembrance is sometimes created with the intent of fostering a civically restorative, or morally reparative, reorientation toward a nation's past. In this category, we might consider such projects as the Vietnam Veterans Memorial in Washington and the Berlin Memorial to the Murdered Jews of Europe. But even when we can rightly expect a monument or memorial to help expand what we can call "conceptual space" for moral deliberation, we must not it expect it to do our moral work for us. In a provocative and important discussion of the Vietnam Veterans' Memorial, Charles Griswold is deeply critical of the project for its failure to answer questions "as to whether the war was just in conception and execution; whether the warriors (and non-warriors) are absolved of moral *responsibility*; and whether an apology is due on several fronts." Yet it is not clear that the memorial—or any memorial—could have made any progress toward promoting national reconciliation if it had attempted to answer those questions. Still further, the memorial was a prerequisite for creating a public forum in which it might be possible to address the sort of questions that Griswold poses. It is true that Americans have (still) mostly deferred difficult and morally necessary debate about the Vietnam War. But even the most morally compelling instance of the civic art of remembrance can only be a catalyst for moral debate and action, not a replacement for it. As I argued in chapter 3, moral inquiry and argument are interpretive and dialogic practices. Even when an instance of civic art is a *successful* catalyst for moral discussion, it cannot conduct the actual moral scrutiny that might lead to constructive moral action.

At this point, one may wonder whether encouraging the production and preservation of civic art is an invitation to create and disseminate propaganda. But along with W. E. B. Du Bois and George Orwell, I believe that all art is propaganda—in the sense that all art seeks to shape the way we perceive and understand the world, and often to determine behavior as well.[52] It is certainly essential that we remain vigilant in distinguishing morally defensible from morally impermissible instances of propaganda. But even art with morally permissible or admirable aims is still propaganda, at least as (reasonably) defined by Garth Jowett and Victoria O'Donnell: the deliberate systematic attempt "to shape perceptions, manipulate cognitions, and direct behavior" in accordance with the creator's aims.[53] As I acknowledged at the outset, civic art can be morally reprehensible when

embedded in cultural narratives that falsify history; that stigmatize, marginalize, and intimidate minorities; or that promote
hatred and violence toward anyone construed as "other." We
must vigorously and consistently reject civic projects enmeshed
in such narratives, if we want to avoid the fascist aestheticization
of politics that Walter Benjamin famously condemned.[54]

Some critics may still object that all memorials are obsolete.
It may be argued, for instance, that they are fundamentally antidemocratic and thus unsuited to contemporary political life. Yet
when the civic art of remembrance helps to communicate democratic virtues, it can be a critical source of democratic solidarity and stability. Other critics may agree with Lewis Mumford
that monuments and memorials represent fixity and death,
instead of a commitment to the growth and renewal that drive
human progress.[55] But the civic art of remembrance can be a
means of constructively reshaping an exclusionary national
identity into a more inclusionary identity.[56] Moreover, when
informed by narratives that express humane regard for persons—
combining the acknowledgment of human suffering with the
affirmation of human dignity—the civic art of remembrance can
provide catalysts for reflection that supports moral accountability and promotes social hope. We have good reasons to deny
places of public honor to civic art that undermines our capacity
to imagine a better future—although we should often consider
relocating it rather than destroying it. Yet we have equally good
reasons to value democratically constructive civic art as a fundamental public good. We ought to encourage it in multiple forms,
support lively debate about its meaning and value, and take reasonable measures to ensure its thoughtful preservation.

5

LANGUAGE MATTERS

We die. That may be the meaning of life. But we do language.
That may be the measure of our lives.
—Toni Morrison

5.1 LANGUAGE ACTIVISM AS IMAGINATIVE REFRAMING

I argued in chapter 4 that, to create space for justice, social movements may need to engage in aesthetic activism, challenging art and artifacts that symbolically sustain narratives that objectify, stigmatize, and dehumanize some social groups. But such narratives can legitimize exclusion, oppression, and even violent repression only by virtue of the language they contain. Hence many social movements are critically concerned to challenge socially influential linguistic forms (words, phrases, sentences, prefixes, and suffixes) and sometimes the grammatical rules and norms that govern them.[1] This chapter thus explores what is often called "language activism." I focus on efforts to imaginatively reframe important domains of social reality by eliminating some of the social biases and epistemic deficiencies shaping dominant linguistic forms and their governing norms.

It must first be noted, all too briefly, that language activism may take two additional forms that will not be discussed in detail here. Some language activists attempt the "exorcism" of terms that have historically been used to denigrate, demean, and diminish members of marginalized minority groups.[2] These projects—sometimes called reclamation projects—start by assuming that even though certain labels can be used to wound the groups targeted by them, those groups can sometimes limit, or even eliminate, their power to wound by collectively using the problematic labels on their own terms. These efforts have had varying levels of success. They have been particularly unsuccessful in regard to labels that have been used to denigrate and demean certain ethnic and cultural groups.[3] Moreover, even though some forms of language activism can be carried out on behalf of an affected group, "reclamation projects" cannot. They can succeed only when carried out by members of the targeted group themselves, and only if the reclamation deprives the word of its derogatory force coming from *any* speaker (not just members of the group itself). Despite these limitations, however, some formerly derogatory terms have been deprived of their power to wound and have occasionally become useful for grounding constructive affirmations of the group's internal solidarity. Some words describing sexual orientation—perhaps especially "gay" and "queer"—seem to have been transformed in this way.[4]

Second, some social movements pursue "language justice" as an array of concerns regarding the preservation of linguistic diversity.[5] One set of concerns focuses on how to achieve language justice when multiple language groups exist within larger political communities. Should such communities accord equal recognition to all the languages within their borders? Should they provide special support for linguistic minorities? Is it unjust to adopt one official (or "first") language that everyone in the community will be expected to learn and use? A second set of concerns centers on the question of what constitutes a just response to the global phenomenon of endangered languages. This problem becomes increasingly urgent with time. By current estimates, a quarter of the world's approximately seven thousand languages have fewer than a thousand remaining speakers, and, going forward, about every three months one such language will die with its final speaker.[6]

Though neither the reclamation projects nor the language justice work is central to this chapter, both kinds of activism can be critical to realizing some of the aims of social justice. Nonetheless, this chapter focuses on language activism as part of the broader project of imaginatively reframing a particular social reality. The discussion will explore three historically significant examples in which language activism has exposed the failure of language to express and promote justice—understood, in keeping with the argument of this book, as humane regard for persons. The examples include two challenges to biases and inadequacies that have shaped linguistic forms and practices: the work of the women's movement to find terminology that concisely connects unwanted sexual advances with their unjust effects, and the efforts of the African American freedom struggle to reject the "discourses of exclusion" that supported Jim Crow segregation. The third example focuses on the human rights activism of international jurist Raphael Lemkin. I will discuss the circumstances that led to Lemkin's coining of the concept of *genocide*, not only exposing the failure of language to name a moral evil, but for the first time creating a category under which that moral evil could be recognized and responded to as a crime.

Social movements, and the moral visionaries who sometimes shape them, rarely have occasion to address fundamental background questions about precisely how language distorts or disguises the social reality they hope to change. This chapter will thus consider how philosophy can help to provide constructive answers to those questions. Moreover, since participants in social movements rarely have the opportunity for sustained reflection on the advantages and disadvantages of language activism, the chapter will conclude with a few relevant observations about the limitations of language activism as a vehicle for imaginative reframing of the social world. It is important to understand why those who seek to make space for justice must sometimes seek to reform socially dominant narratives and not just the concepts on which those narratives may rely.

5. 2 LANGUAGE AND THE CHANNELING OF "ATTENTION"

In the essay "Terministic Screens," literary theorist and philosopher Kenneth Burke makes a claim about language that has considerable force in many domains of human concern: "Even if a given terminology is a *reflection* of reality, by its very nature as a terminology it must be a *selection* of reality; and to this extent it must function also as a *deflection* of reality." Burke contends that because language can be used to reflect, select and deflect reality, any given nomenclature or terminology functions as a "terministic screen" or filter—directing our attention "into some channels rather than others." One consequence of the varied ways in which language "channels" attention, Burke continues, is that considering a choice between different terms for characterizing some object or phenomenon is like looking at different photographs of an object taken with different color-filters. The object does not change from one photograph to the next. But because the filters channel light in different ways, the photographs will reveal "notable distinctions in texture, and even in form."[7]

With this account, Burke offers the outlines of a compelling picture of how language works as "symbolic action" to shape observation. Burke is certainly not the only philosopher to argue that we can "do things" with language or that the language in which we do things shapes what we observe. But the metaphor of language as a filter directing attention in some directions rather than others invites us to consider the roles that imagination can play when we simply want to redirect attention, but especially when we seek to improve the terminology meant to characterize significant aspects of human experience. For instance, through the cognitive activities that constitute *epistemic* imagination we can reflect on the advantages and disadvantages of different "terministic filters" by comparing the experiences that might be enabled, and considering the possible social worlds that might result, when we adopt one term rather than another. Drawing on the workings of *sympathetic* imagination, we can try to focus attention on the problem of what it might be like to inhabit the social worlds that revisions of language might produce. Recognizing the importance of such projects and understanding, more broadly, how human beings "do language," as Toni Morrison puts it, has been central to the constructive work of many social movements.

The power of language to function as a filter is especially apparent when we are deciding how to characterize some *novel* phenomenon or development. For instance, social scientists and other observers agree that economic life is being fundamentally changed by developments in digital technology that have hastened automation, increased reliance on artificial intelligence, and enabled workers to do more of their work remotely. But there is ongoing disagreement about how to characterize resulting changes in relationships between workers, customers, and resources. As journalist Gordon Lichfield notes, a wide range of terms has been considered—including such phrases as "platform economy," "gig economy," "networked economy," "sharing economy," and "on-demand economy." But none of these terms accurately sums up all the relevant developments. Further, whatever term or terms become culturally dominant, those linguistic forms will have profound implications for how we understand the rights of workers and consumers, for instance, and how we structure regulatory mechanisms affecting the way companies collect, use, and store data.[8]

Yet it is not only in seeking to name a new development that we confront the filtering effects of language. Indeed, as Burke observes, the nature of our terms always affects the nature of our observations, "in the sense that the terms direct the attention to one field rather than another." For example, if we use the phrase "online instruction" to describe the project of conducting educational activities during a pandemic, we convey something quite different from what is conveyed by the phrase "remote learning." At the very least, the latter term directs attention away from the instructor as a critical shaping presence in the educational project. In a different sort of case, some critics disparage as mere "political correctness" concerns about the social and political effects of language used to characterize and categorize human beings in certain contexts. But terms like "differently abled" and "undocumented worker" direct attention to vastly different characteristics of persons than are foregrounded by terms such as "disabled" and "illegal alien." Moreover, those differences are not irrelevant to the role that each term might play in shaping the social world and affecting the experiences of those who inhabit it. The upshot of these consideration is that language matters, and that it matters a great deal to the work that progressive social movements do.

5.3 LINGUISTIC RELATIVISM, SOCIAL CONSTRUCTIONISM, AND THE "VOICE OF THE OPPRESSED"

Detailed consideration of specific linguistic inadequacies and their proposed remedies must be preceded by an important caveat: acknowledging the power of language to select, reflect, and deflect reality need not—and in Burke's case does not—involve *either* linguistic relativism, as a claim that people's perceptions are entirely dependent on their language, *or* "strong" social constructionism, as a claim that reality is "nothing but" a social construction determined by the language we use. Burke certainly held that much of what we take to be observations of reality "may be but the spinning out of possibilities implicit in our particular choice of terms."[9] Yet, contrary to many influential interpretations of his view, Burke never argues that there is no reality independent of language, or that we might somehow be permanently trapped in a "prison house" of language—which relativism and strong constructionism typically imply. His view, to reiterate its central point, is that language reflects, selects, and deflects *reality*. Moreover, the problem here is not just that we misinterpret Burke if we read him as either a linguistic relativist or a "strong" social constructionist.[10] The real danger is that such misinterpretations obscure a powerful implication of Burke's project: we can fully acknowledge the role of language in shaping observation without denying that we can perceive anything independent of language or holding that there is nothing independent of language to perceive.

We must not underestimate the extent to which the projects of constructive social movements are deeply inconsistent with the commitments of linguistic relativism and strong social constructionism. First, both of these positions threaten to collapse into the view that there can never really be important truths about human experience that language has not (yet) captured. Of course, human beings initially learn to express even their most fundamental beliefs and desires through terminology that is dominant in the cultures that help to form them. But it does not follow from this fact that there might not be something important about human experience that a particular set of practices fails to articulate, or even actively masks by the absence of appropriate terminology for it. In several influential arguments in *Contingency, Irony and Solidarity*, Richard Rorty insists otherwise. There is "no prelinguistic consciousness to which language needs to be adequate," he argues, and there is nothing "deep within human beings" that might be distorted or damaged in the process of certain kinds of socialization. The human subject, he claims, "is simply whatever acculturation makes of it."[11] Indeed, for Rorty, persons are "centerless networks of beliefs and desires whose vocabularies are determined by historical circumstance."[12]

Rorty usually insists that these claims simply express commitment to a familiar, "non-reductive" physicalism about persons and their psychological states.[13] Moreover, his conception of the self as "simply" a centerless network of beliefs and desires is a well-entrenched component of many postmodernist theories, as well as an element of some theories of mind accepted by contemporary analytic philosophers.[14] But the conception of language that Rorty associates with these positions makes it difficult to understand some of the most important projects of second- and third-wave feminism. Recall, for instance, that Betty Friedan intended *The Feminine Mystique* to provide a label for the then unnamed unhappiness and dissatisfaction that she believed many women experienced under the cultural constraints in place in post–World War II America. She took the dissatisfaction to be real, despite the fact that it initially had no name.

Further, as discussed in chapter 2, Nancy Hirschmann makes a compelling case for the centrality to second-wave feminism of consciousness-raising sessions in which women might learn to articulate central aspects of their experience in a feminist vocabulary that would replace the patriarchal filters of culturally conventional language. Some of those linguistic "filters" effectively denied important aspects of some women's experiences—for instance, that some women had strong ambitions for success in the world outside the home, and that some might not be "fulfilled" by having children. Rorty would no doubt insist that these sessions were simply replacing one "vocabulary" with another, without getting any closer to a language-independent truth about the harms that patriarchal oppression produces or about the nature of women's experience of that harm. But we must ask whether this stance can make sense of the work that the women's movement has actually done, or of the terms on which that work has been carried out.

In his essay on "Feminism and Pragmatism," Rorty sought to frame Catherine MacKinnon's work as a project of pure "redescription." He argued that MacKinnon's (admitted) belief in the historical contingency of various conventional assumptions about sexuality and "femininity" counted as good evidence for his interpretation. Yet in the process of developing this interpretation, Rorty defends some deeply problematic assertions. In particular, he contends that "we pragmatists have to identify most of the wrongness of past male oppression with its suppression of past potentiality rather than in [*sic*] its injustice to past actuality."[15] But even a sympathetic reader might ask: "past potentiality" for what? We can also wonder about the scope of "most" in the phrase "most of the wrongness" and about how to characterize the "rest" of the wrongness. In addition, is the "rest" of the wrongness injustice to "past actuality," and if so, how does one draw the dividing line? But most important, to hearken back to my discussion in chapter 3, Rorty's characterization is inconsistent with MacKinnon's own account of her project. Recall that she insists that women are "human beings in truth, if not in social reality," and that she understands the concept of sexual harassment to be a more accurate expression of certain aspects of women's social experience than the concepts it replaced. This shows that like most (if not all) critically reflective feminists, MacKinnon believes that the wrongness of patriarchal oppression is a function of the real injustice that it does to real selves who virtually always have a "deep" sense that the oppression they have experienced is wrong—whether or not they can always adequately name the oppression when it occurs.

There is a second problematic implication in linguistic relativism and strong social constructionism: the readiness of those who defend these views to conclude—as Rorty expresses it—that victims "do not have much in the way of language" and that "there is no such thing as the 'voice of the oppressed." Rorty even argues that the task of putting victims' experience into language must "be done for them by somebody else."[16] Yet there is no good evidence for the sweeping nature of such claims. To be sure, some individuals may be so overwhelmed by the experience of oppression that they require assistance in putting the reality of their experience into language. Some may even develop "adaptive preferences" as a way of limiting unhappiness (and quieting the tendency to express it) by adjusting many of their central desires and expectations to a life that limits their choices and possibilities. But, in any oppressed group, there are always people who are not overwhelmed by oppression—and who manage to develop few, if any, adaptive preferences for it. Even in those social contexts that have come closest to functioning as what Erving Goffman might have called a "total institution"—chattel slavery and concentration camps, for instance—there are always people who are not overwhelmed by their condition, and who form few, if any, adaptive preferences. That is, there are always people, who—despite oppression—manage to retain a sense of their own worth and a belief in the value of their own agency, as well as the capacity to put those understandings into language. As Orlando Patterson argues in *Slavery and Social Death*, "There is absolutely no evidence from the long and dismal annals of slavery to suggest that any group of slaves ever internalized the conception of degradation held by their masters. To be dishonored—and to sense, however acutely, such dishonor—is not to lose the quintessential human urge to participate and to want a place."[17]

It is tempting to think that any captive's sense of their own worth would have been reflected in large-scale rebellions or widespread escape. Indeed, as some commentators have noted—and as this writer can confirm—some contemporary African Americans still harbor a secret shame at the thought that more African-descended slaves did not openly rebel or escape chattel slavery in America. But Edward Baptist urges, in *The Half Has Never Been Told: Slavery and the Makings of American Capitalism*, that, by the mid-1820s, enslavers had built a slave-trading system that, in various ways, made most forms of resistance almost "impossible to carry out successfully." He goes on to argue, however, that there is voluminous evidence—perhaps especially in the extensive testimony of former slaves themselves—that most "chose survival," that their survival required "solidarity," and that this solidarity allowed them "to light their own way by building a critique of enslavers' power that was an alternative story about what things were and what they meant."[18] It is important, moreover, that testimony of survivors will virtually always be more reliable than that of external commentators (like Rorty) on the question of whether victims' experiences and stories must be told for them by someone else. One of the most compelling sources of support for this claim is Viktor Frankl's remarkable exploration, in *Man's Search for Meaning*, of the psychological traits that made some people able to retain a robust sense of identity and agency despite the horrifying experience of imprisonment in a Nazi death camp.

The voices of those who retain a robust sense of identity and agency can become "audible" in many different ways: for instance, in quiet resistance or overt rebellion, in the symbolic work of art or the theoretical work of engaged social criticism. But, as Baptist suggests, the pathways through which any agent proves willing and able to express resistance will surely be dependent on the means by which a "near-total" institution seeks to suppress such resistance. Still further, as many participants in social movements have argued, the work done by those with the strongest voices to enable us to hear the weakest voices is vitally important. bell hooks argues in her book *Talking Back: Thinking Feminist, Thinking Black,* that finding a voice—and, in fact, not having it thrust on one from "outside"—is an essential part of any liberation struggle. Indeed, hooks continues, for the oppressed and the exploited, finding their own voice is "a necessary starting place."[19]

The discussion of Martin Luther King and Vaclav Havel in chapter 2 noted that people who have been oppressed are most likely to *find* their voice as the outcome of collective action—in particular, as the outcome of their collective self-assertion as political agents. In some of her recent work, Judith Butler has developed a distinctive version of this insight. Those who are familiar with Butler's early work on the social and linguistic formation of gender and sexuality might presume that, on her view, we can never break free of the linguistic norms that form "the subject." Much like Rorty's theory about how "vocabularies" work, Butler's views about the power of linguistic norms have seemed—as Nussbaum expressed it—to encourage political "quietism and retreat." But in *Notes Toward a Performative Theory of Assembly*, Butler has explored the political potential of "assembled' groups who—in spite of previous racial, ethnic, or economic exclusion—become capable, collectively, of disrupting power, including the power of linguistic norms. Through these disruptions, Butler urges, they become able to make themselves heard and felt in politically consequential outcome. One of the most compelling features of Butler's account is her observation that social media sometimes play a critical role in allowing people who live under authoritarian regimes to find their voices through collective resistance and rebellion.[20]

In different ways, then, Havel, King, hooks, and Butler offer compelling challenges to Rorty's contention that social change could ever be just a matter of replacing one "vocabulary" with another. Their work makes it reasonable to assume that we can acknowledge the shaping power of language and yet also believe that social change helps to constructively reshape reality. Acknowledging the power of language to initially shape human identity and agency is, in many respects, a defensibly "weak" social constructionism. Any plausible theory of how language works must acknowledge that the social realities within which we are shaped are unavoidably framed by linguistic forms, practices, and norms that help determine the social and political boundaries of our everyday lives. It must also be emphasized that these boundaries, and the linguistic phenomena that help produce them, are often remarkably resistant to change. But we can change the language that limits space for justice if we come to understand the varied paths by which it channels social "attention." This is why the work of language activists who seek to document and alter these paths is critically important. The rest of this chapter will explore the implications of this stance for three different, though often related, kinds of efforts to provide conceptual space for justice: (a) attempts to identify and define unaddressed wrongs and injustices by naming them; (b) efforts to replace language that severs the links between injustice and its effects; and (c) efforts to replace language that actively masks injustice and wrongly legitimizes institutions and practices that sustain it.

5.4 THE POWER AND PROMISE OF NAMING AN UNNAMED WRONG

Like many of the projects that progressive social movements pursue, most genuinely constructive efforts to provide conceptual space for justice are fundamentally collective projects. But, as I urged at the conclusion of chapter 1, moral visionaries and innovative leaders have sometimes played an essential—and even outsized—role in the constructive evolution of social movements and their projects. Nowhere is this more evident than in the influence of jurist and human rights activist Raphael Lemkin in shaping the development of the international human rights movement. Lemkin is best remembered as the legal scholar who coined the term "genocide," providing the first official account of its meaning in his book *Axis Rule in Occupied Europe: Laws of*

Occupation, Analysis of Government, Proposals for Redress (1944). The term is introduced in a section entitled "Genocide—A New Term and New Conception for Destruction of Nations": "'New conceptions' require new terms. By 'genocide' we mean the destruction of a nation or of an ethnic group. This new word, coined by the author to denote an old practice in its modern development, is made from the ancient Greek word *genos* (race, tribe) and the Latin *cide* (killing), thus corresponding in its formation to such words as tyrannicide, homicide [*sic*], infanticide, etc."[21]

There had been a felt need for such a term for some time before Lemkin published *Axis Rule in Occupied Europe*. One of the most consequential expressions of that need came in 1941, when Winston Churchill delivered a radio address in which he alluded to atrocities being committed by the Nazis—including mass executions of Soviet Jews—during the surprise invasion of the Soviet Union. Churchill declared, correctly, that "we are in the presence of a crime without a name."[22] As Lemkin had learned while still a student at the University of Lvov in the 1920s, as long as such atrocities were not recognized as a crime in international law, there was little hope of getting an effective worldwide response to their commission. Lemkin became preoccupied with the problem—beginning with his dissatisfaction with how the international community had responded to the atrocities that Turkey committed against Armenians from 1915 to 1916.[23] Three years after Churchill's "crime without a name" address, but even before the full scope of Nazi atrocities came to light, Lemkin introduced the concept of genocide in the hope of laying the foundation for a new understanding of, and a robust international response to, a terrible but complex crime:

"Genocide does not necessarily mean the immediate destruction of a nation, except when accomplished by mass killings of all members of a nation. It is intended rather to signify a coordinated plan of different actions aiming at the destruction of essential foundations of the life of national groups, with the aim of annihilating the groups themselves. The objectives of such a plan would be disintegration of the political and social institutions, of culture, language, national feelings, religion, and the economic existence of national groups, and the destruction of the personal security, liberty, health, dignity, and even the lives of the individuals belonging to such groups.[24]

Lemkin's project was something quite different from what some philosophers call "conceptual engineering": the project of assessing and improving concepts that have historically been central to various kinds of philosophical inquiry.[25] What philosophers describe as conceptual engineering is essentially an effort *to improve representation* by refining or replacing concepts. In contrast, the linguistic innovation embodied in Lemkin's work was part of a project *to improve the world* by articulating the nature and consequences of a serious crime. Moreover, like virtually all such projects that are intended to make a difference in the world—and that are genuinely capable of doing so—Lemkin's innovation was not the product of philosophical speculation about proper representation. It was rather the outcome of a lifetime of engaged moral inquiry that could only have emerged from what Michael Walzer describes as "workmanlike social criticism and political struggle."

Lemkin's social criticism and political struggle began in earnest in 1933 when, as an international jurist in prewar Poland, he recommended to the League of Nations a proposal to outlaw acts of "barbarism" and "vandalism." He then continued to practice law in Warsaw until the Nazis invaded Poland in 1939, at which time he joined the resistance. After he was injured, he fled to the United States (in 1941) and eventually became a legal advisor to the U.S. chief prosecutor at Nuremberg. Over the course of his career, he actively sought fundamental change in international law, mainly through institutions like the United Nations that emerged at the end of the Second World War. During this period, he learned that forty-nine members of his own family had been killed in the Holocaust. It was apparently also during this period that he came to think that notions like "barbarity" and even "mass murder" were simply inadequate to capture the idea of targeting a group of people for elimination, and that any project of doing so was not strictly speaking a war crime but an attack of the very humanity of the people targeted for destruction[26]. Lemkin's most lasting contribution was getting the United Nations to adopt the *Convention on the Punishment and Prevention of Genocide* in 1948—even though the United States did not ratify the convention until 1988, and disagreement about elements of Lemkin's definition continues to this day.

Why does Lemkin's personal story matter to this argument? It is only when we understand the scope of his active and deeply engaged leadership in getting international recognition of genocide as a crime that we can understand some of the most important sources of moral progress. Lemkin's story shows, in particular, that the power and social promise of naming a wrong typically emerges only under two conditions. First, the new name must be rooted in a detailed, richly textured understanding of what is at stake in putting it forward as an appropriate characterization of an unnamed phenomenon. Only when it is rooted in such an understanding can a new name both reflect and select reality in the most informative way and effectively help to prevent dangerous "deflections of reality" made possible by less informative terminology. Such a richly textured understanding can typically emerge only out of engaged social criticism and political struggle. Second, the morally and politically progressive insights generated by the name must eventually be broadly disseminated if they are to affect the world. Philosophy is not (and cannot be) the principal vehicle through which this dissemination occurs.[27] Philosophy might, of course, be a vehicle for getting a new word placed in an influential dictionary. But only socially and politically engaged moral inquirers—which philosophy rarely produces—can do the critical work of disseminating progressive moral insights in ways that have the potential to change the world that accepts them.

Lemkin's story also helps us identify the main characteristics of engaged moral inquirers, especially when it is considered alongside stories of the life and work of figures like Gandhi, King, and MacKinnon. Such figures share four main characteristics: First, they typically have a committed personal engagement with the everyday consequences of the moral concepts and arguments they advance. Second, they must almost always have shown that they are willing to assume great personal risk in order to advance the causes they advocate. This means that to be an engaged moral inquirer is, by definition, to be a forceful moral advocate as well. Third, engaged inquiry qualifies as moral only when the inquirer is committed to the idea that deliberate exposure of others to the risk of harm is acceptable only as a morally necessary, though deeply regrettable, means for combatting oppressive and unjust moral practices. But finally, engaged moral inquirers recognize the importance of drawing on modes of communication and forms of persuasion that do not privilege discursive reason-giving and argument. For instance, MacKinnon often appeals to the vision of a social world in which no one experiences sexuality in an alienated form. King famously imagined a world in which people would be judged by "the content of their character" rather than the color of their skin. Lemkin imagined a world in which we would not only punish genocide but find ways to prevent it. It is also important that some deeply engaged moral inquirers—including Gandhi, King, and Chavez, have been willing to offer their own practice, and even their own lives, as embodiments of the insights they hope to disseminate. Socrates is one of the few philosophers to qualify as an engaged moral inquirer in the sense described here.

The legal theorist Richard Posner once argued that contemporary moral philosophy lacks the "intellectual vitality" and "emotional power" to have any substantial influence over the processes that produce real social change, mainly because its practitioners are unwilling to rely on forms of persuasion that "bypass our rational calculating faculty." Indeed, Posner claims that the influence of the most successful "moral entrepreneurs," as he calls them, is never a function of the quality of their arguments but of their skill at "nonrational" and even "irrational" persuasion.[28] There is an unexpected element of truth in this provocative, if in some ways misguided, claim. In particular, as I have argued, there certainly are important differences between the methods of the academic moral philosopher and those of the engaged moral inquirer. Two of those differences are most important: the engaged moral inquirers' willingness to endure great personal risk in order to defend the positions they hold, and their readiness to rely on modes of communicating moral insights that do not rely on discursive reason-giving and argument.

Posner rightly recognizes the engaged moral inquirer's readiness sometimes to "bypass" discursive argument. But we must not misunderstand the breadth of projects that fit in this category. Some efforts to bypass discursive argument in political life may well be meant to strengthen the appeal to nonrational emotions like impulsive anger and fear. Other attempts to bypass discursive argument turn out to produce political effects that are not just nonrational but irrational. In one of the most instructive accounts of such a phenomenon, the sociologist and psychiatrist

Jonathan Metzl has shown that some white Americans have come to accept a conception of their identity so shaped by antipathy to nonwhite others that they are essentially "dying of whiteness"—rejecting social policies that might promote their own well-being, in order to make sure that nonwhite "others" don't benefit.[29]

Yet some appeals to imagination that are not in any sense nonrational or irrational work, at least initially, by bypassing discursive argument. When a defender of human rights asks us to imagine a world in which it is possible to prevent genocide, she is asking us to rationally consider what it would mean to live in a world where people are not targeted for destruction because of their membership in a particular racial, ethnic, or religious affinity group. Such efforts rest on the idea that once we understand that any group could be singled out in this way and can conceive of what it means to actually be singled out in this way, we can surely see the rationality of getting one's government to sign onto the *UN Convention on Punishment and Prevention of Genocide* and to pursue its implication with integrity.

Equally important, the sort of figure who is likely to make the kind of "irrational" appeal Posner has in mind is unlikely to qualify as an engaged moral inquirer in the sense defended here. One of Posner's aims was to defend a deep skepticism about morality, a skepticism expressed by his readiness to describe Hitler as a "moral entrepreneur" who sought to narrow the bounds of altruism, unlike Jesus or King, who sought to expand them. But Hitler's appeals to xenophobic hatred and fear, along with the large-scale atrocities that were methodically and systematically built on that hate-filled xenophobia, are simply incompatible with the idea of moral inquiry and advocacy defended here. Of course, as chapter 3 argues, engaged moral inquirers sometimes rely on the disruptive power *of suffering* as a means to generate humane insight and support for a society shaped by humane regard for persons. But trying to generate compassionate concern for suffering is a fundamentally different project than encouraging the large-scale violence, war, and murder that constituted genocide and crimes against humanity.

Finally, Posner's claims that moral philosophy cannot play *any* substantive role in shaping social change simply are not supported by the facts. First, even if academic moral philosophers can only be "part-time" inquirers and advocates in the world beyond the academy—perhaps by such activities as teaching in prisons, participating in ethics committees in hospitals, serving as consultants to government agencies—the work that they do in such roles can have a substantive influence.[30] Second, the content of narrowly "academic" philosophical moral inquiry may include such projects as the study of traditions of moral argument, analyses of the quality of moral arguments, exploration of the implications of central moral concepts, and sometimes a kind of "engineering" of moral concepts that is meant to offer more defensible understandings of moral experience. All of these projects can be of value to the work of social movements. Third, as I argue more fully in chapter 8, academic philosophy is sometimes most valuable for its capacity to enrich moral and political imagination by offering inspiring and hopeful visions of societies shaped by a genuine concern for justice.

5.5. ADVANCING JUSTICE BY RECONNECTING INJUSTICE WITH ITS EFFECTS

One of the most crucial means by which language deflects attention from injustice is by severing the connection between offending actions (and their sustaining institutions) and the harmful consequences of those actions and institutions. In an influential essay entitled "Action and Responsibility," the philosopher Joel Feinberg succinctly described the phenomenon that enables this kind of separation between actions and their consequences. There is a "well-known feature of our language," Feinberg contends, "whereby a man's action can be described almost as narrowly or broadly as we please." He called this feature of language the "accordion effect" because "an action, like the folding musical instrument can be squeezed down to a minimum or else stretched way out."[31] When the language we use to describe some action functions as a "stretched out" accordion might, it can allow our characterization of the action to include its most important effects, as when we say that "Peter startled Paul," instead of "Peter opened the door causing Paul to be startled." Feinberg noted that "more often than not our language obliges us by providing a relatively complex action word for the purpose" of succinctly characterizing actions in ways that capture their most important effects. In Feinberg's example, the verb "to startle" serves as just such a complex verb.

Yet for centuries there was no complex action word or phrase to adequately characterize the nature and consequences of sexual coercion at work. Indeed, as I briefly noted in chapter 4, in the absence of appropriate terminology, unwanted sexual advances and what Reva Siegal has described as "unwanted sexual relations imposed by superiors on subordinates at work" were treated as phenomena that could be engaged in with social and legal impunity.[32] Moreover, background cultural assumptions made it difficult to enlarge conceptual space in ways that might allow for a different response. Unwanted sexual advances and relations were sometimes treated as a "necessary cost" to be borne by women—either because of their subordinate status (as chattel slaves or low-paid wage labor), or because women who dared to seek paid employment outside the home deserved to be put "in their place." In other contexts, sexual coercion at work was deemed an "unavoidable" response of employers who supposedly found the employee "attractive," or who (allegedly "understandably") assumed that the conduct was something the female employee "really wanted," despite her objections. Finally, certain kinds of sexual coercion were passed off as "just a joke"—to which female targets of the coercion were simply overreacting.

As we might expect, the attention-deflecting dominance of such characterizations, which served to conceptually separate the coercive conduct from the harm it caused, were usually accompanied by troubling assumptions about who bears responsibility for addressing the conduct's effects. The governing assumption was that it was essentially a woman's responsibility either to flee the situation in which such coercion was occurring or to tolerate the conduct without complaint if fleeing the coercive situation was not feasible or was perhaps even physically impossible. The conditions that might make toleration necessary could include such devastating circumstances as chattel slavery, and severe economic hardships. But, in the 1970s, as more and more women began to speak up about what it meant to experience sexual coercion at work—even those with the economic and political "means" to flee—it became clear that sexual coercion at work could be devastating for women in virtually any social and economic circumstances. Even if they managed to find appropriate employment after leaving, those who fled the coercion had to absorb the distress of the coercion itself, overcome the trivialization, humiliation, and intimidation· often used to silence their complaints, and face the fact that the only way to be free of sexual coercion was to leave their employment.[33]

The irony of this last point was rarely lost on those who experienced the coercion, particularly as the emergent concept of sexual harassment was just beginning to change the way we characterized the offending conduct. Thus, in an interview with a reporter for the *New York Times* in 1975, one young woman who was working in a restaurant to put herself through college wondered: "Why do women have to put up with this sort of thing anyway? You aren't in a position to say 'get your crummy hands off me' because you need the tips, that's what a waitress job is all about. Women are the ones who are punished. They have to leave a job because of a man's behavior and the man is left there, sitting pretty."[34] Regrettably, there can still be highly visible failure to acknowledge the doubly punitive nature of demanding that the target of sexual coercion at work must either tolerate the conduct or try to find other employment. In summer 2016, thirty years after the Supreme Court's unanimous sexual harassment decision in *Meritor Savings Bank v. Vinson* (1986), the man who would become the forty-fifth president of the United States was asked how he would respond if his own daughter were sexually harassed at work. He replied, "I would like to think she would find another career or find another company if that was the case."[35] Of course, as Reva Siegal might argue, coming from a presumed billionaire, this response suggests that it is not possible to fully appreciate the nature and harms of sexual harassment unless we understand the connection between sexual coercion at work and a social order that (typically) "situates sexual relations between men and women in relations of economic dependency between men and women."[36]

Yet the widespread acceptance and use of the concept of sexual harassment must surely be recognized as an important part of the project of making space for justice. To begin with, it now seems unlikely that anyone could collapse the "accordion of description" and take us back to the culturally widespread denials of morally and legally significant connections between sexual coercion at work and harmful consequences for the targets of that coercion. Moreover, the social and political effects of the accordion-stretching concept of sexual harassment support claims made by some theorists of women's social movement activism that certain kinds of language activism have genuine "revolutionary potential."[37] In this way, the emergence of the concept of sexual harassment can serve as something of a model for language activism in other efforts to make conceptual space for justice. It should encourage broader questions about how and where existing linguistic forms might serve to deflect our attention from significant instances of injustice.

Any socially constructive consequences that a given instance of language activism is likely to have will never be immediate, and some culturally prominent forces may remain recalcitrant in the face of linguistic change. Even in the twenty-first century, after all, an influential political leader could talk about sexual harassment in terms that suggested a return to cultural assumptions of the 1970s. Equally important, since new words or phrases are always integrated into the social world *even as that world is changed by their acceptance and use*, disagreements about how to define some new linguistic form, as well as about how to apply it, will emerge again and again. As Reva Siegal has noted: "The regulation of sexual harassment, and debates over it, imbue workplace interactions with new significance" and "macro and micro transformations in the ecology of work change the meaning of particular overtures, actions and utterances."

But even as the introduction of new linguistic forms may generate new sources of disagreement, and perhaps even new forms of social conflict, it can also generate unexpected instances of agreement with the potential to break down cultural barriers that have seemed impermeable. In spring 2018 the *New York Times* published a record of an especially unlikely example of this possibility: a conversation between Catherine MacKinnon and the conservative news host and former Miss America Gretchen Carlson reflecting on how to build constructively—in spite of some political divides—on the social changes made possible by the emergence of the concept of sexual harassment.[38] Thus language matters not only because it has the power to affirm insufficiently acknowledged links between certain kinds of conduct and its consequences, but because it has the power to encourage new socially constructive connections between people. The #MeToo revolution is a recent critical reminder of the power of language to help reshape the social world.

5.6 THE LIBERATORY POTENTIAL OF REJECTING LANGUAGE THAT LEGITIMIZES INJUSTICE

Yet the use of language to deny the connection between unjust actions and their effects is not the only means by which language serves to deflect attention from injustice. In her Nobel lecture in 1993, Toni Morrison observed that there are myriad ways in which language can be used in service of subjugation. She lamented, in particular, the "waste of time and life that rationalizations and representations of dominance [have] required" as "lethal discourses of exclusion blocking access to cognition for both the excluder and the excluded."[39] Morrison rightly urges that "discourses of exclusion" seek to "limit knowledge." Social movements have taught us that some of the most persistent "discourses of exclusion" attempt to mask the truths of social exclusion and oppression by purporting to legitimize those institutions, policies, and practices that are central to sustaining exclusion and oppression.

No term has more fully functioned to mask the truth of oppression than the phrase "separate but equal," which emerged as one of the terminological screens relied on to defend Jim Crow segregation in America. Yet despite the efforts of those who sought to defend the constitutional acceptability of the separate-but-equal concept, some of those who were subject to the concept's consequences retained a robust sense of their own worth and the value of their own agency, as well as the capacity to put those understandings into the language of resistance and political struggle. It was thus that, at the end of the nineteenth century, leaders of the African American freedom struggle in New Orleans, Louisiana, turned to the legal system to challenge the constitutionality of Jim Crow laws. One of those challenges—to the Louisiana Railway Accommodations Act of 1890—went all the way to the U.S. Supreme Court, in the case *of Plessy v. Ferguson* (1896). The Louisiana Act had declared that in order to "promote the comfort" of its passengers, all the railroad lines in the state were required to provide "equal but separate accommodations for the white and colored races." In an effort to have the law declared unconstitutional, an early Civil Rights Association—the New Orleans Citizens' Committee—recruited a man named Homer Plessy to violate the law. Prefiguring the example of Rosa Parks nearly six decades later, Plessy was arrested.

When the Supreme Court finally decided the case, they produced what C. Vann Woodward famously called the "national decision against equality."[40] The majority held that as long as the relevant facilities and accommodations were truly equal, racial segregation would not violate the constitutional guarantee of equal protection of the law, and that racial segregation was not an intrinsic barrier to providing equal accommodations. But the most important element of the argument for the majority's decision is this (now) infamous analysis of the plaintiff's position: "We consider the underlying fallacy of the plaintiff's argument to consist in the assumption that the enforced separation of the two races stamps the colored race with a badge of inferiority. If this be so, it is not by reason of anything found in the act, but solely because the colored race chooses to put that construction upon it."[41] The stance in this passage is not an ordinary lie. Insofar as it addressed the plaintiff, and those whose interests he represented, the stance was a kind of judicial "gaslighting": an effort to silence further legal complaint about segregation by trying to undermine the plaintiff's confidence in their understanding of reality.[42] But insofar as the opinion addressed the white American majority, it was an assurance that the court would not destabilize the system of beliefs, actions, and institutions that sustained white supremacy. By insisting on the constitutionality of the phase "separate but equal," the court effectively also declared its intention to preserve the narrative that underwrote white America's affected ignorance about the reality of American apartheid.

The *Plessy* court's gaslighting effort did not shake the plaintiff's confidence in his understanding of reality. Moreover, the social activists who were in the vanguard of the twentieth-century African American freedom struggle never relinquished what Antonio Gramsci might have called their "good sense" about the real nature and consequences of American racial apartheid. Groups such as the Citizens of Committee of New Orleans, created in 1891 to mount the constitutional test in *Plessy*; the Niagara Movement of 1905, which eventually led to creation of the NAACP; and the Montgomery Improvement Association, which from 1955 to 1956 coordinated the Montgomery bus boycott, never doubted that they accurately understood the ugly truth of American racial oppression. The *Plessy* court's effort to sustain white supremacy was far more effective. It took the Supreme Court another fifty-eight years to acknowledge a *part* of the ugly truth in *Brown v. Board of Education* (1954). Ironically, some of the most powerful arguments in *Brown* rested on the testimony of African American social scientists Kenneth and Mamie Clark, whose research revealed some of the damage done by the "badge of inferiority" created by school segregation.

But even after the decision in *Brown* and, indeed, long after passage of the Civil Rights act of 1964 and the Voting Rights Act of 1965, the movement away from the *Plessy* court's decision against racial equality remains uneven and—despite the obvious progress—incomplete. One reason is that the formal structures of southern de jure segregation were never the only important source of racial injustice in America. In January 1966, just months after passage of the Voting Rights Act, Martin Luther King, Jr., moved his family into a modest dwelling on the west side of Chicago to mark the beginning of the Civil Rights Movement's effort to tackle de facto segregation in the North. Scholars and city residents continue to disagree about whether the Chicago Freedom Movement could be called a success. But it is worth remembering that during the summer of 1966, in response to violent anti-Black protests, King declared that "the people from Mississippi ought to come to Chicago to learn how to hate."[43] The civil unrest that exploded in response to King's assassination in 1968 and the brief but intense strength of support for the Black Panther Party that followed in the wake of that unrest are vivid reminders of how persistent the effects of American apartheid have been. Still further, even in the first decade of the twentieth century, as some observers were proclaiming Barack Obama's election as president as proof that America was on the path to becoming a "postracial society,"

Obama held his first inaugural celebration in what was then—
and what apparently remains—one of the most racially strati-
fied cities in America. The effects of that stratification, repeated
in many of America's urban centers, are fairly clear: significant
numbers of African Americans lack equal access to employment,
safe and affordable housing, quality health care, and quality education, and many remain subject to significant injustice at the
hands of the local police and in the national system of carceral
control.

There has clearly been significant progress for some segments
of Black America, in such domains as electoral representation,
access to higher education, and the breaking down of some long-
standing barriers to representation in high-status professions.
Moreover, this progress has been made possible by the efforts of
the many people and groups who have fought to reject slavery
and segregation. The effort to dismantle the structures of de jure
segregation—beginning with the rejection of the discourses of
exclusion that supported Jim Crow—has been a critical element
of that work.

However, given the continued strength and depth of de facto
segregation, the socially transformative effects of the work begun
in *Plessy* should not have been expected, alone, to make space
for racial justice in America. Several overlapping, socially dominant narratives have persistently conferred a spurious legitimacy
on institutions, policies, and practices that sustain the compli-
cated social reality that constitutes de facto racial segregation.
American racial injustice is sustained by a complex social imaginary: composed of founding myths that unreflectively venerate
figures who accepted racist assumptions; unexamined claims
about American moral "exceptionalism"; and myopic interpretations of history that sometimes owe more to affected ignorance than to empirical fact. Even the most successful project of

replacing biased and epistemically inadequate linguistic forms could never have matched the social and political reach of America's socially dominant racial narratives. Reshaping the social world sustained by this structure of belief and attitudes is a project of immense proportions.

But, as I will show in the following chapter, social movements have often taken on the challenge of critiquing complex social imaginaries. These efforts to imaginatively reshape some of the central narratives that constitute these social imaginaries have produced important lessons for political thought as well as political practice. Chapter 6 will explore the most important of these insights.

6

JUSTICE AND THE NARRATIVE IMAGINATION

Stories have been used to dispossess and to malign. But stories can also be used to empower. . . . Stories can break the dignity of a people. But stories can also repair that broken dignity.

—Chimamanda Ngozi Adichie

6.1 WHY NARRATIVE MATTERS TO SOCIAL MOVEMENTS

Alasdair MacIntyre observes, in *After Virtue*, that we begin life occupying social roles defined by narratives we did not produce. We must learn what these roles prescribe, he rightly urges, "if we are to understand how others respond to us and how our responses to them are apt to be construed."[1] Ironically, some of the most socially consequential roles regarding race, ethnicity, gender, and socioeconomic status are described by deceptively pithy phrases such as "the happy slave," "the untamable savage," "the undeserving poor," "the model minority," and "intrinsically fulfilling motherhood." Understanding what these roles prescribe and how they fit into the narratives by which they are framed can be a demanding task, since they are shaped by tangled webs of historical interpretation and complex layers of stigmatizing stereotypes.

Being initiated into roles defined by stigmatizing narratives can be arduous, often in ways that are opaque to a cultural outsider. Failure to understand the narrative construction of race in America led Hannah Arendt to claim, in her essay "Reflections on Little Rock" (written in 1958), that Black Americans who allowed their children to participate in school desegregation efforts were shamelessly exploiting those children in pursuit of a political goal.[2] But, as Ralph Ellison observed, those parents were aware that the effort had "overtones of a rite of initiation"—indeed, of a "confrontation of the terrors of social life with all the mysteries stripped away." Yet "in the outlook of many of these parents . . . the child is expected to face the terror and contain his fear and anger precisely because he is a Negro American. Thus, he's required to master the inner tensions created by his racial situation, and if he gets hurt—then his is one more sacrifice. It is a harsh requirement, but if he fails this basic test, his life will be even harsher."[3]

This chapter argues that if we hope to eliminate such unjustly asymmetrical rituals of sacrifice to make space for justice, we must actively challenge narratives that give spurious legitimacy to unjust social institutions and practices.[4] This means that social movements must be ready to engage in what I call *narrative activism*. They must endeavor to revise and sometimes to replace narratives underwriting ways of life that unjustly limit agency, deny human dignity, and marginalize and oppress some social groups. MacIntyre may have been right to argue that "we are never more (and sometimes less) than the co-authors of our own narratives."[5] But any group content to be less than coauthors of its defining narratives will be doomed to a perpetually marginalized and disempowered status. The most effective progressive social movements have been guided by the realization that the only narratives that can empower a people and affirm their dignity—to borrow Chimamanda Adichie's formulation—are narratives they have themselves helped to tell.

Yet narrative activism is never a matter of simply telling and disseminating a new story. This is because the narrative dimensions of any society's social imaginary, in Charles Taylor's sense, are exceedingly complex. Recall that a social imaginary, as Taylor defines it, is the "common understanding" that underwrites a society's common practices and grounds the shared sense of their legitimacy, and that it is preserved and transmitted though "images, legends, and stories."[6] But in any large and complex society, the social imaginary will be shaped by multiple, intersecting narratives that overlap and diverge in unexpected ways. Challenging the influence of any one narrative may thus require challenging the effects and implications of others with which it intersects. Eventually, the process may even require reframing the goals that the relevant social movement was seeking to achieve through its activism.

Thus, for instance, narratives about gender that must be challenged in order to achieve genuine liberation for women will intersect with narratives about class in potentially problematic ways. This lesson emerged in late twentieth-century America, as many women who were socioeconomically well placed took advantage of expanded opportunities to work outside the domestic realm. These women were frequently able to pursue these opportunities only because less well-off women, who faced persistently constrained opportunities for employment, took on relatively insecure—and sometimes poorly compensated—work as housekeepers and as caregivers for the children of women who were better off. It quickly became clear that if the liberation of women were to be more than liberation for affluent women, it would require the women's movement to promote attention to economic inequality and to the idea that affordable childcare is a public good. Accepting new framing narratives may thus require social movements to see themselves differently, even as they seek to change the world around them.

One very dangerous combination of intersecting narratives in American life frames the concept of "the model minority," which is frequently used to characterize Asian Americans. On first reflection, the concept might seem to be a benign celebration of Asian Americans' apparent academic, economic, and professional success.[7] But the stereotype came into existence in the 1950s and began to gain social currency in the 1960s, as an implicit critique of African American social activism. It thus intersects unavoidably with negative narratives depicting African Americans as angry and inclined to complain and protest, rather than to work hard and sacrifice. On the model minority narrative, most Asian Americans—allegedly unlike most African Americans—are quiet, hard-working, seeking to assimilate rather than critique society, and unlikely to protest very much when they are victims of injustice.

The resulting narrative construct poses three important difficulties. First, it ignores important differences between various Asian American subgroups with regard to cultural heritage and traditions, socioeconomic status, and even academic success. Studies that disaggregate subgroups within the larger population reveal remarkable variability in life experiences and socioeconomic outcomes.[8] Second, the model minority construct is never more than an expression of relative valuing. It is not a way of expressing *humane regard* for Asian Americans as intrinsically worthy of respect for their human dignity and compassionate concern for their susceptibility to suffering. This relative valuing takes a dangerous turn when political figures encourage latent anti-Asian racism to emerge as a social force, as some did in response to the COVID-19 pandemic. The resulting anti-Asian violence has reasserted a vicious prejudice that had been temporarily suppressed as a way of condemning African Americans. The danger of violence is exacerbated by xenophobic narratives of "others" who are not "like us"—perhaps taking social and economic benefits that do not belong to "them." Third, except for reparations provided as a response to the internment of Japanese Americans during World War II, the model minority construct has supported policies and practices that have mostly rewarded Asian Americans for not protesting injustice—for being "quiet" and not complaining or fighting back. Taken together, these considerations suggest that being celebrated as the model minority has never been more than a mixed blessing, since the practice is inextricably linked with racist and anti-immigrant prejudice.

Although socially consequential narratives often serve to legitimize injustice in robust ways, revising and replacing those narratives will not obviate the need for resistance and activism of other kinds. Inequalities in social, political, and economic power are equally essential to shoring up unjust institutions and challenging these inequalities will usually be just as critical as narrative activism to ensuring that progressive social change can be substantive and lasting. But in this regard, narrative activism is no different from all the other methods and tactics used by social movements. Sit-ins, boycotts, occupations of public space, and efforts to reshape the political aesthetics of public space by challenging problematic public monuments can be important for bringing public attention to a movement's claims and interests. Yet these strategies cannot alone produce and sustain substantive social change. Moreover, the narrative activism that has furthered the aims of successful social movements has never been confined simply to challenging the narrative schemes accepted by socially and politically dominant groups. It has sometimes been just as important to change the narratives shaping the self-understandings of those in socially marginalized groups—especially if those narratives are entangled, as they often are, with the disempowering beliefs accepted by dominant groups. As I urged in chapter 2, projects of narrative self-reframing are often critical to encouraging a group's constructive understanding of its own political agency. Narrative self-framing is also indispensable to showing that it might be important for members of the group to exercise their agency either through active participation in a social movement or at least through robust support for others who do. As Martin Luther King, Jr., urged in *Stride Toward Freedom*, the early formation of the Civil Rights Movement depended on the gradual emergence of a new understanding of the possibilities of African American political agency.

Still further, even a movement seeking radical or revolutionary change will at some point need to rely on narrative activism to craft a picture of itself and its goals capable of attracting participants to the movement. This truth was brought home by Solidarity activists in late 1970s Poland, who were encouraged and emboldened by Vaclav Havel's essay "The Power of the Powerless." Moreover, the need for narrative self-reframing can be especially urgent as a response to government efforts to undermine a group's support. In the late 1960s the FBI's Counterintelligence Program (COINTELPRO) sought to misrepresent commitments of the Black Panther Party in order to weaken their support among non-Black allies, and among middle-class Black Americans who thought they could support many of the party's goals, if not its methods.[9] The party's constant struggles to reclaim its own narrative—sometimes even within its own ranks—should remind us that narrative activism matters in unexpected contexts. More broadly, philosophers and political theorists who hope to understand and encourage the pursuit of social justice cannot afford to overlook or discount the multifaceted transformative powers of narrative activism.

The word *narrative*, as used here, draws on common understanding: referring to any recounting of actions, events, and states of affairs in a manner that gives them a compelling shape and meaning. Implicit in common understanding is the recognition that our imaginative capacities are critical to constructing effective and engaging narratives, even about matters of fact. Hence any social movement's efforts at narrative activism will demand a complex, collective exercise of narrative imagination. But what is "narrative imagination"? In *Cultivating Humanity*, Martha Nussbaum asserted the importance to stable political life of cultivating the citizen's narrative imagination, by which she meant the ability "to think what it might be like to be in the shoes of a person different from oneself, to be an intelligent reader of that person's story, and to understand the emotions and wishes and desires that someone so placed might have."[10] Progressive social movements have shown that it is just as important to cultivate the capacity to *construct* compelling narratives that convey the facts, and reveal the faces, of injustice and that encourage humane insight into what might be required to remedy injustice. Narrative imagination, therefore, must be understood to have two crucial aspects. It involves the ability to be an intelligent and empathetic "reader" of others' stories, as Nussbaum contends, but it also involves the capacity to construct and present a compelling account of one's own story and of the stories of those with whom one recognizes socially consequential affinities.

What are the features of narrative itself that make it so important to the work of social movements? Narrative is the most important means that human beings have—whether through words, images, or some combination of words and images—of giving *meaning* to diverse perceptions, observations, and experiences. As psychologist Donald Polkinghorne observed in *Narrative Knowing and the Human Sciences,*

> narrative is the fundamental scheme for linking individual human actions and events into interrelated aspects of an understandable composite. For example, the action of a narrative scheme joins the two separate events "the father died" and "the son cried" into a single episode, "the son cried when his father died." Seeing the events as connected increases our understanding of them both—the son cares for his father, and the father's death pains the son. Narrative displays the significance that events have for one another.[11]

This capacity to concisely articulate meaningful connections makes narrative especially important to social movements. Iris Young has argued that communicating through narrative can be particularly valuable in large, culturally complex societies where, as Young observes, "knowledge of others may be largely mediated by statistical generalities," and where "there may be little understanding of lived need or interest across groups." In such conditions, we may even want to follow Young in holding as a *norm* of political communication that "everyone should aim to enlarge their social understanding by learning about the specific experience and meanings attending other social locations."[12] Young rightly concedes that narrative discourse is not a substitute for political argument in which we provide reasons that can be evaluated by reference to salient facts and plausible scientific and social-scientific theories. But any attempt to offer such reasons takes place within discursive contexts shaped by the narrative construction of social meaning and value. Moreover, the narratives that frame political argument and deliberation have sometimes evolved to deny any social significance or political value to the legitimate needs and interests of certain social groups. Members of socially dominant groups may then take such narratives to license ignoring the claims and interests of marginalized groups or denying that they can be the source of politically legitimate reasons. Social movements must therefore cultivate the constructive dimension of narrative imagination if they are to counter the disenfranchising antidemocratic effects of such narratives.

6.2 HOW SOCIAL NARRATIVES CREATE MEANING AND VALUE

Successfully addressing these effects demands a deeper understanding of how social narratives help to create socially dominant understandings of meaning and value. As a start, we must recognize that social narratives create social meaning along several dimensions. In the most basic dimension, they create meaning by connecting events: shaping dominant understandings of the historical salience of particular eras, episodes, and events and emphasizing the contributions of particular people to eras, episodes, and events that are important in the life of the group. In so doing, they perform a second important function by helping to create and sustain a group's collective identity over time, in particular by preserving basic understandings of who "belongs" and who doesn't. Third, social and political narratives provide cultural "instruction" about socially desirable and acceptable belief and action: framing gender roles; shaping normative expectations about phenomena such as race, ethnicity, and class; defining the benefits and burdens of age; and foregrounding civic virtues believed to be essential to the continued existence of the group. Finally, socially influential narratives often evolve, over time, as part of a complex effort to explain and to justify the institutions and practices in which socially desired beliefs and actions have a place. Taken together, these considerations show that socially influential narratives create social meaning by shaping a group's sense of its history, its collective identity, its normative expectations governing belief and behavior, and its basic understandings of the nature and justification of its core practices and institutions.

Polkinghorne reminds us that narratives create meaning by connecting actions, events, and states of affairs *in time*: "The son cried when his father died."[13] But the temporality of socially influential narratives can be hidden, or effectively erased, if the roles they define come to function as ahistorical constructs important mainly for their usefulness to "explain" history. This is how the notion of the happy slave functioned in antebellum narratives. Slavery was portrayed as beneficial for enslaved persons because they supposedly "needed" the civilizing influence of Euro-American cultures. In this picture, history was something that unfolded around the slave, allegedly in response to the slave's "essential nature," rather than a process in which the slave might participate as an independent agent. This is why the publication and dissemination of fugitive slave narratives proved to be so important to the abolitionist movement. As I show more fully below, these narratives refuted the idea of the happy slave not just by providing first-person accounts of the cruelties, indignities, and violence of slavery, but by insisting on respect for the rational agency of enslaved persons and the depth of their desire to determine their own place in history.

Reflecting on differences between the picture of the social world associated with the narrative of the happy slave and the vision embodied in narratives provided by ex-slaves themselves leads to a critical insight about how narrative works. Like the more elemental linguistic forms out of which they are constructed, narratives inevitably select and deflect elements of the reality they purport simply to reflect. But in contrast to simple linguistic forms, narratives do not simply channel attention to one set of observational data rather than another, they actually impose an order on observations and experiences that has the potential to influence—and sometimes drastically constrain—the way we understand and respond to new observations and experiences. To adapt Burke's terminology, narratives function as complex epistemic "filters" or "screens," imposing an unavoidably *perspectival* order on observations and experiences. When the perspectives embodied in socially dominant narratives serve to filter out, or screen out, certain facts or experiences regarding human lives, they can be used as means of denying moral and political validity to the claims and interests of those whose experiences they screen out.

The perspectival order embedded in a narrative may even serve to support practices and policies meant to deny some people's humanity. This was true of the many anti-Black narratives that appeared in successive waves of white supremacist propaganda in Europe and America, in defense of chattel slavery and colonialism. It was also true of the racist narratives constructed by the Nazis' anti-Jewish propaganda machine that, even before adoption of the Nuremberg Race Laws in 1935, helped to create a climate in which violence and brutality against Jews were tolerated and even encouraged. Still further, as anthropologist and novelist David Treuer has written, the effort to dehumanize Native Americans shaped the narratives framing the idea of the "untamed and untamable savage," which was used for centuries to justify seizures of Indian lands, spoliation of natural environments in which Native peoples might prosper, and outright massacre, as in the massacre at Wounded Knee in 1890.[14]

The problem is not that dehumanizing narratives involve the *perspectival* filtering of reality. Perspectival filtering is an unavoidable feature of any narrative construction. Even those narratives that are most likely to yield humane insight, and that may offer an enlarged and morally comprehensive understanding of the world, are unavoidably perspectival. Rather, the problem is that socially influential narratives have too often filtered reality in ways that offer morally as well as epistemically inadequate perspectives: screening out relevant information in ways that allow members of dominant groups either to actively deny or to affect morally culpable ignorance of the humanity of others.

Polkinghorne is certainly right to emphasize that the narrative filtering of reality sometimes produces genuine "narrative knowing." Moreover, there are contexts in which narrative framing increases understanding in ways that strongly support the pursuit of justice. Philosophers such as Iris Murdoch, Cora Diamond, and Martha Nussbaum have sought to explain the nature, sources, and value of this kind of narrative knowing, reminding us that "ordinary" empirical knowledge about material facts can be insufficient to ensure sound ethical judgment or defensible political deliberation.[15] Their work has convincingly shown that sometimes practical reasoning functions well only when we seek the kind of insight that might come from a work of fiction, an autobiography, or even just an empathetic stance toward the lived experience of an actual distant "other." As I argued in chapter 3, this is because what we sometimes most need to understand and acknowledge is the humanity of the other, and to respond to the other with *humane regard*: that critical combination of respect for others' rational agency and compassionate concern for their capacity to suffer. In such contexts, engaging and compelling narrative framings of experience can be essential to conveying the knowledge, which Young aptly calls "situated knowledge," that is necessary for defensible moral reasoning and political deliberation.

The fact remains, however, that socially influential narratives are sometimes obstacles to knowledge and understanding because the perspectival order they impose on experience helps to suppress the facts, and obscure the faces, of injustice. Social movements cannot make room for justice unless they are willing to subject such narratives to careful scrutiny, and that scrutiny must go beyond seeking to determine whether the narratives are, on the whole, true, or false. Even if they contain truths, what additional important facts might these narratives be omitting? Who is celebrated or denigrated by these narratives and why? Are the beliefs and actions they recommend genuinely worthy of recognition? Of course, even in societies ostensibly committed to freedom of speech and tolerance of dissent, socially dominant groups will often be resistant to such questions. But only by seeking serious answers to questions about how social narratives create beliefs about who and what has value can social movements expose, and constructively challenge, the kind of epistemic filtering that limits humane insight into the facts and faces of social injustice.

The epistemically inadequate filtering of reality is not the only important means by which social and political narratives may distort dominant understandings of the facts and faces of injustice. A second source of narrative distortion is a phenomenon that Nelson Goodman characterizes as a discrepancy between "the order of telling" and the "order of occurrence." This narrative "twisting of time," as Goodman describes it, can be epistemically benign when the order of telling makes no real difference to "the basic identity or narrative status" of a story.[16] For example, consider what will result if several people are asked to recount what happened in an Olympic marathon, but some people start their narratives with the outcome of the race (eventually filling in details about how the race was won) while others start from the beginning of the race (preferring to build suspense in narrating the outcome). Goodman argues that, in such contexts, these varied retellings could all present "very much the same story" of who won the marathon and effectively preserve the story's basic core. Though Goodman does not pursue the matter, we might add that in such cases the narrative twisting of time is not only benign but often reveals the epistemic value of the varied insights that can emerge when narrators do not all feel compelled to follow the "direction of time."

Goodman nonetheless acknowledges that the narrative "twisting of time" is sometimes an obstacle to understanding the order in which narrated events actually occurred. Indeed, some failures to follow the direction of time may so fully obscure the true core of the story that they can lead us to get the order of events entirely wrong. He asks us to consider, for example, what it would mean to be presented with a series of snapshots of an automobile moving slowly down an otherwise empty road. Since we would have no way of determining the relationship of the car to any stationary objects or to a real landscape, and since a car can in fact go backward or forward, Goodman urges that it would not be clear whether the car in the photographs was being driven forward or backward.[17]

Of course, we often value the narrative twisting of time in fiction, for instance, in the modernist works of writers like Virginia Woolf, James Joyce, and William Faulkner. But when socially consequential narratives survive as temporally "twisted tales," in Goodman's phrase, they preserve no record of the social and historical "landscape" by reference to which we can determine the order in which significant events in the narrative actually occurred. The result can be a narrative that not only obscures understanding but also seems to justify outcomes that most of us would identify as injustice if we could only determine the order in which narrated events actually occurred. In a particularly influential example of a socially consequential twisted tale, the narrative that defines women as "naturally" more nurturing than men, and as therefore better suited for—and more likely to thrive in—domestic life than economic life, has often been used to justify the underrepresentation of women in certain kinds of social roles and professions. The narrative that frames the concept of intrinsically fulfilling motherhood suppresses facts about the social and historical landscape by reference to which we could understand the role of persistent gender discrimination in producing underrepresentation of women in certain social roles and in professions in the "public" realm. One of Virginia Woolf's most important contributions to social thought, in *A Room of One's Own*, was to insist that claims about the "intrinsic" deficiencies of women writers were rooted in a twisted tale that disguised the role of gender discrimination in limiting women's access to the conditions of literary achievement. The story that Wolff challenged is just one example of the damaging twisting of time that contaminates too many socially dominant narratives.

The remainder of this chapter will explore some efforts of social movements to challenge the twisted tales and epistemically inadequate filters that shape too many socially and politically influential narratives. The discussion will focus on two kinds of *narrative activism*: (a) challenges to narrative schemes that deny or ignore important facts about subjection to oppressive and disempowering practices and institutions; and (b) challenges to inaccurate or incomplete historical judgments that distort collective memory and encourage exclusionary and xenophobic collective identities.

6.3 THE EMANCIPATORY POTENTIAL OF NARRATIVE ACTIVISM

The publication and dissemination of the texts that we now call slave narratives—the abolitionist project that began in the middle of the eighteenth century and continued into the beginning of the twentieth—is perhaps the most important example of narrative activism in human history. It is certainly the best example we have of what I call *emancipatory narrative activism.* This label is not meant to suggest that slave narratives could have directly resulted in emancipation. Just as the most thoughtfully designed public monument cannot itself engage in moral inquiry, even the most accurate and richly textured narrative cannot directly produce desired social change. Yet, at their most effective, autobiographical slave narratives achieved three significant goals. First, they provided situated knowledge of the realities of life as an enslaved person. Second, they offered humane insight into the moral standing of enslaved persons: displaying their rational agency, as well as depicting their suffering. Third, they constituted narrative acts of resistance that, in various ways, asserted the case for emancipation and full citizenship. As acts of narrative resistance, as literary scholar and historian William L. Andrews has argued, they also became a critical means by which the authors could effectively declare themselves free.[18] Autobiographical slave narratives were thus invaluable weapons in cultural and conceptual battles against slavery, as well as in the overarching project to affirm the dignity and moral worth of those who had been subjected to slavery.

At the center of this complex project of narrative activism were 102 book-length narratives written by former slaves during the antebellum period.[19] From the beginning, these narratives were often met with challenges to their authenticity. Proslavery critics charged that they were the handiwork of white abolitionist editors who were not interested in disseminating the truth of slavery but in producing one-sided antislavery "propaganda." Some critics even denied that African-descended slaves could possibly have achieved the level of literacy, the powers of self-reflection, and the capacity for recollection necessary to produce a compelling narrative. Moreover, skepticism about the authenticity of the narratives was not confined to antebellum critics, since well into the twentieth century, influential historians insisted that slave narratives could not be deemed reliable sources of historical evidence. The position of Ulrich Phillips, in his account of *Life and Labor in the Old South* (1929), is emblematic of this skeptical approach, with its insistence that "ex-slave narratives . . . in general were issued with so much abolitionist editing that as a class their authenticity is doubtful."[20] It was not until the late 1960s and early 1970s that a significant number of historians began to think that there might be something problematic about this stance. One consideration that helped inspire confidence in the evidentiary value of at least some slave narratives is that, for an important subset of the core texts, important details could be confirmed by publicly available facts, often including the evidence of the authors' own speeches, sermons, and letters. A significant remainder of the core group of narratives were edited by figures whose integrity is convincingly defended by historian John W. Blasingame.[21]

Frederick Douglass was especially concerned to put the authenticity of his autobiographies beyond dispute. In a letter reproduced in the preface to *My Bondage and My Freedom*, the second of his autobiographies, he insisted that "there are special reasons why I should write my own biography, in preference to employing another to do it. Not only is slavery on trial, but unfortunately, the enslaved people are also on trial. It is alleged, that they are, naturally, inferior; that they are so low in the scale of humanity, and so utterly stupid, that they are unconscious of their wrongs, and do not apprehend their rights."[22] Henry Louis Gates rightly contends that such claims show how important literacy became to most black abolitionists and that slave narratives not only offered evidence of the cruelty and tyranny of slavery but also "bore witness to the urge of every black slave to be free and literate."[23] The passage also confirms Gates's claim that no slave narrative was ever simply an autobiography of a single individual. Each individual's narrative, Gates argues, was also a "communal utterance": a "collective tale" intended to help validate the claims of *every* black slave to merit emancipation and inclusion as full citizens in America. In my view, autobiographical slave narratives could play this role because they expressed the authors' refusal to passively cooperate with the injustices of slavery. In a powerful anticipation of a stance defended a century later by Martin Luther King, Jr., a critical assumption of Douglass's autobiographies was his conviction that to cooperate with the oppressor is ultimately to provide the oppressor with—in King's phrase—a "convenient justification" for oppression.[24] It is thus through the narrative act of resistance to oppression that the autobiographical slave narratives did some of their most important conceptual and moral work of asserting the dignity and moral worth of enslaved people.

But Douglass's stance diverges from King's in one significant respect. Unlike King, Douglass was willing to allow that violent resistance—he sometimes called it "rebellion"—can be justified, and sometimes even required, as a first resort in the effort to assert one's dignity in the context of extreme oppression. Some of the most arresting passages in Douglass's autobiographies describe an episode in which Douglass vigorously fights back against the violence with which the slave "breaker" Covey attempts to subdue and degrade him. In such passages, as philosopher Bernard Boxill has argued, Douglass shows his readiness to recommend violent resistance "not simply because it may force the slave masters to give up slavery, but because it denies them the semblance of a rational justification for slavery."[25] This stance has generated lively debate among Douglass's philosophical interpreters—particularly Bernard Boxill and Frank Kirkland—about the relationship of Douglass's stance to William Lloyd Garrison's project of "moral suasion" with which Douglass was at one point in his life associated.[26] Moral suasion, as Garrison conceived of it, was a fundamentally *nonviolent*, and essentially *nonpolitical*, effort to bring the reader (or listener) to a realization of the moral wrongs of slavery. Did Douglass, the mature abolitionist thinker, believe that violent resistance could be a special form of moral suasion?

My view is that he did not. In 1859, four years after the publication of *My Bondage and My Freedom*, Douglass insists that John Brown was "perfectly sane and free from merely revengeful passion," but in terms that treat violent resistance as a morally necessary last resort against slavery, rather than as implicitly a form of moral argument against it. He contends that Brown

> has attacked slavery with the weapons precisely adapted to bring
> it to the death. Moral considerations have long since been

exhausted upon slaveholders. It is in vain to reason with them. One might as well hunt bears with ethics and political economy for weapons, as to seek to "pluck the spoiled out of the hand of the oppressor" by the mere force of moral law. Slavery is a system of brute force. It shields itself behind might, rather than right. It must be met with its own weapons.[27]

Of course, in this regard, Douglass's approach has much in common with that of Nelson Mandela, who accepted that the intertwining of nonviolent strategies at one stage with violent resistance at another could be a morally defensible element of the struggle to end South African Apartheid.

Yet whatever the moral status of violent resistance in Douglass's thought, his autobiographies provided a powerful account of what it meant to be subjected to chattel slavery. That feature of his narratives connects them with the role that slave narratives, more generally, played as part of the (generically non-Garrisonian) moral argument against slavery. Viewed in this light, as Elizabeth Anderson has argued, slave narratives constituted a powerful challenge to the epistemic injustice embodied in proslavery narratives.[28] By providing situated knowledge of the cruel injustices of slavery, as well as humane insight into the experience of being subject to those injustices, slave narratives used the printed word to fight back against proslavery efforts to discount the testimony of former slaves and to suppress the ugly truths of slavery. In my view, in so doing, they once again showed how important social movements have been to the project of articulating the critical moral insight that social justice demands humane regard for persons. The narratives were compelling statements of the need to condemn the slave system's failure of compassionate concern for human suffering, as well as its failure to respect the rational agency and moral standing of enslaved persons as human beings.[29]

To the non-Garrisonian abolitionist, it was always clear that ending slavery would ultimately demand more than narrative activism. This was well understood by those prominent black abolitionists who, shortly after the Emancipation Proclamation, called for freedmen to join the cause of the Union in fighting the Civil War. Douglass was especially vehement in issuing this call, urging that "the iron gate of our prison stands half open. One gallant rush from the North will fling it wide open, while four millions of our brothers and sisters shall march out into liberty."[30] Among the first to answer Douglass's call were those—including Douglass's two sons—who would eventually constitute the Massachusetts 54th Regiment, whose efforts in the battle of Fort Wagner would later be depicted in Saint Gaudens's memorial in Boston.[31] Yet the fact that counternarratives produced by the abolitionist movement did not, alone, end slavery does not diminish the moral and political value of the narrative activism of which they were a part. What it shows is that an institution on the scale of American chattel slavery, which was so deeply embedded in the American way of life, had to be challenged on multiple fronts.

When the participants in a social movement decide to take up narrative activism, they engage in an activity that carries unexpected risk. Although narrative activism is often welcomed as an indispensable source of situated knowledge and testimony, some portion of one's audience may always try to dismiss one's testimony not merely as inaccurate, but as unworthy of serious attention or even entirely lacking in credibility.[32] Proslavery critics and skeptical historians of slavery were often motivated by straightforward prejudice to dismiss the testimony of slave narratives. But the readiness to dismiss narrative activism as unserious can reflect that skepticism of "anecdotes and images" that I discussed in chapter 4. Some skeptics believe that anyone who offers a narrative rather than a discursive argument in support of important claims and interests is "unscientific" and insufficiently interested in reliable documentation by empirical data. Such dismissals can be especially harsh —and sometimes epistemically unjust—when they discount the testimony of socially marginalized individuals for whom personal narrative is the only means of entering their testimony about injustice into the public record.

The risk of being disbelieved is greatest when a significant portion of one's audience accepts some version of the Rortyan view discussed in chapter 5: the idea that victims "do not have much in the way of language." Those who accept such a view will assume that anyone who has the capacity to construct an orderly and compelling narrative of unjust treatment and then to publicly present it with clarity and confidence could not really have been harmed by the treatment they describe. In practice, the risk of being subject to such judgments has been greatest when women describe persistent domestic abuse, or when they try to characterize long-running patterns of sexual harassment or discrimination in the workplace. It is as if any woman who is strong enough to make a coherent accusation of this kind of wrongdoing—and to thereby fight back against it—could not possibly have been harmed by the conduct being described. This is especially likely, as Francesca Polletta and Pang Chen have argued, if one's narrative of victimization intersects with a socially influential narrative that effectively denies that one could ever really be a victim of sexual harassment or abuse —for instance, the narrative of "the strong black woman."[33] In such cases, the claim is often disbelieved because the claimant is deemed incapable of being harmed in the manner being described. This disbelief thereby becomes another failure of humane regard.

Yet despite these persistent risks, narrative activism has always been—and to this day remains—an important element of the women's movement. Narrative activism was critical to the emergence of the concept of sexual harassment and its gradual evolution as a concept of cultural and legal importance; women had to be willing to break the silence imposed by socially dominant narratives that had constructed unwanted sexual advances at work as a necessary cost of seeking employment outside of the home. This is a reminder that, before the concept gained cultural and legal currency, one of the most important functions of women's narratives of sexual harassment was raising women's own consciousness that what they were experiencing was a form of gender oppression and a special kind of employment discrimination. The role that narrative activism played in this process confirms Young's contention that politically consequential narratives can be a vital means of "articulating collective affinities," and that this role is just as valuable to progressive social movements as conveying "situated knowledge" to socially dominant majorities.[34] The role of narrative activism in articulating collective affinities has been especially important in the emergence of the online activism that helped to drive the #MeToo Movement. More broadly, whatever the inherent risks of narrative activism, it remains a valuable method of entering important testimony about the facts and faces of injustice into the public record.

I have so far discussed three functions that may be served by emancipatory narratives: (1) conveying situated knowledge to dominant majorities, (2) articulating collective affinities, and (3) carrying out acts of narrative resistance. But there is a fourth important function that draws on an idea implicit in some narrative conceptions of the self: that, through narrative, we can have the capacity to "remake" ourselves.[35] Translating this idea to the collective projects of social movements, it has been argued that marginalized groups may be able to "remake," or "re-create," themselves by virtue of the stories they tell of their past, but *only if* they do so in (sometimes difficult) conversation with others who have been dominant forces in shaping that past. A provocative example of this fourth kind of emancipatory narrative activism has recently emerged in the nonfiction writing of David Treuer, who grew up as a member of the Ojibwe tribe on the Leech Lake Indian reservation in Minnesota.

Treuer's emancipatory project begins with the assumption that the ways in which a group tells its own story of reality "shapes that reality: the manner of telling makes the world."[36] He then argues that if Native Americans continue to tell the story of their past "as a tragedy," they may consign themselves to a tragic future. He contends in *The Heartbeat of Wounded Knee: Native America from 1890 to the Present*, for instance, that the Massacre at Wounded Knee in 1890 was not the end of Native America— even though it was certainly a brutal expression of the desire of expansionist forces in America to exterminate the Indian. Finally, as, for instance, in the book *Rez Life: An Indian's Journey Through Reservation Life*, Treuer posits that Native Americans will not fully comprehend the possibilities of a hopeful future until they appreciate, and vehemently reiterate to Americans as a whole, what they have contributed to the development of American society, but also what was unjustly taken from them as America came to take its current form. In articulating some of the contributions that have been undervalued, Treuer argues that

> Indian reservations, and those of us who live on them, are as American as apple pie, baseball, and muscle cars. Unlike apple pie, however, Indians contributed to the birth of America itself. The Oneida were allies of the Revolutionary Army who fed U.S.

troops at Valley Forge and helped defeat the British in New York, and the Iroquois Confederacy served as one of the many models for the American constitution. . . . Indians have been disproportionally involved in every war America has fought since its first.[37]

In discussing the injustice that, in his view, needs to be redressed, Treuer has recently argued that because America's national parks were founded on land that once belonged to Indian tribes—often created only after they "were removed, forcibly, sometimes by an invading army" and other times following treaties signed under duress—they ought to be returned. On the basis of this contention, Treuer has become a forceful advocate for what he describes as the "Return of the National Parks to the Tribes."[38]

Treuer thus claims to provide a communal narrative appropriate to guide Native America's constructive self-remaking. Of course, it involves assertions that many non-Native Americans will surely contest. But elements of Treuer's narrative might also be contested by some Native Americans themselves: there are 564 federally recognized Indian tribes in America, and it is far from obvious that they will all agree with Treuer's assessment of their past, or with his account of the requirements for a hopeful future. But emancipatory narratives are often contested; the possibility that such narratives are likely to generate disagreement is thus not a consideration against narrative activism. Indeed, the conversations generated by contested counternarratives can often be a critical catalyst for serious and constructive reflection about the requirements of social justice.

I stress that my conception of emancipatory narratives does not treat the production of most intentionally fictional narratives as a central component of the narrative activism in which social movements engage. To be sure, as I argued in chapter 3, art has the capacity to produce humane insight and sometimes to point the way to constructive social change. I also maintained, at the

212   MOVEMENTS AND COLLECTIVE IMAGINATION

end of chapter 1, that authors of fiction often contribute signifi-
cantly to the cultural and intellectual labor that helps to make
social change possible. But with very few exceptions—in works
such as Harriet Beecher Stowe's *Uncle Tom's Cabin*, Sinclair Lewis's *The Jungle*, and even Douglass's own fictional work *The Heroic
Slave*—fictional narratives are rarely understood or intended by
their authors as *fundamentally* contributions to the contentious
politics of social movements. There is no doubt that fiction sometimes generates responses that influence political outcomes.
Nor is there any doubt that novelists and short-story writers from
communities that have experienced discrimination, marginalization, and oppression often gladly acknowledge the power of
their work to offer insight into the nature of that experience, and
to help display the need to address the injustices that shape it.
Still further, the contemporary writer Tobias Wolff is probably
correct in claiming that "the most radical political writing is that
which makes you aware of the reality of another human being":
"Good stories slip past our defenses—we all want to know what
happens next—and then slow time down and compel our interest and belief in other lives than our own, so that we feel ourselves in another presence. . . . Writers who can make others,
even our enemies, real to us have achieved a profound political
end, whether or not they would call it that."[39] Yet when a writer's primary goal is to tell a good story, that writer's efforts do
not constitute narrative activism in the sense discussed here.

6.4 CORRECTING THE HISTORIES THAT
ARE PRESENT IN "ALL THAT WE DO"

James Baldwin once urged that "the great force of history comes
from the fact that we carry it within us" and, indeed, that it is

"present in all that we do." He goes on to claim that "it could scarcely be otherwise, since it is to history that we owe our frames of reference, our identities and our aspirations."[40] The most effective social movements have understood this and thus have often sought to make room for justice by challenging historical interpretations that distort collective memory and encourage exclusionary and xenophobic collective identities. Such efforts have been a key element of progressive social movements at least since the start of the twentieth century, when the historian Carter G. Woodson, along with the Association for the Study of Negro Life and History, worked to create America's first "Negro History Week" in 1926. Negro History Week gradually gave way to Black History Month in the United States and then in the United Kingdom.[41] The example set by these projects has encouraged a wide range of narrative activism across the globe. A central focus of this activism has been rectifying inaccuracies in historical interpretations and filling in gaps in historical knowledge regarding the cultural contributions, experiences, and achievements of minority populations and women—groups who have often been undervalued, and sometimes virtually ignored, by dominant accounts of history.

As might be expected, these projects are frequently sources of social conflict. In the United States, for instance, numerous "culture wars" have flared up around such questions as what constitutes a defensible account of the nation's beginnings (1776 or 1619) and what obligations the nation might have incurred to acknowledge and repair various moral wrongs (reparations for slavery, or restoration of land to Native Americans). In Australia, "history wars" have erupted around the question of how to characterize the colonization of Australia and its effects on indigenous people who predated European colonists and settlers.[42] Criticism of the narrative activism at the center of such "wars" sometimes focuses on concerns about the allegedly socially divisive character of its historical interpretations. But the most vehement criticisms charge that narrative activists fail to understand the true nature and purpose of history. The objection is that narrative activism wrongly deems it appropriate to use history as a means to promote political ends, and that such efforts are likely to produce politicized and partisan history that is intellectually suspect and socially dangerous.[43] According to these critics, history should be an objectively valid recounting that makes the past intelligible in ways that might constructively inform the present—though it need not do so. It is then claimed that injecting the interests of social movements into the framing of historical interpretations will prevent the proper pursuit of this goal.

But history and human interests are fundamentally intertwined, and it is impossible for the histories we produce not to be shaped by those interests. The past does not present itself to an inquirer as a fully constituted truth just waiting to be adequately grasped and articulated. Even our decisions about what events or episodes need explanation will reflect various interests of the inquirer, as will our assumptions about what constitutes a satisfactory explanation of those events. As Joel Feinberg has argued, "Intelligibility is always intelligibility *to* someone, and understanding is always *someone's* understanding."[44] Feinberg urges that historians must posit explanations of the causes of events against a background of beliefs about what constitutes "ordinary" or routine conditions of everyday life, and that an important subset of such beliefs will inevitably change with time and place. This strongly suggests that one of the principal reasons that historical explanations differ over time, and from place to place, is that what we might call our "epistemological interests" in explaining things differ, and our historical explanations reflect those differences.

Moreover, when we consider historical subjects that are central to our society's social imaginary, the epistemological interests and assumptions that shape the histories we produce are inextricably linked with socially and politically consequential interests. A late twentieth-century controversy regarding the legacy of Thomas Jefferson vividly illustrates the point. In 1997 historian Annette Gordon-Reed published a meticulously documented book, *Thomas Jefferson and Sally Hemings: An American Controversy*, which argued that we could not understand Jefferson's legacy, or fully comprehend the complex truths of American slavery, unless we took seriously the claim that Jefferson had fathered as many as six children by an enslaved woman named Sally Hemings.[45] The claim included the assertion that Jefferson had been involved in a physical relationship with Hemings for nearly four decades and on two continents. Many historians had long insisted that these assertions, first made by one of Jefferson's political enemies in 1802, could not possibly be true. Indeed, in the very year that Gordon-Reed's book was published, an influential television documentary interviewed several historians who vigorously rejected the idea, with one of them declaring it a "moral impossibility."[46] The lone exception was the African American historian John Hope Franklin, who observed that the presence of so many "mixed-race" and "mulatto" people in the American South showed that sexual relationships between slaveholders and slaves must have been common, and that since Hemings would have been "subject to [Jefferson's] exploitation in every conceivable way," there was no reason not to believe that the claims about Jefferson's relationship with Hemings might be true.[47]

A year later an article published in the journal *Nature* reported on a Y-chromosome haplotype DNA study of Hemings's descendants that helped to substantiate at least some of the paternity claims. Two important addenda addressed the challenges of drawing the right conclusions in the case.[48] Less than two years after the original *Nature* article appeared, the Thomas Jefferson Foundation (the institution that owns and operates Monticello) published a report concluding that "the DNA study, combined with multiple strands of currently available documentary and statistical evidence" indicates a high probability that Jefferson fathered at least one and "most likely all six of Sally Hemings' children appearing in Jefferson's records."[49] The DNA studies thus helped to override the resistance of those whose interests in preserving the "purity" of Jefferson's legacy had led them to consistently discount testimony from undervalued subjects. But initially it was the narrative activism of Gordon-Reed, in particular, that took their testimony seriously, resisted implausible claims about "moral impossibility," and ultimately helped to give rise to the scientific studies. This complex episode thus challenges the idea that narrative activism about history can simply be dismissed as nothing but the expression of purely "political" special interests. Narrative activism may sometimes be the only means of exposing the narrow political interests that have consistently distorted the histories that we all, ultimately, have an interest in finally getting right.

The episode also confirms the wisdom of Hans Gadamer's claim, in *Truth and Method*, that the questions historians raise about the past are always strongly influenced by their place in history, and particularly by their era's preconceptions and prejudices.[50] Of course, in this regard, it is entirely likely that some of the preconceptions that led historians to dismiss claims about Jefferson and Hemings involved stigmatizing assumptions about race and ethnicity—some of which Jefferson himself expressed in some of his notorious claims about race in *Notes on the State of Virginia*. But many historical treatments of the story reflect what

Nietzsche would have called an "antiquarian" reverence for the past—a reverence that produced a dogged and irrational resistance to the idea that one of America's "founding fathers" could possibly have been involved in the kind of relationship posited by the Hemings story.

What makes evaluating the merits of historical interpretations so challenging is not just that historians' interests and the preconceptions of inquiring subjects always shape the questions that they pose. There is the additional fact that, like every narrative, historical narratives and interpretations are inevitably and unavoidably perspectival, even when historians convincingly aim at an ideal of "disinterested" (that is, non-self-interested) reflection. This is why the twentieth-century Dutch historian Pieter Geyl insisted that history is "an argument without end." Geyl acknowledged that any given historian may take a particular historical judgment to be "the only possible conclusion to draw from the facts" and that she may even feel "sustained and comforted" by a sense of "special kinship" with the past. Yet the judgment "will have no finality," Geyl contends, because a historian can see the past "only from a point view," and it is always possible to challenge the accuracy and completeness of that point of view. Geyl denied that this ought to lead to a relativistic interpretation of what is involved in doing history, and he rejected the idea that history's unavoidably perspectival character might diminish its epistemic value. Indeed, he confidently asserted that "any one thesis or presentation may, in itself, be unacceptable, and yet when it has been jettisoned, there remains something valuable. Its very critics are that much richer."[51]

In the contemporary moment, many societies are plagued by a widespread refusal to acknowledge that careful scrutiny of a historical judgment with which we disagree might yield a deeper understanding of the histories we already carry "within us."

Instead, a sizable portion of the citizens of many societies have an antiquarian reverence for the familiar stories that are often, at best, only partially true. This leads them to simply reject any narratives that run counter to the "official story" of the past, especially if the counternarratives implicate one's society in conduct that ought to generate reactive sentiments, such as moral guilt and shame. In a contemporary American example, this kind of recalcitrance has shaped some influential reactions to the so-called 1619 project, initiated by the *New York Times*, which asks Americans to imagine what it might mean to put the realities of American slavery at the center of the American story. Indeed, in summer 2020 U.S. senator Tom Cotton summarily declared that slavery was nothing more than "a necessary evil" and began a concerted effort (on that basis) to deny federal funds to school districts that seek to teach any aspect of the claims of the 1619 project.[52]

To be sure, the 1619 project has been challenged by a range of critics on the political "left" as well as the "right." Some of these criticisms have focused on disagreements about how to interpret the facts. For instance, the historian Nell Painter contends that the twenty Africans who were brought to Virginia in 1619 were bought and sold not as slaves, but as indentured servants with a fixed term. Painter contends that it was only in the period from the 1660s to the 1680s that changes in the laws began the terrible process of "turning 'servants' from Africa into racialized workers enslaved for life."[53] Still other critics have challenged what they take to be a deep "pessimism" in the 1619 project, particularly pessimism about the possibility that anti-Black racism can ever be disentangled from the fiber of American society. Critics plausibly worry that this is the kind of pessimism that suppresses progressive social movements and effectively acquiesces in a kind of political quietism.

Yet it is one thing to resist the 1619 project on the grounds that it gets the history wrong, or that it offers an unduly bleak and socially dangerous picture of the future. It is a vastly different thing to dismiss the entire endeavor of challenging the official American story on the grounds that there could be no real need for further national reckoning with the evils of slavery. This attitude is of a piece, I contend, with the broader effort to silence discussion about many morally unseemly elements of America's past regarding marginalization and stigmatization of various groups throughout American history. In school districts around the United States, for instance, momentum is growing for efforts that give families the right to "opt out" of curricula shaped by the concerns of Black history. Such efforts seem part of a larger project in some circles to turn away from painful truths of America's past.

But there are two other important sources of resistance to such calls to come to terms with a painful national past—both of which are global in reach, even if they take different forms in different national contexts. The first is a deep and profound anger toward cultural and political elites. In America, this anger is often expressed in the form of an allegation is that members of the elite classes have ignored white economic hardship and betrayed white Americans by paying too much attention to the struggles of nonwhite Americas. According to a study by the Pew Research Center in 2019, versions of this anger toward political elites are fueling support for (allegedly) antiestablishment leaders around the globe. This anger takes on a particularly problematic tone when it is compounded by the second source of resistance to the demand to scrutinize a morally problematic past: the growth in xenophobic populism offering narratives that put fear and resentment at the center of the history that many people carry within. In many contexts, especially where concerns about immigration have been heightened, there is fear of allegedly "losing one's place" in society and resentment at those one comes to believe are taking "one's place." In countries that also have a history of legally sanctioned discrimination and oppression against some groups, these feelings of fear and resentment take a complex turn: marginalized and stigmatized people who want to tell a story in which they have been victimized now become the victimizers. The tendency to be motivated in these ways by fear and resentment will often be exacerbated by economic stagnation, changes in the nature of work, and cynical manipulation by authoritarian political groups who may circulate conspiracy theories that give socially alienated people a false sense of being able to render this complex world fully intelligible.

What should progressive social movements do in this challenging moment? The first step is to recognize that when sizable numbers of people understand themselves through narratives that purport to license feelings of resentment and victimization, we will often confront what philosopher Luvell Anderson calls a "gap in shared hermeneutical resources."[54] That is, there will be contexts in which we think we are engaged in genuine communication about the meaning and importance of a particular event—say, a police killing of an unarmed African American man—and yet we soon discover that conflicting narratives deprive us of important cognitive tools for coming to a shared understanding of what happened and why. This inability to come to such an understanding of certain events can be a serious obstacle to communicating rationally about the nature, sources, and existence of injustice. It thereby diminishes the likelihood of creating constructive conditions for pursuing a just and genuinely shared political life. Thus the second step that progressive social movements should take is to consider what it might take to repair the hermeneutical divides, and whether social movements can play a role in that project. As a start, progressive movements may want to consider whether it is possible to tell the truth about the facts of social injustice without, at the same time, denying important facts about the social and economic alienation—and sometimes even hardship—shaping the lives of at least some on "the other side" of the divide who are being asked to confront those facts. Progressive movements may also want to consider whether it is possible to find rhetorical strategies for talking about accountability to remedy injustice without producing an unrelenting shame that sometimes shuts down the willingness to seek a remedy.

But it must be stressed that people on the other side of the hermeneutical divides are not necessarily motivated primarily by economic dislocation and hardship. They may be swayed by dystopian narratives that mischaracterize important social facts and draw on xenophobia and scapegoating. The result is often a hardening of political resistance to the idea that injustice might even exist in their societies. Chapter 7 will show that the challenges posed by these narratives are a function of the emotions and other affective responses on which the narratives depend, and the cognitive biases and stigmatizing stereotypes that discourage scrutiny of the narratives' content. But the chapter also explores the possibility that the political dominance of the fear and resentment embedded in dystopian social narratives can be overcome by the constructive power of political hope.

III

THE IMPORTANCE OF
POLITICAL HOPE

7

THE EMPIRE OF AFFECT
AND THE CHALLENGE OF
COLLECTIVE HOPE

I hope indeed; but hope itself is fear
Viewed on the sunny side . . .
— Christina Rossetti

7.1 DEEP NARRATIVES, INTERPRETIVE
DIVIDES, AND COLLECTIVE HOPE

The chapters in part 2 argued that constructive social movements can make space for justice only when they can harness the powers of imagination in three critical domains. Aesthetic imagination matters because symbolic expressions of collective memory communicate a society's understanding of who "belongs" and is therefore worthy of humane regard. Epistemic imagination matters because it generates linguistic forms that shape any given social world and profoundly influence our experience of it. Narrative imagination matters because its constructions create social meaning, shape collective identity and social roles, and legitimize central institutions and practices.

The concluding chapters of this book will argue that making space for justice also involves constructively exploiting the political possibilities of hope. King once observed that "Every step towards the goal of justice requires sacrifice, suffering and struggle; the tireless exertions and passionate concern of dedicated individuals."[1] He also understood that no one could endure such sacrifice and struggle unless they could sustain hope for moral repair and renewal in the world. But while some varieties of hope are important because they support projects of social change, social movements focused on justice must eventually join the search for a collective, socially constructive hope that might stabilize institutions capable of securing humane regard. King and Mandela both understood the importance of such hope, though they had different visions of the work needed to help produce it.

Both varieties of hope are deeply intertwined with imagination: they depend on the ability to consider unfamiliar possibilities and perspectives, and to engage in novel reflection on what is actual and familiar. This means that the rhetoric of imaginative transformation is a critical dimension of political discourse and communication. It also means that a persistent challenge confronting movements seeking justice is learning how to strike the right balance between rhetoric that demands redress for injustice and rhetoric that opens up the possibility of social reconciliation. Political hope is sometimes most important for its capacity to serve as an antidote to fear, anger, and despair. This is why contemporary efforts to ground political hope in the fear, anger, and despair of socially dominant groups pose a singularly destructive challenge to political stability and to the search for a socially constructive, collective hope that might be open to the claims of justice.

But we cannot understand the possibility of such collective hope unless we can first envision the possibility of a robust shared understanding of the social world. Further, the members of a complex, modern society cannot actually *have* a common hope unless they can articulate shared goals and shared interpretations of how to achieve them. It must thus be acknowledged that chapter 6 concluded with a potentially dispiriting observation: contemporary social movements and their intended audiences often confront an interpretive gulf—what Luvell Anderson describes as a "hermeneutical impasse"—that prevents them from achieving shared understanding of important aspects of the social world.[2] A persistent inability to transcend such impasses will be a substantial obstacle even to showing that injustice exists, let alone persuading others that it can be remedied, and convincing them that they ought to be part of the effort. We can bridge the underlying interpretive divides only if we can understand their sources, and this understanding, as Martha Nussbaum urges, requires us to be thoughtful and empathetic readers of at least *some* stories of people with whom we disagree. The challenge is that participants in some social movements may be wary of exhortations to seek empathetic understanding. They may fear that such projects can lead an inquirer to identify with, or be "indoctrinated" by, central commitments of the lives they come to understand. They may also worry that the inquirer will end up being too ready to forgive, excuse, or even justify everything associated with such a life—even, for instance, when it involves deep intolerance of marginalized groups.

Yet, in response to the first set of worries, while we sometimes achieve understanding that strengthens our capacity to view unfamiliar others with humane regard, even the most humanizing understanding is fundamentally different from identification with, or acceptance of, the way of life of those we come to understand. Some people who contemplate an unfamiliar way of life may make the "evaluative leap" from understanding to identification and approval.[3] But such leaps occur only when those making the leap were already inclined to do so. As William James suggests in his analysis of "conversion" in *The Varieties of Religious Experience*, a plausible candidate for an evaluative leap must have a sense of some "incompleteness or wrongness" from which she is "eager to escape," and some "dimly imagined" alternative ideal that she hopes to achieve.[4] When someone is "converted" to another way of life, it is thus because they discovered something in that way of life that answered to something already existing in themselves.

To address the second set of concerns, we must start by rejecting the familiar, but unfortunate, saying that "to understand all is to forgive all." J. L. Austin is reported to have said that there are times when understanding "might just add contempt to hatred."[5] In so doing, understanding will actually strengthen attitudes that block forgiveness rather than those that promote it. Jerome Neu also observes that understanding doesn't lead directly to excusing, because understanding may "produce a perception of the insult behind an injury. The mere fact that a person's behavior had causes (and here it is important . . . that causes can include reasons) does not lift responsibility."[6] Finally, if understanding does not directly lead to excusing, it certainly cannot directly lead to justifying. It is true that to understand an unfamiliar way of life is to find some of the conduct that it sanctions intelligible, by coming to understand its underlying reasons. Yet explanation is still distinct from justification. A teacher may understand that a student who submitted a plagiarized assignment did so to avoid being penalized for a late submission. But making an action intelligible does not justify it. Justification depends on the quality of people's reasons, and we can sometimes reject their reasons as morally unacceptable, or as poorly grounded in empirical facts, even though we understand how those reasons issued in the relevant conduct. Justification also depends on the "fit" between people's reasons and their conduct, and we do not have to accept others' assertions that their conduct displays the proper fit. If a police officer uses deadly force that looks disproportionate to the threat posed by a suspect, we do not have to accept the officer's claim that the killing was nonetheless an appropriate response to the alleged offense.

Mindful of these important distinctions between understanding, on one hand, and approving or justifying, on the other, the sociologist Arlie Hochschild has fully embraced the kind of interpretive project that Nussbaum recommends. Hochschild's influential book *Strangers in their Own Land: Anger and Mourning on the American Right* draws on the resources of narrative imagination to understand consequential developments in American politics. Although the book focuses on the emergence of Tea Party conservatism in the American South, the analysis offers conceptual tools that can be useful for addressing interpretive divides in many other contexts. The most important tool is Hochschild's concept of the "deep story": "A deep story is *a feels-as-if story*—it's the story feelings tell, in the language of symbols. It removes judgment. It removes fact. It tells us how things feel. Such a story permits those on both sides of the political spectrum to stand back and explore the *subjective prism* through which the party on the other side sees the world. And I don't believe that we understand anyone's politics . . . without it. For we all have a deep story."[7] Hochschild's deep story concept has special value for social movements—as well as for political philosophy—not just because it affirms the social and political importance of narrative, but also because it rightly contends that some consequential narratives may tell us relatively little about the way the world really is but a great deal about people's affective responses to the way they believe it to be. Hochschild thus acknowledges the reality of what I call the *empire of affect*: the fact that our political judgments and actions are powerfully, and unavoidably, influenced by our affective responses to, and orientations in, the world. Indeed, much of Hochschild's recent work has sought to show that emotion underwrites many of our most important political beliefs and judgments.

I refer to affective responses, rather than more narrowly to emotions, because our political beliefs and judgments are not shaped by "ordinary" emotions alone. On my account, there are three distinct categories of affective response: (a) ordinary emotions, (b) volitional attitudes and dispositions, and (c) affective orientations. The category of *ordinary emotions* includes both "primary" emotions, such as fear and anger (often considered to have a strongly "automatic" dimension), as well as "secondary" emotions, such as compassion, pride, and object-oriented hope (which seem to depend more fully on cognitive activity and less on "feeling"). The realm of *volitional attitudes and dispositions* includes affective responses such as commitment and resilience, which tend to incline us toward certain kinds of actions, and reluctance and reserve, which tend to delay or discourage action. Finally, the category of *affective orientation* includes negative orientations such as despair, but also the positive orientation that we can call "positional hope." The modifier "positional" is intended to capture the fact that some kinds of hope involve "standing firm" on the conviction that something good or desirable can happen—even in the most challenging of times—and that one might be an effective part of the efforts that bring it about.

Hochschild is clearly committed to taking these phenomena seriously, and, as I have urged, the concept of the deep story is a clear expression of that commitment. Yet in *Strangers in Their*

Own Land, Hochschild never really explains what it is about any story that "feelings tell" that makes that story "deep." The most salient fact about the story through which she explains the emergence of the Tea Party is that it clearly reveals some of the tellers' deepest and most fundamental hopes and fears. Thus I suggest that this is what makes a story a deep story. As Hochschild characterizes the deep story that emerged from her interviews, it was initially told mainly by older, white, predominantly male Americans who understand themselves as having waited patiently "in line" for their turn to realize the "American Dream," only to discover that (allegedly) undeserving others were "cutting the line" ahead of them. This is thus, fundamentally, a story of diminishing hopes, but perhaps even more fully of increasing fears of the loss of social standing. But adding insult to injury, on this narrative, the "line-cutters" have been aided by elites who have realized the Dream yet seem to delight in taunting those who are being "passed over" with unsympathetic accusations of backwardness, racism, and misogyny.

Hochschild suggests that the story gradually gained currency with wider audiences that included (some) white women and (many) younger white males because it seemed to express their feelings of status-loss and their fears that the American Dream might be out of reach. In this vein, it is worthy of note that this very American deep story about diminishing hopes and fears of status-loss has analogs in other national contexts. Those stories have been thought to explain the outcome of the UK vote on Brexit in 2016, as well as the rise of populist authoritarianism in a number of Western democracies. Taken together, what these stories tell us is not just deep truths about the hopes and fears of particular social groups, but the equally deep truth that hope and fear are the two components in the affective dimension of human life that are most important to shaping political life.

Of course, Hochschild is certainly not the first theorist to foreground the centrality of hope and fear in political life. Modern Western political philosophy originated with Thomas Hobbes's contention, in the *Leviathan*, that the only thing that can prevent life from degenerating into a war of all against all is "fear of death; desire of such things as are necessary to commodious living; and a hope by their industry to obtain them."[8] But Hobbes assumed that political life can be grounded only in individualistic, atomistic hopes for the means of "commodious living," and he presumed that such hope supports stable political life only because—and only as long as—it suppresses our fears of violence, conflict, and death. Hobbes and many of his successors failed to appreciate an important truth that organic intellectuals like King, Havel, and Mandela clearly understood. That truth is that it is possible to generate a kind of political hope that is genuinely collective and promotes political stability not simply by suppressing fundamental fears, but by allowing us to transcend those fears in an expansive and socially constructive way. To realize that possibility, it will be necessary to draw on the work of constructive social movements, the constructive rhetoric of their visionary leaders, and theories defended by psychologists, philosophers, and social thinkers who believe that some varieties of hope are not just servants of our deepest fears. But the point is that hope can be a powerful expression of the fact that human beings do not have to be dominated by fear, and political life can reflect that fact.[9]

Since fear is often thought to be a primary emotion, activated almost automatically at a rudimentary level of the nervous system, some neuroscientists believe that it will consistently "dominate" secondary emotions like object-oriented hope (and, presumably, affective orientations like positional hope).[10] It is also important that the mechanisms that produce fear, mechanisms through which we defensively react to danger and to what we take as serious threats of harm, have an adaptive and protective value. Fear operates quickly, and that is sometimes a very good thing. Still further, the pathways by which it is possible to produce *collective* fear seem to be less complex—because they are less dependent on cognitive capacities and "higher" mental processes—than the pathways by which we might generate collective hope. The combined weight of these considerations might be thought to undermine the project of producing a collective hope that will not simply be overpowered by collective fear.

Yet some recent work in cognitive science and social psychology has begun to confirm what visionary leaders of social movements have long understood: there really are identifiable and accessible pathways to collective and socially constructive hope.[11] We follow these paths when we appeal to people's capacity to accept a shared social identity; when we encourage the readiness to interpret important episodes and events in light of that identity; and when we assist efforts to articulate shared goals and then to collaborate on collectively imagining what the world might look like if those goals were realized. To be sure, in the midst of deep social conflict that tends to lead to a dearth of shared hermeneutical resources, it is not initially obvious how complex modern societies might produce the robust shared identity on which this project of creating collective hope depends. I suggest that, as a generic project, it will require many citizens of complex multicultural societies to honestly confront the distance between the deep stories they accept and the real truths about how their societies currently work, and why. In the American context, what will be required are substantive civic conversations, modeled on the "Citizen Assemblies" developed by theorists of deliberative democracy but dedicated to considering how reflective Americans of goodwill might come to a factually defensible, shared understanding of the nature and consequences of America's past.

7.2 HOPE AS THE "SUNNY SIDE" OF A COMPLEX PAIRING

But we cannot understand the possibility of a socially constructive and robust collective hope until we have a more basic understanding of hope itself. In the spirit of the epigraph with which this chapter begins, I urge that we cannot understand hope itself unless we acknowledge that hope and fear are essentially interrelated. Baruch Spinoza's analysis of emotions in his *Ethics* offers an insightful—if provocative—account of this interrelatedness. As he understands the relationship, "hope is simply an inconstant joy arising from the image of something in the future or in the past about whose outcome we are in doubt. Conversely, fear is an inconstant sadness which also arises from an image of something that is in doubt."[12] We may want to resist Spinoza's claim that hope originates as a form of joy and fear as a form of sadness, but he is surely correct to posit that, at its core, hope is the "sunny side"—in Christina Rossetti's phrase—of the dyad constituted by hope and fear.[13]

Spinoza's analysis proves especially compelling in the *Treatise Theological-Political* when he reflects on some political implications of the dyadic relationship between hope and fear. He contends, for instance, that because the human capacity of judgment is limited, and "the good things of fortune" for which we have "a boundless desire" are uncertain, we can "fluctuate wretchedly between hope and fear" in ways that make us vulnerable to superstition and manipulation.[14] This claim has unexpected contemporary resonance as we struggle with the challenge of controlling the spread of wild conspiracy theories and "alternative facts." But Spinoza also reminds us that hope is the most politically constructive aspect of the affective dimension of human life and therefore urges that laws should always be designed so that "people are restrained less by fear than hope of something good which they very much desire; for in this way everybody will do his duty willingly."[15]

Yet the political value of hope is not exhausted by its potential to promote political stability. The practice of constructive social movements has shown that hope is also a central element of the moral psychology that makes their projects possible. In fact, hope is sometimes *most* important for its tendency to support attitudes that sustain the pursuit of justice: including the conviction that social problems have realizable remedies; confidence in our capacity to constructively pursue those remedies; and commitment to the value of such pursuits even when we confront adversity. Of course, social movements typically pursue their aims through contentious politics, as I noted at length in chapter 1. This means that there will be important differences between the varieties of hope that undergird socially transformative projects conducted by social movements and the kind of hope that is likely to be a principal source of political stability. Consider, for instance, the kind of hope that might sustain a commitment to justice even in the face of great adversity. In a critical passage from *Disturbing the Peace*, Vaclav Havel described this kind of hope "above all as a state of mind, not a state of the world. Either we have hope within us or we don't; it is a dimension of the soul; it's not essentially dependent on some particular observation of the world or estimate of the situation. Hope is not prognostication. It is an orientation of the spirit, an orientation of the heart; it transcends the world that is immediately experienced and is anchored somewhere beyond its horizons." Still further:

> Hope, in this deep and powerful sense, is not the same as joy that things are going well,. . . but, rather, an ability to work for something because it is good, not just because it stands a chance to succeed. The more unpropitious the situation in which we demonstrate hope, the deeper that hope is. Hope is definitely not the same thing as optimism. It is not the conviction that something will turn out well, but the certainty that something makes sense, regardless of how it turns out.[16]

This conception of a hope that originates beyond the "horizons" of experience is profoundly different from the hope that might be counted on to support stable political life, which is likely to be very much rooted in objects *in* the world. This suggests that hope is a complex affective response that comes in many different varieties.

In fact, hope is such a complex phenomenon that, historically, there has been substantial disagreement on the question of whether *any* variety of hope could really be an emotion. Many medieval and many early modern thinkers certainly believed that hope was a fundamental emotion.[17] Yet some later accounts in experimental psychology did not even include hope in their catalogs of the emotions. More recently, some psychologists have held that hope is a secondary emotion that, as C. R. Snyder has urged, is essentially dependent on cognitive activity.[18] But it seems unlikely that this conception can illuminate the positional hope that Havel describes. We can best explain disagreements about the affective status of hope, and find plausible commonality across the varieties of hope, only if we presume that emotions are just one category of significant affective response, and that the phenomena we can intelligibly describe as hope will be found in more than one category.

Given all this complexity, is there any way to concisely express what unites all the phenomena that seem to merit the label "hope"? I believe that there is, and I understand the core idea in a version of a view that philosophers sometimes call the "standard account." On my version of that account, hope is "expectant desire": a stance that combines wanting or desiring something to happen or be true with thinking that it could really happen or be true.[19] Some contemporary philosophers will object that this definition captures only the most superficial aspects of hope and that any plausibly substantive hope always has the "aura of agency." On this objection, any defensible definition should include the idea that hope always involves a readiness to act in pursuit of the object of our hope.[20] But, surely, we can hope for things over which we cannot have—or rationally expect to have—any control. For instance, when one hopes that a friend will be in remission after her cancer treatment ends, one is not in any way implicating one's own agency, since the outcome of treatment will be determined by phenomena over which one has no control. Yet it is entirely appropriate to hold that the concerned friend in the example has an object-directed hope for her sick friend to return to good health.

Yet although we can articulate the "essence" of hope, varieties of hope may differ along several dimensions. We must ask, first, whether an instance of hope is an ordinary secondary emotion, a volitional disposition, or an affective orientation. But five additional characteristics can be significant: the source of the hope; the object of the hope; the strength of any probability judgments on which hope may rest; the quality of the reasons that might support those judgments; and the extent to which hope is directly linked to a readiness to act. On the sources of hope, we can recall Havel's view that there is a kind of hope that originates in something that transcends experience. Some thinkers have even held that hope might be "inborn." Erich Fromm believed, for instance, that "we start out with hope," and that once life begins, "the vicissitudes of environment and accident begin to further or block the potential of hope."[21] Hopes can also differ with regard to their objects: one can hope for some material object or gain, or for the realization of some state of affairs. Moreover, while hope is mainly future-oriented, it sometimes focuses on past eras or events, as when one hopes that someone did not suffer a painful demise. The fourth and fifth characteristics of hope concern how likely it is that our object-directed hopes will come to fruition, and the reasonableness of any such judgments of probability. We rely on these considerations to determine whether some instance of hope is reasonable.

The final consideration directs us to acknowledge, as I urged earlier, that there are genuine cases of hoping that do not have the "aura" of one's own agency. It might be objected that these are cases of wishful thinking rather than hoping. But in contrast to hope, one can wish for things that are not possible—as one might wish that one could have been a citizen of Athens during the age of Pericles. Even when an object-directed hope concerns some past event, such as hoping that someone did not suffer a painful demise, hope is always rooted in the conceptual realm of possibility. It is especially important to distinguish between hoping and wishing, since failing to appreciate the difference makes it too easy to confuse hope with optimism. As Havel rightly insisted, hope is not the same thing as optimism. Optimism is generally expecting that good things will happen, and sometimes even expecting that the things we most desire will happen. But having hope must sometimes be compatible with being prepared for the worst that could happen. In our individual lives, as well as in political life, we are sometimes called on to summon up such hope when we confront serious crises. Optimism may actually prove to be obstacles to hope in such contexts, if it serves to mask the reality of the adversity we face.

The philosopher Jonathan Lear has described a phenomenon that he calls "radical hope" to capture one way in which hope can be consistent with being prepared for the worst. Lear believes that radical hope can emerge only if one is willing to contemplate the worst that could happen yet still remain open to the "bare idea" that something good could still happen.[22] Viktor Frankl seems to describe just this kind of openness in *Man's Search for Meaning* when he discusses the process by which some survivors of Nazi concentration camps avoided the psychopathology of despair.[23] This is also the stance that sustained Nelson Mandela during twenty-seven years in prison—a fact that is richly revealed in his letters and in pivotal passages from his autobiography, *Long Walk to Freedom*. In an especially moving passage from that book, Mandela describes his participation in the custom of naming a grandchild: "The name I had chosen was Zaziwe—which means 'hope.' The name had special meaning for me, for during all my years in prison hope never left me—and now it never would. I was convinced that this child would be a part of a new generation of South Africans for whom apartheid would be a distant memory—that was my dream."[24] The hope that sustained Mandela during his time in prison, not unlike the hope that sustained Frankl and others though the terrors of the concentration camp, seems to be a variant of that "orientation of the heart" that Havel describes. It is the kind of hope that persists in spite of experiences that might be expected to extinguish hope if we assume (wrongly) that the only kind of hope that makes sense is hope that seeks empirical "evidence" for reasons to persist.

What I am calling positional hope has important affinities with the phenomenon that Martin Luther King described when he insisted on the possibility of sustaining "infinite hope" even in the face of disappointment. To be sure, King's certainty that infinite hope could be sustained despite the violence and intimidation that confronted participants in the Civil Rights Movement was rooted in the belief that the "arc of the universe bends toward justice" and in his conviction that the secular and the religious alike could agree with him. We may wonder whether it is still possible to adopt King's orientation of infinite hope as we confront the global threat of the deconsolidation of established democracies, the emergence of autocratic leaders who actively seek to undermine the structures of democratic governance, and moral backsliding in states that once seemed to be beacons of freedom and equality. My own view is that infinite hope—as a species of positional hope—is still possible, and that we don't need to be able to show where it is actually "anchored" in order to understand its possibility.

7.3 APPRECIATING THE RHETORIC OF HOPE

As I argued at the end of chapter 1, the work of generating progress toward justice always depends on the physical labor, material sacrifice, and political struggle of communities of concern and action. Some people who constitute those groups are officially members of formal, or even loosely structured, social movements, but many are not. Moreover, as I reiterated in section 7.1, through synchronous or asynchronous collaborations, the imaginative reframing of the world to make space for justice can sometimes be successfully carried out as collective projects. But, especially in times of conflict or crisis, the imaginative reframing of the world in service of *hope* is deeply dependent on the rhetorical skill of a visionary leaders or representatives. Rhetoric, the art of effective speaking or writing to persuade, can be a critical component of the work of constructive social movements. But, in most cases, a movement's most important rhetorical work is usually the province of imaginative and verbally adept individuals.

Rhetoric is rarely given its due in contemporary political thought. As Young argues in *Inclusion and Democracy*, contemporary political philosophers have tended to insist on a "Platonic distinction" between the rational speech that they deem appropriate to political discourse and debate and the "mere rhetoric" that they believe endangers the foundations of rationally defensible political institutions and practices. Young rightly rejects this stance, arguing that an indiscriminate dismissal of all rhetoric as inferior and politically undesirable wrongly denigrates the affective dimension of human experience and unwisely devalues figurative language and symbolic gestures. Young goes on to show that there are contexts in which rhetoric plays crucial positive roles in political communication, especially in democratic societies. Two considerations stand out. The first is Young's insistence that effective rhetoric can sometimes place issues on the agenda for public deliberation that might otherwise be ignored.[25] She doesn't offer examples here, but surely few would deny that one of the most important functions of the "I have a Dream" refrain from King's speech at the March on Washington in 1963 was helping to get the issue of racial segregation on America's national agenda. It was surely an instance of political genius for the gospel singer Mahalia Jackson to interrupt King's reading of his prepared, written speech in order to exhort him to "tell them about the Dream, Martin."

Young also argues that effective rhetoric can sometimes move us from prolonged deliberation about a range of possibilities to focused judgment about which possibility to pursue. In what I take to be a critical example of this process, Franklin Delano Roosevelt's second inaugural address (delivered in 1937) set out the path to the culmination of American progressivism in the policies of the New Deal. A few of the most effective passages are especially instructive:

> I see millions of families trying to live on incomes so meager that the pall of family disaster hangs over them day by day. . . . I see millions denied education, recreation, and the opportunity to better their lot and the lot of their children. . . . I see one-third of a nation ill-housed, ill-clad, ill-nourished.
>
> It is not in despair that I paint you that picture. I paint it for you in hope—because the Nation, seeing and understanding the injustice in it, proposes to paint it out. We are determined to make every American citizen the subject of his country's interest and concern; and we will never regard any faithful law-abiding group within our borders as superfluous. The test of our progress is not whether we add more to the abundance of those who have much; it is whether we provide enough for those who have too little.[26]

Young's interest in such rhetoric would focus attention on its capacity to further the goal of "inclusion" in a discussion-based democracy. But the vehicle through which the second inaugural furthered the goal of inclusion was the imaginative transformation of fear and despair into hope.[27]

The projects that rhetorically gifted orators like Roosevelt undertake confirm the wisdom of Percy Bysshe Shelley's claim, in "The Defence of Poetry," that imagination has the power to lift "the veil from the hidden beauty of the world" and "make familiar objects be as if they were not familiar." An especially compelling example of this power is contained in Roosevelt's first inaugural address, delivered in 1933. Roosevelt took office at a point in the Great Depression when many feared that the economic devastation and social disruptions of the time would arouse massive social unrest and upheaval. Moreover, in some sense, that prospect—and the powerful fears it expressed— would have been the "familiar" response to the extraordinary economic devastation of the Depression. Yet Roosevelt famously insisted that "the only thing we have to fear is fear itself": that "nameless, unreasoning, unjustified terror which paralyzes needed efforts to convert retreat into advance."[28] This is an especially striking instance of imaginative reframing in service of inspiring hope. Here, what would have been a "familiar" response to economic devastation was imaginatively reframed as an "unjustified" and "nameless" terror to be resisted.

In the long term, the rhetoric of Roosevelt's first inaugural gave rise to a resolve that eventually generated hope for constructive change and, in many cases, motivated commitment to pursue that change. But perhaps most important, in the short term it inspired positional hope that prevented the devastation of the era from generating unrelenting despair. Roosevelt's rhetoric could have this transformative power because it acknowledged that destructive fear would be the immediate and "familiar" reaction, even as it invited the listener to understand those circumstances in a new and constructive light. Like many such speeches, Roosevelt's first inaugural invites us to treat an occasion of social uncertainty—and even social crisis—as an opportunity to create new and better modes of social life. Such speeches imaginatively transform occasions in which fear, anger and despair would be familiar reactions into unexpected opportunities to contemplate social renewal. This is the process exemplified in the Gettysburg Address, when Lincoln asserts that the sacrifice and loss of the Civil War could provide the opportunity for a "new birth of freedom." It is also evident in the ways in which King's "I have a Dream" refrain transforms righteous indignation and condemnation of segregation into hope for racial equality.

King's speech is a reminder that the transformative rhetoric of hope is an important element in the tradition of the "black jeremiad" that has been so central to African American political thought. In this tradition, what must be transformed into hope is rarely fear but the righteous indignation of the speaker and of those on whose behalf she can plausibly claim to speak. Some instances of this tradition focus more intently than others on righteous indignation. Thus Frederick Douglass's denunciation of the continued existence of slavery is the dominant theme of his speech "What to the Slave Is the Fourth of July" (1852), in which he chastises his fellow Americans for their failure to live up to "the great principles of political freedom and of natural justice, embodied in that Declaration of Independence."[29] In *The Fire Next Time*, James Baldwin's righteous indignation seems to give way more quickly to his hopeful demand for America to eliminate segregation and "achieve our country."[30]

As Richard Rorty suggests, the rhetorical projects of the black jeremiad, like the transformative projects of Lincoln and Roosevelt, are often noteworthy contributions to the American democratic tradition.[31] Significant voices in that tradition have understood the importance to democratic stability of finding ways to imaginatively transform destructive attitudes and emotions like anger and fear into opportunities to contemplate social renewal and hope for the realization of a more just society. Appeals to the secondary emotions of object-focused hope may provide the appropriate vehicle for such reflection, but sometimes it is most important to rhetorically summon up positional hope that does not give way in the face of adversity and crisis.

In an era that often disparages verbal eloquence, many will rightly wonder about the odds of producing many more rhetorically skillful visionaries of hope. Yet the imaginative reframing of uncertainty and crisis in service of hope can sometimes issue from a well-thought-out *nonverbal* gesture. Shortly after taking office as South Africa's first Black president, Nelson Mandela offered just such a gesture with his unanticipated display of public support for the South African Rugby team during the Rugby World Cup in 1995. Many South Africans perceived this as a gesture of racial reconciliation and an expression of hope for the moral renewal of South Africa.[32] Of course, like Lincoln, Roosevelt, and King, Mandela was a person of extraordinary vision and remarkable political wisdom. Holding him up as an exemplar still sets a daunting standard. But the imaginative reframing of uncertainty and crisis can surely be achieved by visionary leaders given to more prosaic words and gestures. The challenge is figuring out where to find such visionaries and then creating cultural space for their messages to be heard.

The intellectual and cultural labor of artists, historians, philosophers, social theorists, and religious thinkers can also contribute to shaping the rhetoric of hope. Indeed, sometimes the most constructive instances of the rhetoric of hope will come from communities that do not actively participate in "contentious politics" at all. Moreover, a writer need not understand her work as a direct contribution to the contentious politics of narrative activism, as discussed in chapter 6, for the work to be able to provide political insight and inspiration to those engaged in the project of reshaping and reconstituting the social world in pursuit of justice.

Ironically, art is sometimes a catalyst for hope by virtue of its capacity to help us vicariously contemplate the "worst that could happen" without requiring the suffering and sacrifice of real people. This means that, as tempting as it might be to prefer *utopian* art, if we care about constructive social change, we must also make room for some kinds of *dystopian* art. The dystopian fiction that we ought to welcome will not seek to produce fear, despair, and uncertainty for their own sakes. Instead, it will be the kind of fiction that confronts us with the inescapable truth that bad things happen but invites us to consider how we might avoid them, along with psychopathology of anger, fear, and despair. A great deal of climate-focused science fiction, for instance, tends to do both of these things. But even when constructively dystopian fiction focuses mainly on avoiding the psychopathology of despair, it can allow us to contemplate and cultivate resilience in the face of despair, and of courage in the face of adversity. In my view, resilience is not only a volitional disposition but a variety of hope that falls midway between the focus of object-directed hope and the stalwart orientation of positional hope. When the main character in Margaret Atwood's *The Handmaid's Tale* discovers the mock-Latin phrase that Atwood translates as "don't let the bastards grind you down," the novel displays a critical virtue of constructive dystopia: its capacity to encourage hope-as-resilience.[33]

My claims about the role of art in creating space for constructive change may seem to treat art as propaganda. But as I argued in chapter 4, in my view, there are good reasons to think that all art is propaganda. Surely the symbolic expression that we call "art" is always provoking us to see and understand the world in some particular way, and at least sometimes to suggest ideas and beliefs that may lead us to act differently from how we would have acted in the absence of our encounter with that work of art.

7.4 REJECTING THE SIMULACRUM OF HOPE

But how should we respond to those dystopian stories that purport to be nonfictional accounts of the real world, although what they are really "about" is the depth of people's diminishing hopes and escalating fears of status loss? Hochschild is right to suggest that these stories matter. The feelings they reveal are real, and humane regard for the people who tell them demands that we try to listen with care. Yet if understanding does not require identification or approval, it also does not require unquestioning silence or political quietism, especially if there is reason to believe that the story we are being told might be woefully inaccurate. There are serious moral and political consequences if, for instance, allegations about large numbers of "line-cutters" and antiwhite elites denying people access to opportunities go unchallenged.

When influential politicians and cultural commentators attempt to articulate a rhetoric of "hope" by appealing to factually questionable dystopian stories, such efforts can only produce a *simulacrum* of constructive hope. What purports to be constructive hope to make one's country "great again," for instance, or to "take back control" from migrants, will be little more than a mix of unsustainable nostalgia and xenophobic loss-aversion masquerading as collective hope. In recent years, the mask has sometimes been lifted in a particularly ugly— and sometimes violent—fashion, when dystopian deep stories become intertwined with the so-called Great Replacement Narrative. This narrative came to worldwide attention as a prelude to the violence that erupted in Charlottesville, Virginia, around a plan to remove a statue of Robert E. Lee.[34] It has also been implicated in mass shootings, in more than one country, that have targeted people on the basis of their ethnicity.

But the growth in acts of terrorist violence is not the only disturbing trend to emerge with the global spread of dystopian "deep stories." In a second trend, fears of status loss have come to dominate concern about diminishing hopes among some socially dominant groups, especially in political discourse and decision-making. Many social scientists were initially unwilling to acknowledge this development. But in a paper challenging the economic focus of the "left behind" thesis initially offered to explain the American presidential election of 2016, the political theorist Diana C. Mutz maintained that "perceived status-threat," not concern about economic hardship, really explained the vote.[35] The tendency for perceived status-threat to dominate "pocketbook" concerns appears to confirm a behavioral theory advanced by Amos Tversky and Daniel Kahneman, in which human beings generally fear loss more than they value success in achieving a goal—perhaps as much as two times more. This means that loss-aversion is often profoundly irrational, as Tversky and Kahneman have claimed.[36] As I noted briefly in chapter 6, Jonathan Metzl has shown that the dominance of perceived status-threat in some communities' decisions about social policy has led them to make choices that lower life expectancy and undermine well-being in their own communities.[37]

But the third, and perhaps most troubling, development in this saga of dystopian narratives is that the dominance of perceived status-threat over diminishing economic hope has increased the political influence of "marginalized status-seekers."

These are people who prefer to create social and political chaos of various kinds, rather than to operate through political processes that they have come to believe (and are too often encouraged to believe) exclude them. Theorists of political behavior have posited that they seek to create chaos as a strategy—a socially dangerous strategy—for seeking status-recognition, and that they are motivated almost entirely by a "need for chaos."[38] In the paper that first articulated this thesis, Michael Peterson, Matthias Osmundsen, and Kevin Arceneaux argued that these marginalized status-seekers are often the most vigorous and indiscriminate disseminators of conspiracy theories and outlandish invented "news" stories. The paper argues that people are motivated by the need for chaos when they feel marginalized and powerless and resent the political institutions and elites whom they blame for their circumstances. The theory is that they seek to produce political chaos as a means of restoring power over their own lives and reasserting their human worth.

Yet marginalized status-seekers have gone beyond merely spreading dangerous conspiracy theories and fake news. In recent episodes, they have gathered together in mobs, sometimes seeking to prove that the theories they have been spreading were true all along, and even trying to permanently silence those who reject their theories. Of course, this is the kind of extra-institutional collective action that informed Gustave Le Bon's claims about the dangers of "the crowd," and we have reason to seek a deeper understanding of its causes and its possible remedies. These developments may lead some critics to object to two claims that are central to this book: my claim that imagination can be a constructive force in political life, and my contention that extra-institutional collective action can often be a socially constructive phenomenon.

To be sure, we must acknowledge the dangers of dystopian stories and conspiracy theories to inspire political chaos and violence. We must also admit that when extra-institutional collective action degenerates into mob violence, it unleashes forces that are fundamentally antithetical to stable political life. Yet we should not therefore reject the *responsible* use of imagination or the socially constructive projects of extra-institutional collectives. The best response to those agents of chaos who can still be reached is to try to remedy the causes of their marginalization and resentment by addressing the social and economic dislocations of contemporary life. But we will need to draw on constructive imagination to do so: for instance, on epistemic imagination as a means of enhancing our problem-solving abilities, and on sympathetic imagination as a source of conflict resolution on the path to social repair. Moreover, we will likely need to strengthen associations of civil society in which the collective action of ordinary citizens might help to reshape local communities that are in disarray. In 1939, during another moment of political crisis, John Dewey suggested a way to think about the kind of projects I have in mind when he defended the concept of "creative democracy." He called for efforts to reinvigorate democracy as "a way of life" that would be "controlled by faith in human nature" and "faith in the capacity of human beings for intelligent judgment and action if proper conditions are furnished."[39] Imagination and the innovation of people in communities of action and concern will be critical to realizing these Deweyan aims in the contemporary social world.

But what is the best way to address less marginalized people who still remain active in conventional political processes, but who are increasingly motivated by perceived-threat rooted in irrational loss-aversion? The most direct mode of address, and the one that seems most compatible with respect for their rational agency, would begin by trying to convince them of how fully their loss-aversion is endangering their own well-being, and to get them consider that the assumptions on which their fears of status loss are based may be incorrect. Of course, as I have consistently acknowledged, people are sometimes hardened in their resistance to self-reflection and can often double-down on their beliefs, when those beliefs are bound up with stigmatizing biases regarding race, ethnicity, and gender, and cognitive biases such as confirmation bias and politically motivated reasoning. In addition, we should not underestimate the possibility that people who vote on the basis of perceived status threat, seeking to protect their political dominance, may believe that they can temporarily exploit marginalized status-seekers to disrupt the functioning of political institutions and processes which they see as denying them their "rightful place in line." But they are making a dangerous bargain when they choose to risk political chaos to try to realize the kind of hopes that actually depend on political stability.

To the fullest extent possible, we should still try to accord respect to those with whom we disagree—even as we acknowledge that it may not be possible to respect the content of their dystopian narratives. Respectful and transparent uses of imagination might prove to be effective means of encouraging people to relinquish the all too durable biases that harden their commitments to unreliable dystopian narratives. From providing opportunities for "low-stakes" encounters with art (in the broadest sense), from encouragement to take part in "high-stakes" civic conversations around history and identity, it is possible to find respectful modes of address, as I argued at greater length in chapter 3. Moreover, the idea of participating in the high-stakes civic projects might be made even more attractive if people can be convinced that such participation is a politically constructive alternative to relying on chaos as political strategy.

Finally, as I will consider more fully in the concluding chapter, constructive social movements can help create a climate in which such civic conversations might have broad appeal. This would involve seeking rhetoric that strikes a sustainable balance between unrelenting demands for immediate redress of injustice and rhetoric that holds out the possibility of appropriate social reconciliation. This is not to deny that even in times of social crisis and upheaval, there is still a role for rhetoric that refuses to be conciliatory in articulating demands for justice. Such rhetoric is sometimes *rationally* necessary because of the "radical flank effect," described in chapter 1, whereby moderate claims for justice are sometimes most effective against the background of more radical demands. Thus, even before the emergence of activist groups intentionally framing their work with the language of "Black power," during the ten years that the activism of Malcolm X and Martin Luther King overlapped (1955–1965) there was a complex—and unexpectedly creative—interplay between King's conciliatory rhetoric and Malcolm X's insistently militant tone.[40]

Equally important, rhetoric that refuses to be conciliatory can sometimes be a *morally* necessary means of voicing claims that have been ignored or actively silenced. In this regard, it should not be hard to comprehend why, in the aftermath of King's assassination, Fred Hampton's insistence that the Black Panthers constituted the vanguard in a true revolution against racial injustice would prove compelling to many African Americans. For many, the violence that took King's life seemed like a violent attack on King's rhetoric of reconciliation and redemption. Moreover, for some, it thereby confirmed Stokely Carmichael's provocative formulation of the Black Power movement's principal objection to King's stance: "It made one fallacious assumption: In order for nonviolence to work, your opponent has to have a conscience. The United States has no conscience."

But even though there is sometimes a defensible role for the rhetoric of resistance over the life of an extended social movement, conciliatory rhetoric is sometimes both rationally and morally required. This is the conclusion that Nelson Mandela came to, upon his release from prison in 1990, when he willingly adopted a conciliatory stance and encouraged others to do so as well, as part of an agreement meant to end South African Apartheid without a bloody civil war. Shortly after Mandela's release, the poet Seamus Heaney likened Mandela's path from violent resister to nation-saving peacemaker to the story of Philoctetes in Sophocles's play of the same name: despite being "wounded and betrayed," Mandela still summoned the capacity of "helping the polis get together again."[41] Heaney understood that Mandela's stance was not just the product of a rational political calculation, but an extraordinary expression of heroism and grace. Indeed, he once described Mandela's intervention as "the *miraculum*." Heaney went on to capture the essence of Mandela's achievement in the poem delivered by the chorus in *The Cure at Troy*, his own verse adaptation of the Philoctetes story. These famous lines from Heaney's poem are a powerful reminder of why Mandela remains both a moral exemplar and a political hero who can be an inspiration to anyone seeking to make space for justice:

History says, Don't hope
On this side of the grave.
But then, once in a lifetime
The longed-for tidal wave
Of justice can rise up,
And hope and history rhyme.[42]

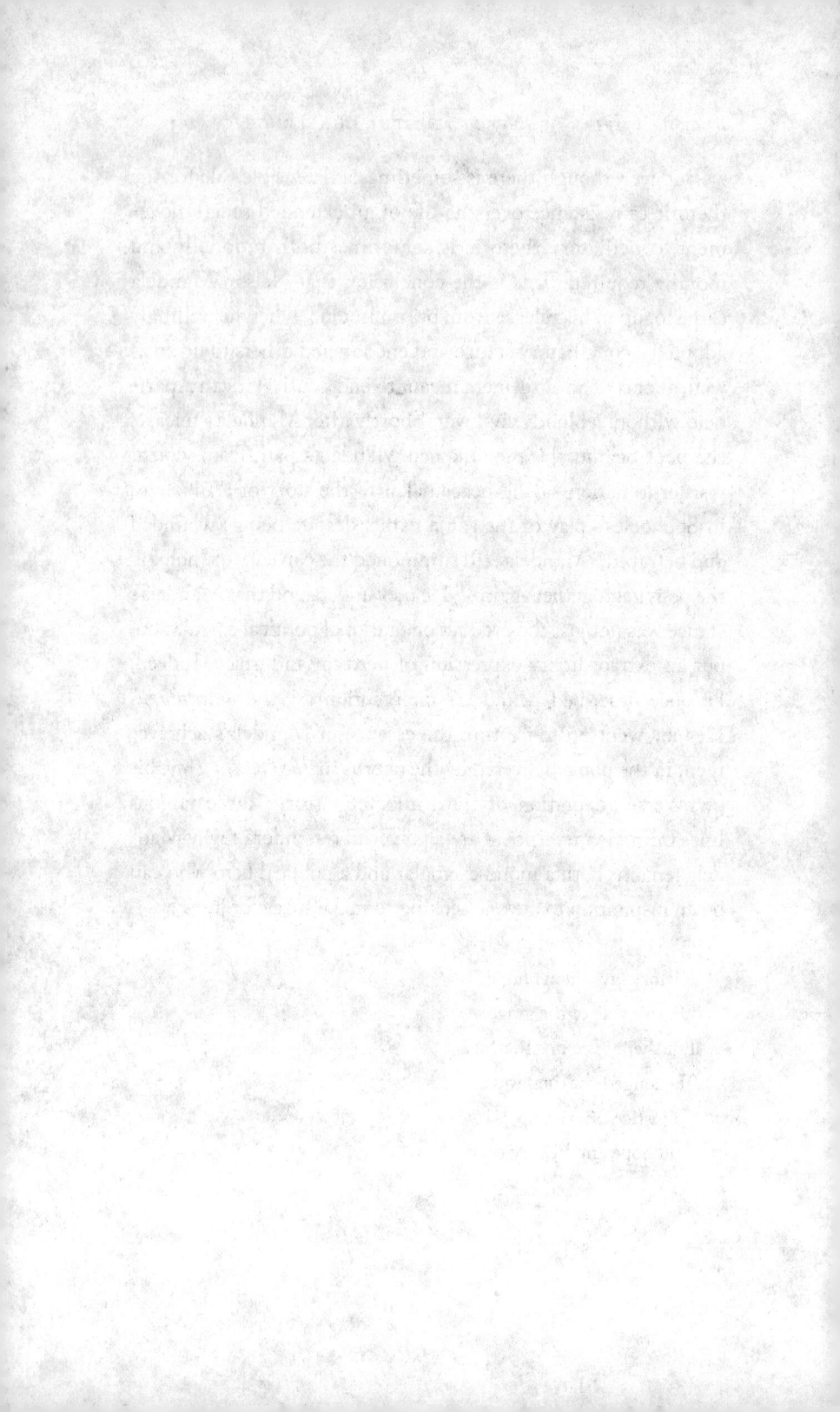

8

HOPE AND HISTORY

Ring the bells that still can ring
Forget your perfect offering.
There is a crack in everything
That's how the light gets in.

—Leonard Cohen

8.1. A STONE OF HOPE

Chapter 7 analyzed the extraordinary constructive power of social movements built on genuine collective hope. But it also explored the destructive power of collective action premised on hate and dystopian fear, and it showed how that power can be intensified when a movement exploits the bare sense of hopelessness of people who feel deeply marginalized. Martin Luther King, Jr., understood that a movement with such characteristics might provide its participants with a "gratifying slogan"; in recent years, such slogans have promised a movement that would make a country "great again," or allow its members to take their country "back" from migrant populations.[1] But King argued, quite plausibly, that a movement built on such foundations could not be expected to last, and that it might produce a great deal of collateral damage in the meantime. He acknowledged that a revolution might be born of despair, as I have argued elsewhere, but he rightly insisted that the results of such a revolution could not be sustained by despair for very long.[2] In one of the most memorable lines from the speech at the 1963 March on Washington, King was emphatic that the Civil Rights Movement needed to "hew out of the mountain of despair a stone of hope."[3]

Some noteworthy contemporary thinkers have proclaimed the "courage of hopelessness" in response to recent political crises. Giorgio Agamben defends hopelessness as the only intelligent alternative to theories people turn to in order to "warm their hearts with empty hopes."[4] Slavoj Žižek endorses hopelessness because what "true courage" requires in times of social and economic crisis is

> not to imagine an alternative, but to accept the consequences of the fact that there is no clearly discernible alternative: the dream of an alternative is a sign of theoretical cowardice; it functions as a fetish that prevents us thinking through to the end the deadlock of our predicament. In short, the true courage is to admit that the light at the end of the tunnel is most likely the headlights of another train approaching us from the opposite direction.[5]

Žižek seems to believe that we must simply resign ourselves to the danger and wait for the crash. That is, the only intellectually defensible thing to do is to look forward to the implosion of late capitalism, and whatever form of social life emerges from the rubble. But King was surely correct about the real-world consequences of this theoretical posture. History has shown that when hopelessness and despair become the dominant forces in any revolution, the mode of life that emerges will be unstable at best, and at worst result in deadly and widespread violence under the guise of progress. Žižek's suspicions of the "fetishes" that drive some contemporary "progressive" politics, and the neoliberal reforms offered as alternatives to those projects, may well be justified. But King's warnings about the dangers of offering hopelessness as an alternative to these efforts is borne out by the Reign of Terror in eighteenth-century France, the violent excesses of Stalinism in the former Soviet Union, and the genocidal horrors carried out by the Khmer Rouge in Cambodia.

Equally important, it is morally unconvincing, and even intellectually disingenuous, to try to represent political quietism as "courage." In an insightful passage from Harper Lee's *To Kill a Mockingbird*, the novel's hero Atticus Finch offers a compelling account of true courage: "It's when you know you're licked before you begin, but you begin anyway and see it through no matter what." This claim echoes one of the most important insights of the constructive social movements discussed in this book: true courage in the face of social crisis and adversity demands hope. Indeed, it must ultimately be rooted in that positional hope that Havel described as a readiness "to work for something because it is good, not just because it stands a chance to succeed." Havel observes that the "more unpropitious the situation in which we demonstrate hope, the deeper that hope is." We can add that the more unpropitious the situation in which social movements seek justice, the truer and deeper the courage they display when they are not deterred. As Seamus Heaney so richly confirmed, this is the kind of courage displayed in Nelson Mandela's readiness to promote peace in South Africa by seeking a constructive balance between demands for justice and openness to the possibility of reconciliation.

8.2 A DELICATE BALANCE

In fact, over the past several decades, social movements have taught us something that political philosophers have rarely even contemplated. They have shown that making space for justice requires a delicate balance between three sometimes quite separate undertakings: (1) projects of reconciliation, (2) efforts to obtain reparative justice, and (3) the pursuit of institutions and practices that create the conditions for a just and flourishing life equally accessible to all. The remainder of this chapter reflects on the implications of this insight for contemporary social movements as well as contemporary political thought. Unfortunately, there can be no algorithm for striking the appropriate balance between these three undertakings, and acknowledging the complexity of the challenge this creates is as critical for political thought as it is for social movements.

As Mandela quickly recognized, in the throes of social crisis, reconciliation can sometimes be the overriding concern. Finding a balance between demands for justice and demands for reconciliation can sometimes be the only means of preventing a civil war. But sometimes it is also the only means of promoting the kind of peace that might eventually allow the creation of a society capable of pursuing the substantive demands of justice. I have adopted Iris Young's notion that the most compelling account of social justice leads to an "enabling conception," on which social justice exists when most people can live relatively free from unnecessary pain and suffering, and they are able to exercise their capacities for choice and action without unwarranted interference, coercion, or violence. But it will not be possible to realize these goals if we settle on the kind of peace that is always hovering on the edge of civil war. King believed that we could achieve the right kind of social peace only by seeking to create a community in which everyone flourishes on the terms of agape, by which he meant "redeeming goodwill" or sometimes "understanding goodwill" toward all.[6] He even supposes that agape might well be the only kind of love that can save human civilization.

Yet, despite his insistence that social movements need to find the "strength to love" in this broad way, King never denied that we must protest injustice wherever we find it. Moreover, his protest could strike the notes of righteous indignation as vigorously as any rhetoric in Douglass's "What to the Slave Is the Fourth of July?" or Malcom X's defiant challenges to what he saw as the persistence of unearned white privilege. Some commentators believe that King's rhetoric became more "radical" and revolutionary after the death of Malcolm X.[7] Yet in the speech "A Time to Break Silence" (1967), his controversial contribution to debate about the Vietnam War, King convincingly presented his calls for a "true revolution of values" as the culmination of a life-long challenge to American materialism and militarism, and to America's resistance to taking a genuinely global perspective on human well-being.[8] King nonetheless remained adamant that we should never treat the protest of injustice as an overriding goal of social activism. As he noted in commenting on the Montgomery bus boycott,

We must remember as we boycott that a boycott is not an end within itself; it is merely a means to awaken a sense of shame within the oppressor and challenge his false sense of superiority. But the end is reconciliation; the end is redemption; the end is the creation of the beloved community. It is this type of spirit and this type of love that can transform opposers into friends. It is this type of understanding goodwill that will transform the deep gloom of the old age into the exuberant gladness of the new age. It is this love which will bring about miracles in the hearts of men.[9]

King thus reminds us that we must seek reconciliation and redemption not simply to prevent the worst that could happen, but to help create the conditions in which we can pursue a just and flourishing social life.

Near the start of chapter 1, I referred to the possibility of striking a constructive balance between the search for justice and openness to reconciliation. Reconciliation is a forward-looking project that may require us to temporarily bracket concerns about injustice and pause the search for policies and institutions that might constitute a remedy. But many insightful participants in social movements came to realize that sometimes reconciliation is not possible if we are too ready to ignore the lingering consequences—sometimes material, and sometimes psycho-social—of certain kinds of harms that have resulted from injustice. Acting on this realization, in the second half of the twentieth century many social movements began to insist that there are circumstances in which we cannot progress toward reconciliation until we give certain backward-looking claims of justice their "due." Giving those claims their due, it was usually argued, meant finding some means of repairing the harms done by grave injustice.

In fact, one of the most remarkable and politically consequential developments to take shape in the second half of the twentieth century was the emergence of a set of phenomena that have come to be known, collectively, as "reparations politics."[10] This phrase names a range of organized political demands for moral repair that have now been made against nations, governments, and their agents, as well as against religious institutions, universities, and corporations. Before 1950, large-scale reparations tended to be limited to postwar compensation between nations. But in the aftermath of World War II and the Holocaust, West German reparations programs introduced the practice of providing national reparations to individual victims as well as to states. Political movements presupposing this idea that groups of "private" persons, and not just nations, can have moral and legal standing to make legitimate reparations demands have now become a truly global phenomenon. Reparations politics have shaped the political landscape from South Africa to South America and from the United States to Eastern Europe.

In an especially critical example, in the belief that a lasting reconciliation would not be possible in South Africa without efforts to repair the deep social and psycho-social wounds of Apartheid, one of the first acts of Mandela's new government was the creation (in 1995) of the Truth and Reconciliation Commission. The TRC was directed to create processes whereby it would be possible to expose the truth about the extent of human-rights violations carried out by the Apartheid regime. But reparations politics includes more than tribunals and truth commissions to reveal the truth and extent of political violence. Reparations may include programs to compensate violations of human rights, citizenship rights, and property rights; programs of material compensation offered to indigenous peoples or other wronged minorities who have been subject to historical injustice; and demands for nations, religious institutions, and even professional societies to issue formal apologies for past injustice.

Demands for reparations are sometimes linked with claims that the wrong in need of repair has been actively ignored, denied, or suppressed. In such cases, the historical denial of harm may be claimed as an additional wrong in itself. The demand for reparations will then include calls for formal acknowledgment of the hitherto suppressed injustice, and public recognition of the sufferings of those subject to the injustices. In this way, the politics of reparation can be also become a politics of recognition: a movement in which those who argue that they have been silenced or ignored seek to have their stories woven into the collective memory and integrated into the public historical record. Occasionally, a demand for recognition may take on something of an independent life, as in the efforts of America's Vietnam veterans to have a national memorial erected in Washington, D.C. But when demands for recognition arise out of demands for the repair of past harm, it is appropriate to treat these demands as important components of the politics of reparation.

Successful efforts to address claims for reparation and recognition can be a powerful expression of moral progress in human affairs. Indeed, in many respects they are evidence of the existence and salutary influence of a complex international culture of human rights. Meeting the demands of the human rights paradigm is virtually always an expression of humane regard: it requires a commitment to the idea of justice as a combination of respect for human dignity and compassionate concern for human suffering. Yet even as we can acknowledge the rise of the politics of reparation as one way of expressing humane regard, profound challenges may attend any effort to defend particular claims for reparations.

One set of challenges involves potential confusion around the notions of responsibility and guilt. For instance, we must be careful to distinguish between the collective responsibility to respond to a wrong and collective guilt for commission of the wrong. In the context of debates about the possibility of reparations for American slavery, for example, recent immigrants who could neither have owned slaves nor supported Jim Crow segregation do not bear any part of the collective guilt for the slavery and its aftermath. But, as the philosopher Thomas McCarthy has urged, there can still be a powerful argument that anyone who benefits from "an unjustly acquired and unjustly distributed" inheritance could well be deemed part of the "collective" that bears responsibility for addressing the wrongs of slavery and its aftermath.[11] Yet anyone who wants to make an argument to support reparations for American slavery must construct an argument that is sensitive to other moral claims that might override a justifiable reparations claim. For instance, perhaps the idea of providing monetary damages in response to the denial of human dignity is potentially incompatible with valuing the victims in a way that respects that dignity.

We must even be willing to ask whether it might sometimes to do more harm than good—even for the wronged parties—to pursue certain kinds of reparations claims. The underlying argument that generates this question should not be conflated with an effort to deny or suppress the wrongs in question. Moreover, in the debate about reparations for American slavery, we must not assume that African-descended people who oppose reparations are guilty of some kind of false consciousness, or that they are simply mouthpieces of racial self-hatred. Influential thinkers of the African diaspora, such as Aime Cesaire, Frantz Fanon, and Orlando Patterson, have raised provocative challenges to the idea that people of the African diaspora ought to support reparations. Near the end of *Black Skin, White Masks*, for instance, Fanon strongly criticized the idea of reparations in postcolonial contexts and urged that the reasoning on which reparations arguments depends is incompatible with the acknowledgment of human freedom.[12] In another example, speaking as a Jamaican American reflecting on the position of "nonnaturalized" African Americans, Orlando Patterson issued the following provocative challenge: "Black Americans can be the first group in the history of mankind who transcend the confines and grip of a cultural heritage, and in so doing they can become the most truly modern of all peoples—a people who feel no need of a nation, a past or a particularistic culture, but whose style of life will be a rational and continually changing adaptation to the exigencies of survival, at the highest possible level of existence."[13] Of course, even those who are ambivalent about reparations for slavery may side with James Baldwin in believing that such a view does not take the effects of history seriously enough. As Baldwin writes: "History . . . is not merely something to be read. And it does not refer merely, or even principally, to the past. On the contrary, the great force of history comes from the fact that we carry it within us, are unconsciously controlled by it in many ways, and history is literally present in all that we do. It could scarcely be otherwise, since it is to history that we owe our frames of reference, our identities, and our aspirations."[14]

8.3 COMING TO TERMS WITH HISTORY

Even if we could produce satisfactory responses to these challenges, there would still be two important unresolved concerns. The first is a concern, articulated by critics such as Jeremy Waldron and John Torpey, that large-scale efforts to address reparation and recognition claims may seriously endanger forward-looking efforts to bring about broadly constructive social change.[15] In Torpey's words, "the global spread of reparations demands and the preoccupation with the past to which it bears witness reflect an unmistakable decline of a more explicitly future-oriented politics."[16] This objection serves, in part, to remind us that the main motivation of constructive social movements is usually reforming or eliminating institutions and practices that endanger a person's chance of exercising their rational agency with minimal interference, and living relatively free of unnecessary pain and suffering.

But the effort to produce a defensible "future-oriented politics" cannot succeed without serious reflection on the past. We must be able to understand whether any present injustices might be functioning as constraints on rational agency, or as obstacles to living a life relatively free of unnecessary suffering. It will often be impossible to understand the nature and scope of the relevant injustices—and ultimately whether they can be remedied—unless we consider the historical events, episodes, and human actions that might have generated them. In short, we must sometimes look backward in order to understand how to constructively move forward. To be sure, a defensible future-oriented politics cannot be focused exclusively on historical injustice. A considerable portion of its projects must address the emerging challenges of (among other things) climate change, the economic and social impacts of globalization, and the social and political consequences of new technologies that have reshaped human reproduction and changed the way we communicate and interact with one another. But even as we address these forward-looking problems, we must remember George Santayana's famous caution about the dangers of repeating the past that we fail to remember. That caveat is just as crucial for those who would create a better future as for those who seek to repair the wrongs of the past.

Still further, the need to consider how hope and history might "rhyme"—in Seamus Heaney's sense—is just as critical for political philosophy as it is for social movements. John Rawls's understanding of what constitutes a fair distribution of the benefits and burdens of social cooperation offers an often-inspiring glimpse of what a just society might look like. But philosophers such as David Lyons and Charles Mills rightly object that

Rawls's view is insufficiently informed by an understanding of the seriousness and scope of American racial injustice.[17] Some elements of Rawls's account of civil disobedience were deeply influenced by what he took King to be arguing in the "Letter from Birmingham Jail." But as Lyons argued, Rawls never fully acknowledged the vast distance between what he described as the problem of "partial compliance" with defensible principles of distributive justice and the oppressive and exploitative social, political, and economic structures that have contributed to making racial injustice so deeply entrenched in America. Lyons makes a powerful case that Rawls wrongly fails to consider that the framework within which political resistance to American racial injustice emerged was neither "nearly just" or even "reasonably just"—to adapt terms from Rawls's account—and that resistance to American racial injustice never needed special moral justification beyond the claim that it was profound injustice.[18]

I have argued elsewhere that Rawls's "refusal of history" in discussing some social consequences of racial injustice can be understood as, in part, Rawls's effort to avoid the rancorous debate about Patrick Moynihan's assertion, in "The Negro Family: The Case of National Action," that some aspects of racial inequality in America were best explained as the product of a "tangle of pathology" in African American communities.[19] For Rawls, an important demand of distributive justice is a requirement to try to mitigate the effects of past bad luck in the distribution of rationally necessary goods—including the kind of family into which one is born or adopted. But critics like Charles Mills rightly object that Rawls never fully acknowledged the scope of what needs "mitigation," because he did not understand the nature and depth of racial injustice.

One of the most important things missing from Rawls's view is an understanding of how fully American political culture has consistently failed to acknowledge that justice demands humane regard, and that every member of society merits that regard. Of course, Rawls's view richly articulates the value of respect, including the importance of self-respect and the idea that a society's basic institutions and practices are not just if they don't help secure the social conditions for self-respect. But as I urged in chapter 3, no Kantian account, even an account that is as morally inspiring as that in *A Theory of Justice* often is, can tell us how to produce the kind of regard that *combines* robust respect with substantive compassion. Moreover, despite continual progress and improvement in American life, there is overwhelming evidence that American political culture still fails to consistently encourage humane regard for members of some social groups. Every now and then we can find reasons for hope, as when the criminal wrongdoing that resulted in the death of George Floyd in 2020 was acknowledged as such because the prosecution succeeded in confronting a jury with the truth of Floyd's humanity.[20] But all too often in contemporary American life, there is a deeply rooted refusal to acknowledge that the members of socially dominant groups are not the only people who deserve humane regard.

But even if we show that a defensible future-oriented politics is fully compatible with taking history seriously, the effort to make hope and history rhyme will confront a second serious objection: the worry, introduced in chapter 6, that a politics too dependent on claims about historical injustice may risk encouraging politicized and partisan history. But as I argued, history and human interests are fundamentally intertwined, and there is no way in which we can fully disentangle them. Moreover, this link between history and human interests need not prevent us from producing and recognizing good and reliable history. To do so, we need to provide what Maurice Mandelbaum once called a "pragmatics" of history: a defensible account of the proper uses of history, and a compelling understanding of the acceptable intersections of history and human interest.[21] I can only suggest the outlines of such an account here. But it would have to begin with two fundamental assumptions: First, one of the most important interests we have in history is a moral interest—that is, an interest in historical explanation that can serve as a vehicle for substantive moral reflection. Second, when this interest is carefully articulated and adequately addressed, we have the capacity to make entirely proper uses of history in political argument and moral reflection.

When we carefully develop the implications of the second assumption, it becomes clear that history adequately serves our moral interests only when it creates genuine possibilities for substantively arguing with the past. Yet historical understanding can create these possibilities only when it embodies an epistemological symmetry with respect to moral praise and moral criticism. To allow moral praise of an interpreted past while denying the possibility of condemning its noteworthy moral failings (as far too many historians, philosophers, and even ordinary people have tended to do) neither serves our moral interests in history nor allows for the possibility of producing adequate and reliable history. Of course, this was one of the most important lessons of the narrative activism undertaken by Annette Gordon-Reed and other scholars with similarly defensible understandings of the pragmatics of history. When the Thomas Jefferson Foundation proved itself ready to approach Jefferson's past in all its moral complexity and to require every visitor to Jefferson's estate to do so (sometimes despite their vocal protests), it rightly recognized the importance of the epistemological symmetry I am urging. In doing so it invited all of us—not just Americans with a moral interest in reliable understandings of the "founding fathers"—to recognize that to be fully human is to be the kind of being who must claim a place in histories that may contain the worst, as well as the best, of human action and organization.

This suggests that we cannot responsibly come to terms with a past that we refuse to confront in all its complexity. At the same time, as Baldwin insisted, we may not be able to escape the "great pain and terror" that often accompany efforts to sincerely confront the history that has "placed one where one is" and "formed one's point of view."[22] Pain and terror may be especially intense when one considers a past that seems to reveal one's guilt, or at least a serious responsibility to help remedy wrongs committed by others whose defining narratives critically intersect with one's own. Further, when pain is linked to the experience of feeling shame while confronting history, it can lead those who feel shame to "shut down" and try to shut out unpleasant historical truths. Alternatively, when the pain of confronting history produces trauma at the thought that one has been, or could have been, subject to serious injustice, this sometimes diminishes hope for transformative social change and encourages a sense of resignation. But these outcomes are not inevitable. In particular, confronting the facts of injustice and victimization sometimes strengthens the resolve to seek transformative change, as it did for so many who viewed the mangled body of Emmett Till.

In *Learning from the Germans: Race and the Memory of Evil*, Susan Neiman warns that confronting the depth of past injustice sometimes hardens everyone's tendencies toward "tribalism" and thereby critically endangers the possibility of constructive discussion about the past.[23] Yet she remains convinced that reflective agents always have the potential to move past all their tribalism, trauma, and pain. An important source of that potential, she argues, is our capacity to reflect on what has transpired in other contexts where the formerly oppressed and former oppressors have learned how to converse in a way that opens up the possibility for moral repair. Neiman is particularly interested to show what Americans might learn from Germans about coming to terms with a past shaped by racial evil, especially on the matter of reparations.

8.4 REMAINING OPEN TO HOPE

But sometimes what we need most, as philosophers like Rorty and social critics like King and Baldwin have understood, is a reason to be engaged by the possibility of moral renewal. In this regard, one of Rorty's most important contributions to the project of creating space for justice is his insistence that political philosophy plays a vital role when it stimulates moral imagination with "new ways of living an individual human life, and new social utopias in which human beings might better flourish."[24] It is in this spirit, I suggest, that we can contemplate Plato's readiness to consider how gender equality might shape the leadership of the ideal polity; Kant's consideration that a federation of sovereign states might secure "perpetual peace"; and Mill's attempt to show that robust respect for individual liberty promotes human progress. Over time, even Rawls came to describe his project as an effort to produce a "realistically utopian" account of a truly just democracy. In so doing, he reminds us that the real tasks of political philosophy are not exhausted by analysis of concepts, or by justification of principles, since moral and political thought should also seek to stir the imagination.

Yet philosophers must not forget that when it comes to making space for justice, we are always part of broader and complex communities of concern and action. To be sure, many who become political philosophers were inspired by the confidence in the authority of philosophy that Marx seems to express in the eleventh Thesis on Feuerbach, when he declares that "philosophers have hitherto interpreted the world; the point, rather, is to change it." But even when philosophers successfully frame some realistic utopia as an alternative to current injustice, making space for the justice we might produce by reference to it is a project that philosophers cannot complete alone. Such projects almost always demand the engaged political struggle of social movements, and those who participate in the movements must remain hopeful that it is possible to realize the possibilities constructed by imagination.

Still further, everyone who is concerned to promote justice must appreciate that the constructive politics capable of realizing justice in the contemporary world cannot simply reproduce the assumptions, practices, and demands of past social movements. It will certainly be important to preserve critical moral insights generated by those movements and to respect the lessons they teach about the roles of imagination and affect in political life. But meeting contemporary requirements for justice as humane regard will require openness to new political strategies, new forms of engaged inquiry, and new collaborations that resist familiar boundaries of race, ethnicity, geography, and even gender. Shortly before his assassination, Martin Luther King was moving toward an understanding of the struggle for justice that embodied this recognition. The extraordinary challenges of contemporary life make this approach more critical than ever. Justice has always demanded institutions, policies, and practices that further humane regard by addressing disabling constraints, including morally indefensible domination; persistent threats to physical security and safety; environmental degradation; poverty and economic insecurity; and limited access to material and cultural conditions of human flourishing. But now we must address these constraints in a world scarred by climate change, divided by epistemic insularity and social mistrust, stifled by increasing economic inequality, and stymied by uncertainty about the social and economic consequences of emerging technology. It will take a great deal of human ingenuity and a strong political will to respond to these conditions, and social movements must become more inclusive communities of concern and action if they are to get their demands for relevant progress on the public agenda.

Making space for justice in this challenging time will also require that all who care about justice remain open to the politically constructive possibilities of hope. This is why I have argued against progressive projects driven by the politics of self-righteous shaming, and by an insistence that the stain of some injustices can never be overcome. As Desmond Tutu urged, openness to constructive hope typically requires openness to the possibility of forgiveness.[25] Indeed, as Hannah Arendt showed in *The Human Condition*, where forgiveness is possible and appropriate, it has the potential to release both the wrongdoer and the wronged from "the predicament of irreversibility."[26] This is because where forgiveness is possible, so are redemption and reconciliation. Some readers will want to resist King's insistence that we need a method of seeking social change that leaves open the possibility of noncoercively transforming and even redeeming our political "opponents"—even those who may have wronged us. But as King maintained, if we cannot hope to ever "win our opponents over," it is unlikely that we will be able to live in a community with them without bitterness and destructive political conflict.

At the other end of the political spectrum, countermovements driven by the politics of fear and resentment are endangering flourishing societies and the humane regard they might provide. This is because the politically constructive possibilities of hope are available only when citizens, generally, resist the seductions of resentment, and the pull of irrational fears, by cultivating a civic virtue that I call "civic grace."[27] Civic grace is a matter of standing ready to relinquish political resentments and bitterness in service of shared political ideals and social goals. It is also a readiness to *seek* shared ideals and goals when social disagreements—and sometimes even histories of deadly social conflict—may initially make it difficult to identify common concerns. It is imperative, here, that we distinguish civic grace from forgiveness. First, unlike civic grace, forgiveness starts from an assumption that there is blameworthy wrongdoing to forgive. Second, in contrast to civic grace, political forgiveness often requires painstaking face-to-face confrontations between those seeking forgiveness and wronged parties contemplating grants of forgiveness. Civic grace can certainly be a prelude to political forgiveness, whenever forgiveness is both possible and appropriate. But civic grace can be a source of social solidarity where forgiveness is irrelevant or unlikely, or where it might fail to acknowledge histories of shared responsibility for cycles of violence and harm that have persistently shaped life in some societies.

Civic grace is essentially a consistent readiness to extend civic goodwill to fellow citizens: even to many of our most determined political opponents, and certainly to potential political allies, whom we may never meet face to face. It is a willingness to treat their interests, agency, and moral standing with respect and to take seriously their capacity for suffering and pain. As Mandela understood, just as democratic life often demands sacrifice and self-transcendence, democracies also depend on the widespread possession of civic grace more fully than any other form of political organization. This is why the steep decline in civic grace in many societies, perhaps especially in America, has helped to strengthen the politics of resentment and endanger democratic stability.

Of course, given the depth of many contemporary political divisions and resentments, we may wonder whether it is possible to recover the sources of civic grace. But the writer E. B. White offers a heartening view:

> Things can look dark, then a break shows in the clouds, and all is changed, sometimes rather suddenly. It is quite obvious that the human race has made a . . . mess of life on this planet. But as a people we probably harbor seeds of goodness that have lain for a long time waiting to sprout when the conditions are right. Man's curiosity, his relentlessness, his inventiveness, his ingenuity have led him into deep trouble. We can only hope that these same traits will enable him to claw his way out. Hang on to your hat. Hang on to your hope. And wind the clock, for tomorrow is another day.[28]

In the spirit of the epigraph from Leonard Cohen's "Anthem," with which this chapter began, this passage reminds us that hope is ultimately the means by which "the light gets in."

NOTES

INTRODUCTION

1. I explain my terminological choices regarding the phrases "social movements," "progressive" and "constructive" social movements, and "backlash" and "countermovements" in chap. 1, sec. 1.2.
2. Michael Walzer, *Interpretation and Social Criticism* (Cambridge, Mass.: Harvard University Press, 1987), 27.
3. John Dewey and James H. Tufts, *Ethics* (New York: Holt, 1909), iv.
4. Ron Eyerman and Andrew Jamison, *Social Movements: A Cognitive Approach* (University Park: Pennsylvania State University Press, 1991), 4.
5. William James, "The Moral Philosopher and the Moral Life," in *Essays in Pragmatism* (New York: Hafner, 1948), 141.
6. David Lyons, "Moral Judgment, Historical Reality and Civil Disobedience," *Philosophy & Public Affairs* 27, no. 1 (1998): 31–49; Sally Haslanger, "Racism, Ideology, and Social Movements," *Res Philosophica* 94, 1 (2017): 1–22; Candice Delmas, *The Duty to Resist: When Disobedience Should Be Uncivil* (Oxford: Oxford University Press, 2018); Christopher LeBron, *The Making of Black Lives Matter: A Brief History of an Idea* (Oxford: Oxford University Press, 2017).
7. The term *universal citizenship* is most famously used by Iris Young in, for instance, "Polity and Group Difference: A Critique of the Ideal of Universal Citizenship," *Ethics* 99, no. 2 (January 1989): 250–74.
8. Frederick Douglass, "What to the Slave Is the Fourth of July?," in *The Portable Frederick Douglass*, ed. John Stauffer and Henry Louis Gates, Jr. (New York: Penguin, 2016).

9. Michele Moody-Adams, *Fieldwork in Familiar Places: Morality, Culture and Philosophy* (Cambridge, Mass.: Harvard University Press, 1997).

1. WHAT IS A SOCIAL MOVEMENT?

1. John S. McClelland, *The Crowd, and the Mob: From Plato to Canetti* (Oxford: Routledge, 1989), 26–35, 151.
2. McClelland, 106.
3. Gustave Le Bon, *The Crowd: A Study of the Popular Mind* (1895; repr., Digireads, 2009).
4. Le Bon, 30.
5. Jeff Goodwin and James J. Jasper, "Editors' Introduction," in *The Social Movements Reader: Cases and Concepts*, 3rd ed. (Oxford: Wiley-Blackwell, 2015), 5–6.
6. The phrase "contentious politics" was coined by Charles Tilly and continues to shape social theory of various kinds. See, for instance, Charles Tilly and Sidney Tarrow, *Contentious Politics*, 2nd ed. (Oxford: Oxford University Press, 2015).
7. Indeed, in my view, it took the recognition that the Civil Rights Movement was shaped by Gandhian ideas and practices to help scholars fully appreciate the extent to which Gandhian satyagraha constituted a counterweight to Le Bon's mistrust.
8. Bayard Rustin, "From Protest to Politics: The Future of the Civil Rights Movement," *Commentary* 39, no. 2 (February 1965).
9. Martin Luther King, Jr., *Stride Toward Freedom*, in *A Testament of Hope: The Essential Writings and Speeches of Martin Luther King, Jr.*, ed. James M. Washington (New York: Harper Collins, 1991), 86.
10. King, 84.
11. Hannah Arendt, *On Violence* (New York: Houghton Mifflin Harcourt, 1970), 54.
12. Erica Chenoweth and Maria Stephan, *Why Civil Resistance Works: The Strategic Logic of Non-Violent Conflict* (New York: Columbia University Press, 2011). See also Chenoweth, *Civil Resistance: What Everyone Needs to Know©* (New York: Oxford University Press, 2021).
13. Gene Sharp, *From Dictatorship to Democracy: A Conceptual Framework for Liberation* (New York: New Press, 1994).

14. Herbert H. Haines, "Radical Flank Effect," in *The Wiley-Blackwell Encyclopedia of Social and Political Movements*, ed. David A. Snow et al. (Hoboken, N.J.: Wiley, 2013). See also Haines, "Black Radicalization and the Funding of Civil Rights," *Social Problems* 32, no. 1 (1984).

15. Herbert H. Haines, *Black Radicals and the Civil Rights Mainstream, 1954–1970* (Knoxville: University of Tennessee Press, 1988).

16. John Rawls, *A Theory of Justice*, rev. ed. (Cambridge, Mass.: Harvard University Press, 1987), secs. 53–39.

17. See Michele Moody-Adams, "Democratic Conflict and the Political Morality of Compromise," in *Nomos* 59 (2018): 186–219, https://www.jstor.org/stable/26786040.

18. Michele Moody-Adams, "The Path of Conscientious Citizenship," in *To Shape a New World*, ed. Tommie Shelby and Brandon Terry (Cambridge, Mass.: Harvard University Press, 2018).

19. King, "Pilgrimage to Nonviolence," in *A Testament Hope*, 36.

20. See Mahatma Gandhi, *Mahatma Gandhi and Leo Tolstoy Letters*, ed. B. Srinivasa Murthy (Long Beach, Calif.: Long Beach Publications, 1987), https://www.mkgandhi.org/ebks/MG_Tolstoy_Letters.pdf/.

21. King, *Stride Toward Freedom*.

22. Moody-Adams, "Path of Conscientious Citizenship," 281–82.

23. Nate Cohn and Kevin Quealy, "How Public Opinion Has Moved on Black Lives Matter," *New York Times*, June 10, 2020, https://www.nytimes.com/interactive/2020/06/10/upshot/black-lives-matter-attitudes.html.

24. The observation is attributed to Laura J. Cooper, labor law professor at the University of Minnesota, who was first quoted by the *Minneapolis Star Tribune* in reference to the case. The quote is reprinted in the epilogue of Clara Bingham and Laura Leedy Gansler, *Class Action: The Landmark Case That Changed Sexual Harassment Law* (New York: Random House, 2002).

25. Iris Young, *Justice and the Politics of Difference* (Princeton, N.J.: Princeton University Press, 1990), 15–38.

26. Iris Young, "Polity and Group Difference: A Critique of the Ideal of Universal Citizenship," *Ethics* 99, no. 2 (January 1989): 250–74.

27. See, for instance, Charles Tilly, Ernesto Castañeda, and Lesley J. Wood, "Social Movements as Politics," in *Social Movements, 1768–2018*,

4th ed. (New York: Routledge, 2020). See also Goodwin and Jasper, "Editors' Introduction," 4.

28. Tilly, Castañeda, and Wood, "Social Movements as Politics," 6.

29. I discuss such movements more fully in chap. 7, sec. 7.

30. Tilly, Castañeda, and Wood, "Social Movements as Politics," 6.

31. It has certainly been argued that trees can have legal standing, including something like legal rights. See Christopher D. Stone, *Should Trees Have Standing? Law, Morality, and the Environment* (Oxford: Oxford University Press, 1972).

32. The meaning of the claim "could take an interest in" is fully compatible with the possibility that one might need to mature, or to develop better comprehension of a good, or even to emerge from a coma in order to understand why a particular thing is in one's interest. Childhood vaccinations can be in a baby's interest even though only after maturing will the baby be able to take an interest in vaccinations. I am grateful to an anonymous reviewer for the example and for noting the importance of this point.

33. Adam Smith, *The Theory of Moral Sentiments*, ed. D. D. Raphael and A. L. Macfie (Indianapolis, Ind.: Liberty Fund, 1982).

34. Katy Waldman, "How Climate-Change Fiction, or 'Cli-Fi,' Forces Us to Confront the Incipient Death of the Planet," *New Yorker*, November 9, 2018. https://www.newyorker.com/books/page-turner /how-climate-change-fiction-or-cli-fi-forces-us-to-confront-the -incipient-death-of-the-planet

35. Mary Parker Follett, "Constructive Conflict" (1925), in *Dynamic Administration: The Collected Papers of Mary Parker Follett* (Mansfield Center, Conn.: Martino, 2013), 30–49.

36. An anonymous reviewer helpfully encouraged me to clarify this point. A useful discussion of compromise in legislative assemblies appears in Amy Gutmann and Dennis Thompson, *The Spirit of Compromise* (Princeton, N.J.: Princeton University Press, 2012).

37. For a detailed discussion of the movement, see Marshall Ganz, *Why David Sometimes Wins: Leadership, Organization, and Strategy in the California Farm Worker Movement* (New York: Oxford University Press, 2009).

38. Linda Martin Alcoff, *The Future of Whiteness* (Malden, Mass.: Polity 2015).

39. See also Michele Moody-Adams, "Democracy, Identity and Politics," *Res Philosophica* 95, no. 2 (April 2018): 199–218.

40. I am indebted to an anonymous reviewer for the importance of stressing this point. Chapter 3 will develop the idea that, in the context of political society, generalized respect for moral value involves humane regard (respect for autonomous agency combined with compassionate concern for the capacity to suffer).

41. James M. Jasper, *The Art of Moral Protest: Culture, Biography and Creativity in Social Movements* (Chicago: University of Chicago Press, 1997).

42. Herbert Storing, "The Case Against Civil Disobedience" (1978), in *Civil Disobedience in Focus*, ed. Hugo Adam Bedau (New York: Routledge, 1991), 85–102, esp. 86–87.

43. Tilly, Castañeda, and Wood, "Social Movements in Politics," 6.

44. The telegram from King is at https://www.biography.com/news/cesar-chavez-martin-luther-king-jr-telegram#. The praise of Kennedy is at https://timeline.com/cesar-chavez-robert-kennedy-vonviolent-justice-california-789f6354682a.

45. David Lyons, "Moral Judgment, Historical Reality and Civil Disobedience," *Philosophy & Public Affairs* 27, no. 1 (Winter 1998): 31–49.

46. For discussion of King's notion of the beloved community and its connection to the work of Josiah Royce, see Gary Herstein, "The Roycean Roots of the Beloved Community," *Pluralist* 4, no. 2 (2009) 92–107; and Rufus Burrow, "The Beloved Community: Martin Luther King Jr. and Josiah Royce," *Encounter* 73, no. 1 (2012) 37–64.

47. Candice Delmas, *The Duty to Resist: When Disobedience Should Be Uncivil* (Oxford: Oxford University Press, 2018), 5 (for example).

48. These traits are part of what I have called the ethos that makes democracy possible. See, for instance, Moody-Adams "Democratic Conflict and the Political Morality of Compromise," 191–92.

49. Moody-Adams, "The Path of Conscientious Citizenship," 275.

50. Martin Luther King, Jr., "The Birth of a New Nation: Sermon Delivered at Dexter Avenue Baptist Church," April 7, 1957, King Papers, Martin Luther King, Jr., Research Institute, https://kinginstitute.stanford.edu/king-papers/documents/birth-new-nation-sermon-delivered-dexter-avenue-baptist-church.

51. Martin Luther King, Jr., "A Time to Break Silence," in *A Testament of Hope*, 240.

52. Ronald Dworkin, "On Not Prosecuting Civil Disobedience," *New York Review of Books*, June 6, 1968. Note that I do not intend to defend Dworkin's stance on prosecuting civil disobedience, just his understanding of disobedience as an exercise in conscientious citizenship.
53. I develop the concept of affected ignorance in Michele Moody-Adams, "Culture, Responsibility and Affected Ignorance," *Ethics* 104, no. 2 (January 1994): 291–309.
54. I defend this claim on different grounds in Moody-Adams, "The Path of Conscientious Citizenship."
55. I briefly discuss some of relevant international movements in chapter 3. For helpful sources, see Adam Roberts and Timothy Garton Ash, *Civil Resistance and Power Politics: The Experience of Non-Violent Action from Gandhi to the Present* (Oxford: Oxford University Press, 2011); Sharp, *From Dictatorship to Democracy*; Chenoweth and Stephan, *Why Civil Resistance Works*; and Peter Ackerman and Jack Duvall, *A Force More Powerful: A Century of Non-Violent Conflict* (New York: St. Martin's, 2000).
56. Manisha Sinha, *The Slave's Cause: A History of Abolition* (New Haven, Conn.: Yale University Press, 2016), 51.
57. Nelson Mandela, *Long Walk to Freedom: The Autobiography of Nelson Mandela* (New York: Little, Brown, 1994).

2. SOCIAL MOVEMENTS AND THE TASK OF DEMOCRACY

1. Christopher H. Achen and Larry M. Bartels, *Democracy for Realists: Why Elections Do Not Produce Responsive Government* (Princeton, N.J.: Princeton University Press, 2016), 4–5.
2. John Dewey, "Creative Democracy: The Task Before Us," in *The Later Works*, vol. 14: *1939–1941. Essays, Reviews and Miscellany*, ed. Jo Ann Boydston (Carbondale: Southern Illinois University Press, 1988), 228.
3. Dewey, 228.
4. Gene Sharp, *From Dictatorship to Democracy: A Conceptual Framework for Liberation* (New York: New Press, 2012), 34–35. Sharp argues that the emergence of direct democracy councils helped to strengthen the Hungarian Revolution of 1956–1857, and that the Solidarity unions

created by Polish workers during the 1980s helped to propel the democratization of Poland. See also Edmund Wnuk-Lipinski, "Civil Society and Democratization," *The Oxford Handbook of Political Behavior*, ed. Russell J. Dalton and Hans-Dieter Klingemann (Oxford: Oxford University Press, 2007), 677–78.

5. Sharp, *From Dictatorship to Democracy*, 62–63.

6. This paragraph draws on my discussion of Wilson's paper in Michele Moody-Adams, "The Path of Conscientious Citizenship," in *To Shape a New World*, ed. Tommie Shelby and Brandon Terry (Cambridge, Mass.: Harvard University Press, 2018).

7. Michael Lipsky, "Protest as a Political Resource," *American Political Science Review* 62, no. 4 (December 1968): 1144, 1145.

8. Vaclav Havel, "The Power of the Powerless" (October 1978), trans. Paul Wilson, available at HAC Bard blog, Hannah Arendt Center, Bard College, https://hac.bard.edu/amor-mundi/the-power-of-the-power less-vaclav-havel-2011-12-23.

9. This observation is from a Solidarity activist named Zbygniew Bujak, who is quoted discussing the impact of Havel's essay at https://hac .bard.edu/amor-mundi/the-power-of-the-powerless-vaclav-havel -2011-12-23.

10. See Aldon Morris, *The Origins of the Civil Rights Movement* (New York: Simon and Schuster, 1984).

11. "Highlander Folk School," in *The Martin Luther King, Jr., Encyclopedia* (Stanford, Calif.: King Institute, 2008, https://kinginstitute.stanford .edu/encyclopedia/highlander-folk-school.

12. One of the best accounts is in "Highlander Folk School."

13. "James Lawson," in *The Martin Luther King, Jr., Encyclopedia*, https:// kinginstitute.stanford.edu/encyclopedia/lawson-james-m.

14. Alasdair MacIntyre, *After Virtue*, 3rd ed. (Notre Dame, Ind.: University of Notre Dame Press, 2007), 216.

15. Manisha Sinha, *The Slave's Cause: A History of Abolition* (New Haven, Conn.: Yale University Press, 2016), 422. Sinha provides an extremely rich account of the slave narrative as an element in a phenomenon she describes as "fugitive slave abolition"; see her discussion, 421–36.

16. Nancy Hirschmann, "Toward a Feminist Theory of Freedom," *Political Theory* 24, no. 1 (February 1996): 59.

17. See David Kyle Johnson, *The Lavender Scare: Cold War Persecution of Gay and Lesbians in the Federal Government* (Chicago: University of Chicago Press, 2004). See also Margot Cannady, *The Straight State: Sexuality and Citizenship in Twentieth-Century America* (Princeton, N.J.: Princeton University Press, 2011).

18. Iris Young, *Inclusion and Democracy* (Oxford: Oxford University Press, 2002).

19. Young, 56.

20. Young, 57–62.

21. John Stuart Mill, *On Liberty in Utilitarianism and On Liberty: Including Mill's 'Essay on Bentham' and Selections from the Writings of Jeremy Bentham and John Austin*, ed. Mary Warnock, 2nd ed. (Oxford: Wiley-Blackwell, 2003).

22. Jonathan Chait, "Tom Cotton Calls Slavery 'Necessary Evil' to 'Development of Our Country,'" *New York Magazine*, July 27, 2020. https://nymag.com/intelligencer/2020/07/tom-cotton-slavery-necessary-evil-development-country-1619-project.html.

23. Guobin Yang, "Narrative Agency in Hashtag Activism: The Case of #BlackLivesMatter," *Media and Communication* 4, no. 4 (2016): 13–17.

24. Yang, "Narrative Agency and Hashtag Activism." See also Karlyn Campbell, "Agency: Promiscuous and Protean," *Communication and Critical/Cultural Studies* 2, no. 1 (2005): 1–19, doi:10.1080/147914204 2000332134.

25. Catherine MacKinnon, "Where #Me Too Came From and Where It's Going," *Atlantic*, March 24, 2019, https://www.theatlantic.com/ideas/archive/2019/03/catharine-mackinnon-what-metoo-has-changed/585313/.

26. The term "butterfly effect" comes from Edward Lorenz, a physicist working in chaos theory. Lorenz discovered that the nonlinear equations that govern weather have such an incredible sensitivity to initial conditions that a butterfly flapping its wings in Brazil could set off a tornado in Texas. For Lorenz, this was a reason to conclude that long-range weather forecasting is fundamentally unreliable. See, for instance, "This Month in Physics History," *APS News* 12, no. 1 (January 2003), https://www.aps.org/publications/apsnews/200301/history.cfm#.

27. Manuel Castells, *Networks of Outrage and Hope* (Cambridge: Polity, 2003), 24, 25.

28. "Tunisia," Freedom House, 2020, https://freedomhouse.org/country /tunisia/freedom-world/2020.

29. Safwan Masri, *Tunisia: An Arab Anomaly* (New York: Columbia University Press, 2017). Regrettably, as of this writing, lingering economic crises and the challenges of responding effectively to COVID-19 have begun to put Tunisian democracy in serious peril.

30. Zeynep Tufecki, *Twitter and Teargas: The Power and Fragility of Networked Protest* (New Haven, Conn.: Yale University Press, 2017), xii.

31. The comic book is still reprinted periodically today: https://www .comixology.com/Martin-Luther-King-and-the-Montgomery-Story /comics-series/12416.

32. Young, *Inclusion and Democracy*, 63–67, 69.

33. John Rawls, "The Idea of Public Reason Revisited," in *Political Liberalism*, exp. ed. (New York: Columbia University Press, 2005).

34. Rawls, *Political Liberalism*, 135–37.

35. Rawls, 213, 214, 442.

36. Rawls, 462, 463.

37. Young, *Inclusion and Democracy*, 78–80.

38. Achen and Bartels, in *Democracy for Realists*, 4–5, cite claims made by people around the globe, as part of the World Values Survey, that living in a democracy is "very important."

39. Mark Lilla, "The End of Identity Liberalism," *New York Times*, November 18, 2016, https://www.nytimes.com/2016/11/20/opinion/sunday/the -end-of-identity-liberalism.html. See also Lilla, *The Once and Future Liberal* (New York: Harper, 2017).

40. Richard Rorty, *Achieving Our Country: Leftist Thought in Twentieth Century America* (Cambridge, Mass.: Harvard University Press, 1998), 90–91.

41. Rorty, 82.

42. Rorty, 99.

43. James Baldwin, *The Fire Next Time* (1963), in *Baldwin: Collected Essays* (New York: Library of America, 1998), 246–347.

44. Rorty, *Achieving Our Country*, 13–14.

45. Gianna Zocco, "Disturbing the Peace of 'Two Not So Very Different Countries': James Baldwin and Fritz Raddatz." *James Baldwin Review* 3, no. 1 (2017): 95.

46. Martin Luther King, Jr., *A Testament of Hope: The Essential Writings and Speeches of Martin Luther King, Jr.*, ed. James M. Washington (New York: Harper Collins, 1991), 582.

3. SOCIAL MOVEMENTS AND THE MORAL LIFE

1. William James, "The Philosopher and the Moral Life," in *Essays in Pragmatism* (New York: Hafner, 1897), 141.
2. This section draws on an early argument in Michele Moody-Adams, "The Idea of Moral Progress," *Metaphilosophy* 30, 3 (July 1999): 171–72.
3. Jeremy Bentham, *Introduction to the Principles of Morals and Legislation* (1789; repr. New York: Hafner, 1948), 2.
4. Immanuel Kant, *Groundwork of the Metaphysics of Morals*, trans. H. J. Paton (1785; repr. New York: Harper and Row, 1964), 8n.
5. Mark Platts, "Moral Reality," in *Essays on Moral Realism*, ed. Geoffrey Sayre-McCord (Ithaca, N.Y.: Cornell University Press, 1988), 287–89, 298–99.
6. C. D. Broad, *Five Types of Ethical Theory* (1930; repr. London: Routledge and Kegan Paul, 1979), 1.
7. Cicero, *De Natura Deorum*, trans. H. Rackham, Loeb Classical Library (Cambridge: Harvard University Press, 1951), 3.38.
8. Michael Walzer, *Thick and Thin: Moral Argument at Home and Abroad* (Notre Dame, Ind.: University of Notre Dame Press, 1994), 2.
9. Michael Slote, "Is Virtue Possible?" *Analysis* 42, no. 2 (March 1982): 70–76.
10. Aquinas, "Is Ignorance a Cause of Voluntariness," in *The Summa Theologica*, part 1–2, question 6, article 8 (Benziger Bros. edition, Thomistic Institute, 1947), trans. Fathers of the English Dominican Province, https://www.ccel.org/a/aquinas/summa/FS/FS006.html#FSQ6 OUTP1. See also Michele Moody-Adams, "Culture, Responsibility and Affected Ignorance," *Ethics* 104 (January 1994): 291–309.
11. Cheshire Calhoun, "Responsibility and Reproach," *Ethics* 99 (1989): 396–97.
12. Catharine A. MacKinnon, afterword to *Feminism Unmodified: Discourses on Life and Law* (Cambridge, Mass.: Harvard University Press, 1987), 216.

13. MacKinnon, "Difference and Dominance," in *Feminism Unmodified*, 32.

14. Nina Totenberg interview with Justice Ruth Bader Ginsburg at the 2018 Sundance Film Festival, https://www.npr.org/2018/01/22/579595727 /justice-ginsburg-shares-her-own-metoo-story-and-says-it-s-about -time.

15. Stacey Sullivan, "War Rape Victims Sue Karadzic for Damages in the US," *Guardian*, August 6, 2000, https://www.theguardian.com/world /2000/aug/06/warcrimes.theobserver.

16. Michele Moody-Adams, *Fieldwork in Familiar Places: Morality, Culture, and Philosophy* (Cambridge, Mass.: Harvard University Press 1997), 74–106; David Cooper, "Moral Relativism," in *Midwest Studies in Philosophy* 3 (1978), special issue, ed. Peter French, Theodore Uehling, and Howard Wettstein; Peter French, *Responsibility Matters* (Lawrence: University of Kansas Press, 1992).

17. Walzer rightly posits that new moral interpretations can sometimes be recognized as likely to promote moral progress. A plausible theory of what constitutes *evidence* of progress in the pursuit of justice might profitably appeal to criteria that Walzer suggests in contemplating the Velvet Revolution. On such an account, an interpretation enables moral progress in social and political life when it interprets as just *only* those institutions and practices that can be preserved with minimal coercion, with minimal reliance on the arbitrary use of power, without extreme violence and brutality, and with genuine concern for formal and substantive equality before the law.

18. Timothy B. Tyson, *The Blood of Emmett Till* (New York: Simon and Schuster, 2017), discusses the recanting.

19. Mamie Till Mobley and Christopher Benson, *The Death of Innocence: The Story of the Hate Crime That Changed America* (New York: One World, 2003), 139–48.

20. James Baldwin, "As Much Truth as One Can Bear," *New York Times*, January 14, 1962.

21. Steve Lerner, *Sacrifice Zones* (Cambridge, Mass.: MIT Press, 2010). It should be remembered, however, that one of the most important early examples of environmental activism emerged in the Love Canal community—after it was discovered that decades of dumping toxic chemicals had essentially poisoned most of that suburban town.

22. Judith Shklar, *The Faces of Injustice* (New Haven, Conn.: Yale University Press, 1990), 14.

23. Iris Marion Young, *Justice and the Politics of Difference* (Princeton, N.J.: Princeton University Press, 1990).

24. I discuss Aquinas's account of affected ignorance in Moody-Adams, "Culture, Responsibility and Affected Ignorance." To situate this notion in the context of recent philosophical work on the problem of ignorance, I note that some of that work focuses mainly on ignorance rooted in group-based privilege and often impersonal institutions and systems, as is the case with Charles Mills's influential paper "White Ignorance," in *Race and Epistemologies of Ignorance*, ed. Shannon Sullivan and Nancy Tuana (Albany: SUNY Press, 2007), 13–38. Aquinas would likely have resisted any effort—as do I—to trace morally *substantive* ignorance (that culpably looks away from social injustice) to impersonal institutions and social structures, because this limits our ability to talk about *culpable* ignorance. I note, further, that some important recent work that explicitly addresses culpable ignorance has focused mainly on epistemic injustice, rather than directly on the broader social injustice discussed in this book. See, for instance, Jose Medina, *The Epistemology of Resistance: Gender and Racial Oppression, Epistemic Injustice, and the Social Imagination* (Oxford: Oxford University Press, 2013), esp. chap. 4.

25. Nicholas Fanden, "Frustration and Fury as Rand Paul Holds Up Anti-Lynching Bill in the Senate," *New York Times*, June 5, 2020, https://www.nytimes.com/2020/06/05/us/politics/rand-paul-anti-lynching-bill-senate.html.

26. See, for instance, MacKinnon, *Feminism Unmodified*, 127–213; and Catharine A. MacKinnon, *Only Words* (Cambridge, Mass.: Harvard University Press, 1993).

27. Susan Sontag, *Regarding the Pain of Others* (New York: Picador, 2003), 96–97.

28. The photographs are the self-immolation of Buddhist monk Thich Quang Duc (Malcolm Browne, 1963), the Saigon execution during the Tet Offensive (Eddie Adams, 1968), the Kent State shooting (John Paul Filo, 1970), and the girl burned by napalm (Nick Ut, 1972). These are helpfully discussed in Camille Ruquet, "The Legacy of American

Photojournalism in Ken Burns' Vietnam War Documentary Series,"
Images/Memoires 41 (2019), https://preo.u-bourgogne.fr/interfaces/647.
29. Susan Sontag, *On Photography* (New York: Picador, 1973).
30. Brent Staples, "The Perils of Growing Comfortable with Evil," *New York Times*, April 9, 2000, https://www.nytimes.com/2000/04/09 /opinion/editorial-observer-the-perils-of-growing-comfortable-with -evil.html.
31. Carolyn J. Dean, *The Fragility of Empathy After the Holocaust* (Ithaca, N.Y.: Cornell University, 2004), 1–15.
32. John Berger, *Ways of Seeing* (London: Penguin and BBC Books, 1972), 8.
33. Berger, esp. chap. 7, pp. 129–54.
34. Courtney R. Baker, *Humane Insight: Looking at Images of African American Suffering and Death* (Urbana: University of Illinois Press, 2017), 5.
35. Baker, 5–6.
36. Mobley, *Death of Innocence*, 134.
37. A reprint reproduction of the *Look Magazine* story is available at https://www.pbs.org/wgbh/americanexperience/features/till-killers -confession/.
38. Jonathan Glover, *Humanity: A Moral History of the Twentieth Century* (New Haven, Conn.: Yale University Press, 2000), 22–25.
39. David Livingstone Smith, *Less than Human: Why We Demean, Enslave and Exterminate Others* (New York: St. Martin's Griffin, 2012).
40. Charles Mills, "Black Radical Kantianism," *Res Philosophica* 95, no. 1 (January 2018): 1–33.
41. Jamil Zaki, *The War for Kindness: Building Empathy in a Fractured World* (New York: Crown, 2019).
42. Daniel Reisel, "Neuroscience of Restorative Justice," TED Talk, March 18, 2014, ttps://www.youtube.com/watch?v=tzJYY2poQIc/. See also Zaki, *The War for Kindness*.
43. John Dewey, *Art as Experience* (New York: Berkeley Publishing Group, 1934); W. E. B. Du Bois, "The Criteria of Negro Art," *The Crisis* 32 (October 1925): 290–97, http://www.webdubois.org/dbCriteriaNArt.html.
44. This account of the painting draws on the Studio Museum of Harlem's description of it. See https://studiomuseum.org/collection-item/heir looms-accessories.

45. Marshall himself comments on the picture in a video commentary from 2012 at https://vimeo.com/45605233, accessed 8/12/2020.

46. Young, *Justice and the Politics of Difference*, chaps. 1 and 4; Axel Honneth, "Recognition and Justice: Outline of a Plural Theory of Justice," *Acta Sociologica* 47, no. 4 (December 2004): 351–64.

47. Young, *Justice and the Politics of Difference*, 39–40.

48. Young, 38.

49. Young, 40. Young goes on to argue that there are five kinds of oppression: "exploitation, marginalization, powerlessness, cultural imperialism and violence."

50. The World Justice Project convincingly treats accountability in government as a critical element of the rule of law. See https://world justiceproject.org/world-justice-challenge-2021/accountable-gove rnance.

51. Shklar, *The Faces of Injustice*, 19.

52. Michelle Alexander, *The New Jim Crow: Mass Incarceration in the Age of Color Blindness* (New York: New Press, 2010).

53. Jessie Eisenger, "Why Only One Top Banker Went to Jail for the Financial Crisis," *New York Times*, April 30, 2014, https://www.nytimes .com/2014/05/04/magazine/only-one-top-banker-jail-financial-crisis .html. For a helpful account of the financial crisis itself, see Michael Lewis, *The Big Short: Inside the Doomsday Machine* (New York: Norton, 2010).

54. Constant Méheut, "Groups Put French State on Legal Notice Over Police Racism," *New York Times*, January 27, 2021, https://www.nytimes .com/2021/01/27/world/europe/france-police-racism.html; Robert Wright, "Race Relations: The Police Battle to Regain Trust Among Black Britons," *Financial Times*, January 6, 2021, https://www.ft.com /content/56e9b6cd-2672-48b5-be7f-673270e8346e.

55. This section is influenced by the comprehensive report about Flint written by Paul Mohai, "Environmental Justice and the Flint Water Crisis," *Michigan Sociological Review* 32 (Fall 2018): 1–41.

56. Rachel Carson, "Statement Before Congress," June 4, 1963, elcarson-council.org/about-rcc/about-rachel-carson/rachel-carsons-statement -before-congress-1963/.

57. Mohai, "Environmental Justice and the Flint Water Crisis."

58. Mohai, "Environmental Justice and the Flint Water Crisis."

59. David Graham, "The Bureaucrats Charged in Flint's Water Crisis," *Atlantic*, April 20, 2016, https://www.theatlantic.com/national/archive/2016/04/flint-water-lead-criminal-charges/479127/.

60. Mitch Smith, "Flint Water Prosecutors Drop Criminal Charges," *New York Times*, June 13, 2019, https://www.nytimes.com/2019/06/13/us/flint-water-crisis-charges-dropped.html.

61. Young, *Responsibility for Justice*, 52.

62. See, for instance, the discussion of the movement's "horizontalism" and insistence on nonhierarchical decision-making in John Ehrenberg, "What Can We Learn from Occupy's Failure?," *Palgrave Communications*, July 4, 2017, 20, https://www.nature.com/articles/palcomms201762.pdf.

63. Philip Randolph Institute, *A "Freedom Budget" for All Americans: Budgeting Our Resources, 1966–1975, to Achieve "Freedom from Want* (New York: Philip Randolph Institute, 1966), 1. For important commentary, see Michael Yates and Paul LeBlanc, *A Freedom Budget for All Americans Recapturing the Promise of the Civil Rights Movement in the Struggle for Economic Justice Today* (New York: Monthly Review, 2013).

64. Martin Luther King, Jr., "A Time to Break Silence," in *A Testament of Hope: The Essential Writings and Speeches of Martin Luther King, Jr.*, ed. James M. Washington (New York: Harper Collins, 1991), 231–44.

65. Miranda Fricker, *Epistemic Injustice* (Oxford: Oxford University Press, 2007).

66. National Nurses United, "Nurses Say Letting Uninsured Patients Die Is No Laughing Matter Following Abhorrent Audience Cheers," press release, September 13, 2011, https://www.nationalnursesunited.org/press/nurses-say-letting-uninsured-patients-die-no-laughing-matter-following-abhorrent-audience.

67. Clarence Page, "Ron Paul's Harsh Definition of Freedom," *Chicago Tribune*, September 18, 2011, https://www.chicagotribune.com/news/ct-xpm-2011-09-18-ct-oped-0918-page-20110918-story.html.

68. National Nurses United, "Nurses Say Letting Uninsured Patients Die."

4. TAKING IMAGINATION SERIOUSLY

1. Ana Lucia Araujo, "Toppling Monuments Is a Global Phenomenon," *Washington Post*, June 23, 2020, https://www.washingtonpost.com

/outlook/2020/06/23/toppling-monuments-is-global-movement-it
-works/; "How Statues Are Falling Around the World," *New York
Times*, June 24, 2020, updated September 12, 2020, https://www.nytimes
.com/2020/06/24/us/confederate-statues-photos.html.

2. Andrew Lawler, "Pulling Down Statues? It's a Tradition That Dates
Back to U.S. Independence," *National Geographic Magazine*, July 1,
2020, https://www.nationalgeographic.com/history/article/pulling
-down-statues-tradition-dates-back-united-states-independence.

3. Benedict Anderson, *Imagined Communities* (London: Verso Press,
2006)), 6.

4. David Miller, *On Nationality* (Oxford: Oxford University Press, 1997),
32–33.

5. Anderson, *Imagined Communities*, 38, 46.

6. Anderson, 8.

7. In fact, conventional views inherited this conception of the explanandum from Hobbes and Locke, whose commitment to contractual
accounts of the origin of political obligation continue to resonate in
contemporary political thought.

8. Ernst Renan, *What Is a Nation and Other Writings*, trans. and ed.
M. F. N. Giglioli (New York: Columbia University Press, 2018).

9. Danielle S. Allen, *Talking to Strangers: Anxieties of Citizenship Since
Brown v. Board of Education* (Chicago: University of Chicago Press,
2004), 25–49.

10. Moshe Halbertal, *On Sacrifice* (Princeton, N.J.: Princeton University
Press, 2012).

11. Charles Taylor, "The Dynamics of Democratic Exclusion," *Journal of
Democracy* 8, no. 4 (October 1998), https://muse-jhu-edu.ezproxy.cul
.columbia.edu/article/16921.

12. David Cameron, "State Multiculturalism Has Failed Says David Cameron," *BBC News*, February 11, 2011, https://www.bbc.com/news/uk
-politics-12371994. Several European nations eventually followed suit
in adopting this language of muscular liberalism.

13. Pope Francis, *Fratelli Tutti*, October 4, 2020, http://www.vatican.va
/content/francesco/en/encyclicals/documents/papa-francesco_2020
1003_enciclica-fratelli-tutti.html.

14. Bruce Ackerman *We the People*, vol. 3: *The Civil Rights Revolution*
(Cambridge, Mass.: Harvard University Press, 2014); Michele

Moody-Adams, "Democracy, Identity and Politics," *Res Philosophica* 95, no. 2 (April 2018): 199–219.

15. John Rawls, *Political Liberalism*, exp. ed. (New York: Columbia University Press, 2005), 41.

16. Samuel Scheffler, "The Appeal of Political Liberalism," in *Boundaries and Allegiances: Problems of Justice and Responsibility in Liberal Thought* (Oxford: Oxford University Press, 2003).

17. John Rawls, *A Theory of Justice*, rev. ed. (Cambridge, Mass.: Harvard University Press, 1987), 144.

18. Charles Taylor, "Democratic Exclusion (and Its Remedies?)," in *Dilemmas and Connections* (Cambridge, Mass.: Harvard University Press, 2014), 124–46; see also Taylor, *Modern Social Imaginaries* (Durham, N.C.: Duke University Press, 2003), 89–190. This part of the chapter draws on my argument in Michele Moody-Adams, "Memory, Multiculturalism and the Sources of Solidarity," in *Interpreting Modernity: Essays on the Work of Charles Taylor*, ed. Daniel M. Weinstock, Jacob T. Levy, and Jocelyn MacClure (Montreal: McGill-Queens University Press, 2020), esp. 231–36.

19. Taylor, *Modern Social Imaginaries*, 23–24.

20. See, for instance, Michele Moody-Adams, "Democratic Conflict and the Political Morality of Compromise," *Nomos* 59 (New York: New York University Press, 2018), 186–219.

21. Some of the most important articles on this topic are collected in an anthology edited by Amy Kind and Peter Kung, *Knowledge Through Imagination* (Oxford: Oxford University Press, 2016).

22. Several classic and contemporary books help us understand the powers of moral imagination. One of the most important works is Adam Smith, *The Theory of Moral Sentiments*, ed. D. D. Raphael and A. L. Macfie (Indianapolis, Ind.: Liberty Fund, 1982). Important recent books include Mark Johnson, *Moral Imagination: Implications of Cognitive Science for Ethics* (Chicago: University of Chicago Press, 1994); and Patricia Werhane, *Moral Imagination and Management Decision* (Oxford: Oxford University Press, 1999).

23. John Paul Lederach, *The Moral Imagination: The Art and Soul of Building Peace* (Oxford: Oxford University Press, 2010).

24. Leslie Stevenson, "Twelve Conceptions of Imagination," *British Journal of Aesthetics* 45, no. 3 (July 2003): 238–58.

25. Peter F. Strawson, "Imagination and Perception," in *Experience and Theory*, ed. L. Foster, and J. W. Swanson (Amherst: University of Massachusetts Press, 1994), 31–54.

26. Amy Kind, "The Heterogeneity of Imagination," *Erkenntnis* 78 (2013): 141–59.

27. Steven Pinker, "One Thing to Change: Anecdotes Aren't Data," *Harvard Gazette*, June 21, 2019, https://news.harvard.edu/gazette/story /2019/06/focal-point-harvard-professor-steven-pinker-says-the-truth -lies-in-the-data/.

28. Mark Twain, *A Connecticut Yankee in King Arthur's Court* (1889).

29. An especially helpful and detailed account of the emergence of the concept of sexual harassment appears in Clara Bingham and L. Gensler, *Class Action: The Landmark Case That Changed Sexual Harassment Law* (New York: Random House, 2002).

30. See Miranda Fricker, *Epistemic Injustice: Power and the Ethics of Knowing* (Oxford: Oxford University Press, 2007).

31. John Berger, *Ways of Seeing* (London: Penguin and BBC, 1972), 8.

32. Berger, esp. chap. 7, pp. 129–54.

33. See John Dewey, *Art as Experience* (New York: Berkeley, 1934; W. E. B. Du Bois, "The Criteria of Negro Art," *The Crisis* 32 (October 1925): 290–97, http://www.webdubois.org/dbCriteriaNArt.html.

34. For fuller development of this claim, see my "Philosophy and the Art of Human Flourishing," in *Philosophy and Human Flourishing*, ed. John J. Stuhr and James Pawelski (Oxford: Oxford University Press, forthcoming).

35. See, for instance, Katy Waldman, "How Climate Change Fiction, or 'Cli-Fi,' Forces Us to Confront the Incipient Death of the Planet," *New Yorker*, November 9, 2018, https://www.newyorker.com/books/page -turner/how-climate-change-fiction-or-cli-fi-forces-us-to-confront -the-incipient-death-of-the-planet.

36. Anne Fowler et al., "Talking with the Enemy," *Boston Globe*, January 28, 2001, reprinted at https://www.feminist.com/resources /artspeech/genwom/talkingwith.html.

37. Citizen assemblies and other tools of deliberative democracy are discussed at length in essays published in James Fishkin and James Mansbridge, eds., *The Prospects and Limits of Deliberative Democracy*,

Summer 2017, https://www.amacad.org/daedalus/prospects-limits
-deliberative-democracy.

38. David Blight, *Race and Reunion: The Civil War in American Memory*
(Cambridge, Mass.: Harvard University Press, 2001), 299.

39. Blight offers an especially detailed account of the process in his chap.
8.

40. Mitch Landrieu, "Speech on the Removal of Confederate Monuments
in New Orleans," *New York Times*, May 23, 2017, https://www.nytimes
.com/2017/05/23/opinion/mitch-landrieus-speech-transcript.html. The
argument is further developed in Landrieu, *In the Shadow of Statues: A
White Southerner Confronts History* (New York: Penguin, 2018).

41. The Southern Poverty Law Center frequently updates information
about how many Confederate statues, symbols, and names remain in
and on public spaces across the United States. The update released in
June 2021 estimates that there are 1,700 such statues, symbols, and
names—800 of which are monuments and statues. See https://www
.splcenter.org/20190201/whose-heritage-public-symbols-confederacy
#findings. The original report, "Whose Heritage? Public Symbols of
the Confederacy" (2016), is available at https://www.splcenter.org/sites
/default/files/com_whose_heritage.pdf (accessed 12/27/2020).

42. Robin A. Lenhardt "Understanding the Mark: Race, Stigma, and
Equality in Context," *New York University Law Review* 79 (2004): 803–
930; See also Bennett Capers, "Rethinking the Fourth Amendment:
Race, Citizenship and the Equality Principle," *Harvard Civil Rights-
Civil Liberties Law Review* 46, no. 1 (2011): 1–50. According to Len-
hart (845), citizenship harms "refer to stigma-related injuries that . . .
have a negative impact on a racially stigmatized individual's ability
to . . . be a full participant in the relationships, conversations, and processes that are . . . important to community life."

43. Chimamanda Ngozi Adichie, "The Danger of a Single Story," TED
Talk, July 2009, https://www.ted.com/talks/chimamanda_ngozi_
adichie_the_danger_of_a_single_story?language=en.

44. Andrea Shea, "16 Statues and Memorials Were Damaged During Sunday's Protests, Including One Dedicated to African American Soldiers," *NPR*, June 3, 2020, https://www.wbur.org/artery/2020/06/03/16
-statues-memorials-damaged.

45. Jonathan W. White and Scott Sandage, "What Frederick Douglass Had to Say About Monuments," *Smithsonian Magazine*, June 30, 2020, https://www.smithsonianmag.com/history/what-frederick-douglass -had-say-about-monuments-180975225/.

46. Dewey, *Art as Experience*, 244.

47. Kirk Savage offers one of the most helpful descriptions of what is distinctive about the monument, in *Standing Soldiers, Kneeling Slaves: Race, War and Monuments in Nineteenth Century America* (Princeton, N.J.: Princeton University Press, 1997) 194–208.

48. William James, "Robert Gould Shaw: Oration by Professor William James," *Essays in Religion and Morality* (Cambridge, Mass.: Harvard University Press, 1982).

49. Kirk Savage, *Monument Wars: Washington, D.C., the National Mall, and the Transformation of the Memorial Landscape* (Berkeley: University of California Press, 2009), 252, 256.

50. White and Sandage, "What Douglass Had to Say."

51. White and Sandage, "What Douglass Had to Say."

52. Du Bois, "The Criteria of Negro Art"; George Orwell, "Charles Dickens," in *All Art Is Propaganda: Critical Essays* (Boston: Mariner, 2009), 47.

53. Garth Jowett and Victoria O'Donnell, *Propaganda and Persuasion*, 5th ed. (Thousand Oaks, Calif.: Sage, 2012), 6–7.

54. Walter Benjamin, "The Work of Art in the Age of Mechanical Reproduction" (1935), in *Illuminations*, ed. Hannah Arendt, trans. Harry Zohn (New York: Schocken, 1997), 241. Benjamin's concerns about the anesthetization of politics are discussed at length in Crispin Sartwell, *Political Aesthetics* (Ithaca, N.Y.: Cornell University Press, 2010).

55. Lewis Mumford, "The Death of the Monument," in *Circle: International Survey of Constructive Art* (London: Faber and Faber, 1937), 263–70.

56. I thank Wolfgang Mann for assistance in refining this point.

5. LANGUAGE MATTERS

1. Anne Pauwels, "Linguistic Sexism and Feminist Linguistic Activism," in *The Handbook of Language and Gender*, ed. Janet Holmes and Miriam Meyerhoff (Oxford: Blackwell, 2003), 550–70.

2. Gregory Coles, "The Exorcism of Language: Reclaimed Derogatory Terms and Their Limits," *College English* 78, no. 5 (May 2016): 424–46.

3. This not just about the so-called n-word but even about labels for various indigenous groups throughout the Americas and in Oceania.

4. Judith Butler, *Excitable Speech: A Politics of the Performance* (New York: Routledge, 1997); see also Coles, "The Exorcism of Language."

5. This discussion draws on the introduction in Will Kymlicka and Allen Patten, *Language Rights and Political Theory* (Oxford: Oxford University Press, 2003); and Philippe Van Parjis, *Linguistic Justice for Europe, and the World* (Oxford: Oxford University Press, 2011).

6. *UNESCO Atlas of the World's Languages in Danger*, http://www.unesco.org/languages-atlas/en/statistics.html.

7. Kenneth Burke, "Terministic Screens," *Proceedings of the American Catholic Philosophical Association* 39 (1965): 88, 89.

8. Gordon Lichfield, "All the Names for the New Digital Economy and Why None of Them Fits," *Quartz*, November 12, 2015, https://qz.com/548137/all-the-names-for-the-new-digital-economy-and-why-none-of-them-fits/.

9. Burke, "Terministic Screens," 89.

10. For a rich and careful account of Burke's thought that resists unsubtle interpretations of Burke as a relativist or a strong social constructionist, see Paul Stob, "'Terministic Screens,' Social Constructionism, and the Language of Experience: Kenneth Burke's Utilization of William James," *Philosophy & Rhetoric*. 41, no. 2 (2008): 130–52.

11. Richard Rorty, *Contingency, Irony and Solidarity* (Cambridge: Cambridge University Press, 1989), 21, 64–65.

12. Richard Rorty, "The Priority of Democracy to Philosophy," in *Objectivity, Relativism and Truth* (Cambridge: Cambridge University Press, 1990), 75–81.

13. Richard Rorty, "Non-Reductive Physicalism," in *Objectivity Relativism and Truth*, 51–55.

14. Of course, Hume's conception offers a critical precursor of this stance.

15. Richard Rorty, "Feminism and Pragmatism," Tanner Lectures on Human Values, December 7, 1990, 26, https://tannerlectures.utah.edu/_documents/a-to-z/r/rorty92.pdf.

16. Rorty, *Contingency, Irony and Solidarity*, 94.

17. Orlando Patterson, *Slavery and Social Death: A Comparative Study* (Cambridge, Mass.: Harvard University Press, 1982), 97.

18. Edward Baptist, *The Half Has Never Been Told: Slavery and The Making of American Capitalism* (New York: Basic Books, 2014), xxvii.

19. bell hooks, *Talking Back: Thinking Feminist, Thinking Black* (New York: Routledge, 2014), 17–18.

20. Judith Butler, *Notes Toward a Performative Theory of Assembly* (Cambridge, Mass.: Harvard University Press, 2015).

21. Raphael Lemkin, *Axis Rule in Occupied Europe: Laws of Occupation, Analysis of Government, Proposals for Redress* (Washington, D.C.: Carnegie Endowment for International Peace, 1944), 79.

22. Winston Churchill, "Broadcast to the World About Meeting with President Roosevelt," August 24, 1941, https://www.ibiblio.org/pha/policy/1941/410824a.html.

23. Samantha Powers, *A Problem from Hell: America and the Age of Genocide* (New York: Basic Books, 2013), 52–103.

24. Lemkin, *Axis Rule in Occupied Europe*, 79.

25. Herman Cappelen and David Plunkett, "A Guided Tour of Conceptual Engineering and Conceptual Ethics," in *Conceptual Engineering and Conceptual Ethics*, ed. Alexis Burgess, Herman Cappelen, and David Plunkett (Oxford: Oxford University Press, 2020), 5–23.

26. Powers, *A Problem from Hell*. This section also draws on my discussion in Michele Moody-Adams, "Moral Progress and Human Agency," *Ethical Theory and Moral Practice* 20, no. 1, special issue: Moral Progress (February 2017): 153–68.

27. On this point, see my "The Idea of Moral Progress," *Metaphilosophy* 30, no. 3 (July 1999): 171–72; and "Moral Progress and Human Agency."

28. Richard Posner, "The Problematics of Moral and Legal Theory," *Harvard Law Review* 111, no. 7 (1998): 1667.

29. Jonathan Metzl, *Dying of Whiteness: How the Politics of Racial Resentment Is Killing America's Heartland* (New York: Basic Books, 2019).

30. Moody-Adams. "The Idea of Moral Progress," 179–80.

31. Joel Feinberg, "Action and Responsibility," in *Doing and Deserving* (Princeton, N.J.: Princeton University Press, 1970), 134.

32. Reva Siegel, "A Short History of Sexual Harassment," in *Directions in Sexual Harassment Law*, ed. Catherine MacKinnon and Reva B. Siegel (New Haven, Conn.: Yale University Press, 2003), 2–28.

33. Enid Nemy, "Women Begin to Speak out Against Sexual Harassment at Work," *New York Times*, August 19, 1975, https://www.nytimes.com/1975/08/19/archives/women-begin-to-speak-out-against-sexual-harassment-at-work.html.

34. Nemy, "Women Begin to Speak Out."

35. Ben Jacobs and David Smith, "Trump Says if Ivanka Was Harassed at Work She Should 'Find Another Career,'" *Guardian*, August 1, 2016, https://www.theguardian.com/us-news/2016/aug/01/donald-trump-sexual-harassment-roger-ailes-fox.

36. Siegel, "A Short History of Sexual Harassment," 9.

37. Christine Mallinson, "Language and Its Everyday Revolution Potential: Feminist Linguistic Activism in the United States," in *The Oxford Handbook of U.S. Women's Activism*, ed. Holly J. McCammon et al. (Oxford: Oxford University Press, 2017), 419–39.

38. Philip Galanes, "Gretchen Carlson and Catherine MacKinnon Have a Few Things to Say," March 17, 2018, *New York Times*, https://www.nytimes.com/2018/03/17/business/catharine-mackinnon-gretchen-carlson.html.

39. Toni Morrison, Nobel Prize lecture, December 7, 1993, https://www.nobelprize.org/prizes/literature/1993/morrison/lecture/.

40. C. Vann Woodward, "The Case of the Louisiana Traveler," http://users.soc.umn.edu/~samaha/cases/van%20woodward,%20plessy.htm.

41. Michele Moody-Adams, "The Legacy of Plessy v. Ferguson," in *Blackwell Companions to Philosophy: A Companion to African American Philosophy*, ed. Tommy L. Lott and John P. Pittman (Oxford: Blackwell, 2006), 306–12.

42. Kate Abramson, "Turning Up the Lights on Gaslighting," *Philosophical Perspectives* 28: (2014): 1–30.

43. Whet Moser, "What Martin Luther King Wanted for Chicago in 1966," *Chicago Magazine*, January 19, 2015, https://www.chicagomag.com/city-life/january-2015/martin-luther-king-jrs-policy-ideas-for-chicago-circa-1966/.

6. JUSTICE AND THE NARRATIVE IMAGINATION

1. Alasdair MacIntyre, *After Virtue*, 3rd ed. (Notre Dame, Ind.: University of Notre Dame Press, 2007), 216.

2. Hannah Arendt, "Reflections on Little Rock," *Dissent Magazine* (Winter 1959): 50, https://www.dissentmagazine.org/article/reflections-on -little-rock.

3. Ralph Ellison, interview, 1965, in *Who Speaks for the Negro?*, by Robert Penn Warren (New Haven, Conn.: Yale University Press, 1993), 343.

4. This echoes the stance articulated by Danielle S. Allen in *Talking to Strangers: Anxieties of Citizenship Since Brown v. Board of Education* (Chicago: University of Chicago Press, 2004). An anonymous reader for the press justly stressed this point.

5. MacIntyre, *After Virtue*, 213.

6. Charles Taylor, *Modern Social Imaginaries* (Durham, N.C.: Duke University Press, 2003), 23–24.

7. Guy Lowe, "The Model Minority Narrative and Its Effect on Asian American Identity and Social Status," in *Modern Societal Impacts of the Model Minority Stereotype*, ed. Nicholas Daniel Hartlep (Hershey, Pa.: IGI Global, 2015), 323–50.

8. Lowe, 330–31.

9. Joshua Bloom and Waldo E. Martin, Jr., *Black Against Empire: The History and Politics of the Black Panther Party* (Oakland: University of California Press, 2016), 5–8.

10. Martha C. Nussbaum, *Cultivating Humanity: A Classical Defense of Reform in Liberal Education* (Cambridge, Mass.: Harvard University Press, 1997), 10–11.

11. Donald E. Polkinghorne, *Narrative Knowing and the Human Sciences* (Albany, N.Y.: SUNY Press, 1988), 13.

12. Iris Young, *Inclusion and Democracy* (Oxford: Oxford University Press, 2002), 77.

13. Paul Ricoeur argues that narrative and temporality are reciprocally related. See Ricoeur, "Narrative Time," in "On Narrative," special issue, *Critical Inquiry* 7, no. 1 (Autumn 1980): 169–90.

14. David Treuer, *The Heartbeat of Wounded Knee: Native America from 1890 to the Present* (London: Riverhead, 2019).

15. See, for instance, Martha Nussbaum, *Love's Knowledge: Essays on Philosophy and Literature* (Oxford: Oxford University Press, 1990); Cora Diamond, "The Difficulty of Reality and the Difficulty of Philosophy," in *Reading Cavell*, ed. Alice Crary and Stanford Shieh (London:

Routledge, 2005); Iris Murdoch, *Existentialist and Mystics: Writings on Philosophy and Literature* (New York: Penguin, 1999).

16. Nelson Goodman, "Twisted Tales," *Critical Inquiry* 7 (1980): 104.

17. Goodman, 105.

18. William L. Andrews, *To Tell a Free Story: The First Century of African American Autobiography, 1760–1865* (Urbana: University of Illinois Press, 1986).

19. William L. Andrews, "North American Slave Narratives: An Introduction to the Slave Narrative," Documenting the American South digital library, University Library, University of North Carolina at Chapel Hill, https://docsouth.unc.edu/neh/intro.html.

20. Ulrich B. Phillips, *Life and Labor in the Old South* (1929; repr. Columbia: University of South Carolina Press, 2007), 219.

21. John W. Blasingame, ed., *Slave Testimony: Two Centuries of Letters, Speeches, Interviews, and Autobiographies* (Baton Rouge: Louisiana State University Press, 1977), xvii, xxxv–xxxvii.

22. Frederick Douglass, *My Bondage and My Freedom*, intro. and notes by David Blight (1855; New Haven, Conn.: Yale University Press, 2014), 7.

23. Henry Louis Gates, Jr., ed., *The Classic Slave Narratives* (New York: New American Library, 1987), ix–x.

24. Frank Kirkland, "Enslavement, Moral Suasion, and Struggles for Recognition: Frederick Douglass's Answer to the Question—'What Is Enlightenment?,'" in *Frederick Douglass: A Critical Reader*, ed. Bill E. Lawson and Frank M. Kirkland (Malden, Mass.: Blackwell, 1999), 247; and Bernard Boxill, "Two Traditions in Africa American Political Philosophy," *Philosophical Forum* 24 (1992): 119–45.

25. Boxill, "Two Traditions," 129.

26. Boxill, "Two Traditions"; Kirkland, "Enslavement, Moral Suasion and Struggles for Recognition."

27. Frederick Douglass, "Capt. John Brown Not Insane," in *The Portable Frederick Douglass*, ed. John Stauffer and Henry Louis Gates, Jr. (New York: Penguin, 2016), 447.

28. Elizabeth Anderson, "The Epistemology of Injustice," *Southern Journal of Philosophy* 58, no. 1 (2020): 6–29.

29. At the same time, as historian Dickson Bruce has argued, even before the Emancipation Proclamation of 1863, and even before the

all-too-brief period of Reconstruction, African American slave narratives helped to enlarge the "public sphere" in American political life by bringing the voices of African Americans into the realm of political deliberation. Though in the antebellum period former slaves could not hold political office or even vote, those who participated in the abolitionist movement—as powerful orators, in political broadsides, and perhaps especially as published authors—were able to ensure that firsthand accounts of the cruelty, violence, and severe hardships of enslavement were entered into the public record. See Dickson Bruce, "Politics and Political Philosophy in the Slave Narrative," in *Cambridge Companion to the African American Slave Narrative*, ed. Audrey Fisch (Cambridge: Cambridge University Press, 2007), 28–43.

30. Frederick Douglass, "Men of Color, to Arms!" March 2, 1863, reprinted in Lincoln Kirstein and Richard Benson, *Lay This Laurel* (New York: Eakins, 1973).

31. It is estimated that by the end of the war, freed Black men and runaway slaves made up one-tenth of the population of the Northern army even though they were only 1 percent of the population of the North. Some observers, including Abraham Lincoln, suggested that their effort may have helped tip the scales in favor of the Union Army.

32. Francesca Polletta and Pang Chen, "Narrative and Social Movements," in *The Oxford Handbook of Cultural Sociology*, ed. Jeffrey Alexander, Rob Jacobs and Phillip Smith (Oxford: Oxford University Press), 487–506. Polletta and Chen offer an account of the risks of narrative activism that bears some similarities to the one here, but my account was developed independently.

33. Polletta and Chen, "Narrative and Social Movements."

34. Young, *Inclusion and Democracy*, 72–78.

35. Jerome Bruner has been an especially prominent figure in defending this claim. See, e.g., "Life as Narrative," in "Reflections on the Self," special issue of *Social Research* 54, no. 1 (Spring 1987).

36. David Treuer, *The Heartbeat of Wounded Knee: Native America from 1890 to the Present* (London: Riverhead, 2019), 452. Treuer is hereby rejecting Dee Brown's famous conclusion (in *Bury My Heart at Wounded Knee*) that Wounded Knee was essentially the beginning of the tragic destruction of Native American civilization.

37. David Treuer, *Rez Life: An Indian's Journey Through Reservation Life* (New York: Grove, 2013), 10–11.

38. David Treuer, "Return the National Parks to the Tribes,"*Atlantic* (May 2021): 30–45.

39. Tobias Wolff, "The Art of Fiction No. 183," interviewed by Jack Livings in *Paris Review*, no. 171 (Fall 2004), https://www.theparisreview .org/interviews/5391/the-art-of-fiction-no-183-tobias-wolff.

40. James Baldwin, "The White Man's Guilt," 1965, reprinted in *Collected Essays* (New York: Library of America, 1998), 722–26.

41. U.S. national recognition came in 1976; UK national recognition, in 1987.

42. Stuart Macintyre, "The History Wars," *Sydney Papers* (Winter/ Spring 2003): 76–83, http://www.kooriweb.org/foley/resources/pdfs /198.pdf.

43. Two important versions of this objection appear in Diane Ravitch, "Multiculturalism: E Pluribus Plures," *American Scholar* 49, no. 3 (Summer 1990): 337–54; and Arthur M. Schlesinger, *The Disuniting of America: Reflections on a Multicultural Society* (New York: Norton, 1991).

44. Joel Feinberg, "Action and Responsibility," in *Doing and Deserving* (Princeton, N.J.: Princeton University Press, 1970), 144.

45. Annette Gordon-Reed, *Thomas Jefferson and Sally Hemings: An American Controversy* (Charlottesville: University of Virginia Press, 1997).

46. *Thomas Jefferson—A Film by Ken Burns*, episode 12, Public Broadcasting System, 1997.

47. In the Ken Burns film, John Hope Franklin, echoing Feinberg's argument, reminds us that assumptions about what is "morally impossible" or "unintelligible" are a function of one's sociohistorical context.

48. Three *Nature* articles are relevant to determining where the original researchers thought the weight of the evidence falls: Eugene A. Foster et al., "Jefferson Fathered Slave's Last Child," November 5, 1998; Eric S. Lander and Joseph J. Ellis, "Founding Father," November 5, 1998; and Eugene A. Foster et al., "Reply: The Thomas Jefferson Paternity Case," letter to editor, January 7, 1999.

49. Thomas Jefferson Foundation, "Research Findings and Implications," *Report of the Research Committee on Thomas Jefferson and Sally Hemings*, January 2000, https://www.monticello.org/thomas-jefferson/jefferson -slavery/thomas-jefferson-and-sally-hemings-a-brief-account/research

-report-on-jefferson-and-hemings/iv-research-findings-and-impli
cations/.

50. Hans Georg Gadamer, *Truth and Method*, Continuum Impacts (London: Bloomsbury, 1982), xx, 245–67.

51. Pieter Geyl, *Napoleon For and Against*, trans. Olive Rentier (Harmondsworth, UK: Penguin, 1949), 15–16, https://archive.org/stream/in
.ernet.dli.2015.202235/2015.202235.Napoleon-For_djvu.txt.

52. See, for instance, "Tom Cotton Calls Slavery 'Necessary Evil' in Attack
on New York Times' 1619 Project," *Guardian*, July 26, 2020, https://
www.theguardian.com/world/2020/jul/26/tom-cotton-slavery
-necessary-evil-1619-project-new-york-times.

53. Nell Painter, "How We Think About the Term 'Enslaved' Matters,"
Guardian, August 14, 2019, https://www.theguardian.com/us-news
/2019/aug/14/slavery-in-america-1619-first-ships-jamestown.

54. Luvell Anderson, "Hermeneutical Impasses," *Philosophical Topics* 45,
no. 2 (Fall 2017): 1–19.

7. THE EMPIRE OF AFFECT AND THE
CHALLENGE OF COLLECTIVE HOPE

1. Martin Luther King, Jr., *Stride Toward Freedom*, in *A Testament of Hope:
The Essential Writings and Speeches of Martin Luther King, Jr.*, ed.
James M. Washington (New York: Harper Collins, 1991).

2. Luvell Anderson, "Hermeneutical Impasses," *Philosophical Topics* 45,
no. 2 (2017): 1–19.

3. This expands on the discussion in Michele Moody-Adams, "What's
So Special About Academic Freedom?," in *Who's Afraid of Academic
Freedom*, ed. Akeel Bilgrami and Jonathan R. Cole (New York: Colum-
bia University Press, 2015), 116–17.

4. William James, Lecture 9, "Conversion," in *The Varieties of Religious
Experience* (Auckland, N.Z.: Floating, 2008), 271–307.

5. The quote is attributed to Austin by Daniel Dennett in *Elbow Room:
The Varieties of Free Will Worth Wanting* (Cambridge, Mass.: MIT Press,
2015), 36n15.

6. Jerome Neu, "To Understand All Is to Forgive Al—or Is It?," in *Before
Forgiving—Cautionary Views of Forgiveness in Psychotherapy*, ed. Sharon

Lamb and Jeffrie G. Murphy (Oxford: Oxford University Press, 2002), 18.

7. Arlie Hochschild, *Strangers in Their Own Land: Anger and Mourning on the American Right* (New York: New Press, 2016).

8. Thomas Hobbes, *Leviathan* (Oxford: Oxford University Press, 2009).

9. One of the most promising and informative contributions to the social psychology underlying such a stance can be found in the essay by Maria Jarymowicz and Daniel Bar-tal, "The Dominance of Fear Over Hope in the Life of Individuals and Collectives," *European Journal of Social Psychology* 36, no. 3 (May 2006): 367–92. For a very different view of fear, which resists the primary/secondary emotion distinction and (implicitly) rejects the idea that nonhuman animals have ("primary") emotions, see Joseph LeDoux, "Coming to Terms with Fear," *Proceedings of the National Academy of Science* 111, no. 5 (February 2014): 2871–78.

10. Jarymowicz and Bar-tal, "The Dominance of Fear Over Hope."

11. Thierry Devos, Lisa A. Silver, Diane M. Mackie, and Eliot R. Smith, "Experiencing Intergroup Emotions," in *From Prejudice to Intergroup Emotions: Differentiated Reactions to Social Groups*, ed. Diane M. Mackie and Eliot R. Smith (Philadelphia: Psychological Press, 2002), 111–33.

12. Baruch Spinoza, *Ethics: Proved in Geometrical Order*, ed. Matthew J. Kisner (Cambridge: Cambridge University Press, 2018), part 3, proposition 18, Scholium, p. 110.

13. Moira Gatens et al., *Critical Exchange—Spinoza: Thoughts on Hope in Our Political Present, Contemporary Political Theory* 20, no. 1 (2021): 200–31. The idea of hope and fear as an affective dyad draws on Moira Gatens's commentary on p. 201.

14. Spinoza, *Treatise Theological-Political*, trans. Jonathan Israel (Cambridge: Cambridge University Press, 2007), 3.

15. Spinoza, *Treatise Theological-Political*, 72.

16. Vaclav Havel, *Disturbing the Peace: A Conversation with Karel Huizdala* (New York: Vintage, 1990), 181.

17. G. K. Averill, G. Catlin, and K. K. Chon, *Rules of Hope* (New York: Springer-Verlag, 1990), 3–4.

18. C. R. Snyder, *Handbook of Hope* (San Diego, Calif.: Academic, 2000). See also Jarymowicz and Bar-Tal, "The Dominance of Fear Over Hope," 368.

19. Michele Moody-Adams, "Moral Progress and Human Agency," in "Moral Progress," special issue of *Ethical Theory and Moral Practice* 20, no. 1 (February 2017): 19.

20. Several contemporary philosophers offer versions of this objection. Three are of special interest to my framing of the problem. Phillip Petit, "Hope and Its Place in Mind," in "Hope, Power and Governance," special issue of *Annals of the American Academy of Political and Social Science* 592 (March 2004): 152–65; Victoria McGeer, "The Art of Good Hope," in "Hope, Power and Governance," special issue of *Annals of the American Academy of Political and Social Science* 592 (March 2004): 100–27; and Adrienne Martin, *How We Hope* (Princeton, N.J.: Princeton University Press, 2014), 4–6.

21. Erich Fromm, *The Revolution of Hope* (Riverdale, N.Y.: American Mental Health Foundation, 1968), 31.

22. Jonathan Lear, *Radical Hope* (Cambridge, Mass.: Harvard University Press, 2006).

23. Viktor Frankl, *Man's Search for Meaning* (Boston: Beacon, 2006).

24. Nelson Mandela, *Long Walk to Freedom: The Autobiography of Nelson Mandela* (New York: Little, Brown, 1994), 495.

25. Iris Young, *Inclusion and Democracy* (Oxford: Oxford University Press, 2002), 63, 67.

26. Franklin Delano Roosevelt, "Second Inaugural Address," Washington, D.C., January 20, 1937, in *Franklin Delano Roosevelt: Great Speeches*, ed. John Grafton (Mineola, N.Y.: Dover, 1999), 57–62.

27. Many commentators have noted, however, that on matters on racial segregation—including such topics as lynching—Roosevelt's policies were often racially myopic: from the failure of New Deal economic policies to really challenge racial segregation, to Roosevelt's personal failure to take seriously the possibility of using the power of the federal government to make lynching a federal crime.

28. Franklin Delano Roosevelt, "First Inaugural Address," March 4, 1933, in *Franklin Delano Roosevelt: Great Speeches*, 28–33.

29. Frederick Douglass, "What to the Slave Is the Fourth of July," 1852, in *The Portable Frederick Douglass*, ed. John Stauffer and Henry Louis Gates, Jr. (New York: Penguin, 2016), 195–221.

30. James Baldwin, *The Fire Next Time* (New York: Dial, 1963).

31. See Richard Rorty, *Achieving Our Country* (Cambridge, Mass.: Harvard University Press, 1998). I discuss the implications for democratic thought of the links between Rorty and Baldwin in my article "Democracy, Identity and Politics," *Res Philosophica* 95, no. 2 (April 2018): 199–218.

32. A lively account of this episode is provided in John Carlin, *Playing the Enemy: Nelson Mandela and the Game That Made a Nation* (New York: Penguin, 2009).

33. Margaret Atwood, *The Handmaid's Tale* (New York: Houghton Mifflin Harcourt, 1986).

34. Laura Charlton, "What Is the Great Replacement?," *New York Times*, August 6, 2019, https://www.nytimes.com/2019/08/06/us/politics/grand-replacement-explainer.html.

35. Diana C. Mutz, "Status Threat, Not Economic Hardship, Explains the 2016 Presidential Vote," *Proceedings of the National Academy of Sciences* 115, no. 19 (May 8, 2018): E4330–39.

36. Amos Tversky and Daniel Kahneman, "Prospect Theory: An Analysis of Decision Under Risk," *Econometrica* 46, no. 4 (1979): 263–91.

37. Jonathan Metzl, *Dying of Whiteness* (New York: Basic Books, 2019).

38. Michael Petersen, Mathias Osmundsen, and Kevin Arceneaux, "The 'Need for Chaos' and Motivations to Share Hostile Political Rumors," *PsyArXiv*, September 1, 2018.

39. John Dewey "Creative Democracy: The Task Before Us," in *The Later Works*, vol. 14: *1939–1941. Essays, Reviews and Miscellany*, ed. Jo Ann Boydston (Carbondale: Southern Illinois University Press, 1988).

40. Peniel E. Joseph, *The Sword and the Shield: The Revolutionary Lives of Malcolm X and Martin Luther King, Jr.* (New York: Basic Books, 2020).

41. Shaun Johnson, "Seamus Heaney: Hope Is Something That Is There to Be Worked For," *Independent*, October 31, 2002.

42. Seamus Heaney, *The Cure at Troy: A Version of Sophocles' Philoctetes* (New York: Farrar, Straus and Giroux, 1991), 77.

8. HOPE AND HISTORY

1. Martin Luther King, Jr., "Where Do We Go from Here?," in *A Testament of Hope: The Essential Writings and Speeches of Martin Luther King, Jr.*, ed. James M. Washington (New York: Harper Collins, 1991), 45.

2. Michele Moody-Adams, "The Path of Conscientious Citizenship," in *To Shape a New World*, ed. Tommie Shelby and Brandon Terry (Cambridge, Mass.: Harvard University Press, 2018), 286–87.

3. One of the most compelling accounts of King's role in the Civil Rights Movement is offered by David L. Chappell, *A Stone of Hope: Prophetic Religion and the Death of Jim Crow* (Chapel Hill: University of North Carolina Press, 2004).

4. Juliette Cerf, "Thought Is the Courage of Hopelessness: An Interview with Philosopher Giorgio Agamben," trans. Jordan Fisher, June 2014, https://www.versobooks.com/blogs/1612-thought-is-the-courage-of-hopelessness-an-interview-with-philosopher-giorgio-agamben.

5. Slavoj Žižek, "Slavoj Žižek on Greece: The Courage of Hopelessness," *New Statesman*, September 2, 2021, https://www.newstatesman.com/world-affairs/2015/07/slavoj-i-ek-greece-courage-hopelessness.

6. Martin Luther King, Jr., "Facing the Challenge of a New Age," in *A Testament of Hope*, 139–40.

7. Peniel E. Joseph, *The Sword and the Shield: The Revolutionary Lives of Malcolm X and Martin Luther King, Jr.* (New York: Basic Books, 2020), 235.

8. Martin Luther King, Jr., "A Time to Break Silence," in *A Testament of Hope*.

9. King, "Facing the Challenge of a New Age."

10. John Torpey, *Making Whole What Has Been Smashed: On Reparations Politics* (Cambridge, Mass.: Harvard University Press, 2006).

11. Thomas McCarthy, "Coming to Terms with Our Past. Part II: On the Morality and Politics of Reparations for Slavery," *Political Theory* 32, no. 6 (December 2004): 750–72.

12. Frantz Fanon, *Black Skin, White Masks* (New York: Grove, 1967), 225–31.

13. Orlando Patterson, "Toward a Future That Has No Past: Reflections on the Fate of Blacks in the Americas," *Public Interest* (Spring 1972): 35–68.

14. James Baldwin, "Unnameable Objects, Unspeakable Crimes," http://blackstate.com/james-baldwin-unnameable-objects-unspeakable-crimes/.

15. Jeremy Waldron, "Superseding Historic Injustice," *Ethics* 103, no. 1 (October 1992): 4–28; John Torpey, *Making Whole What Has Been*

Smashed: On Reparations Politics (Cambridge, Mass.: Harvard University Press, 2006), 5.

16. Torpey, *Making Whole What Has Been Smashed*, 5.

17. Charles Mills, "Theorizing Racial Justice," Tanner Lecture on Human Values, University of Michigan, February 12, 2020; Mills, "Black Radical Kantianism" *Res Philosophica* 95, no. 1 (January 2018): 1–33; and David Lyons, "Moral Judgment, Historical Reality and Civil Disobedience," *Philosophy & Public Affairs* 27, no. 1 (Winter 1998): 31–49.

18. Lyons, "Moral Judgment, Historical Reality and Civil Disobedience,"

19. Michele Moody-Adams, "Reflections on Rawls and Racial Justice," commentary on Charles Mills's Tanner Lecture on Human Values, University of Michigan, February 2020.

20. Tim Arango, John Eligon, and Shaila Dewan, "How the Trial Over Floyd's Death Flipped the Script for Black Victims," *New York Times*, April 24, 2021, https://www.nytimes.com/2021/04/24/us/george-floyd-black-victims.html.

21. Maurice Mandelbaum, "Some Neglected Philosophic Problems Regarding History," *Journal of Philosophy* 49, no. 10 (May 1952): 317–29.

22. James Baldwin, "The White Man's Guilt," reprinted in *James Baldwin: Collected Essays*, ed. Toni Morrison (New York: Library Classics of the United States, 1998), 722–27.

23. Susan Nieman, *Learning From the Germans: Race and the Memory of Evil* (New York: Farrar, Straus and Giroux, 2019).

24. Richard Rorty, "Is Philosophy Relevant to Applied Ethics?," *Business Ethics Quarterly* 16, no. 3 (2006): 375.

25. Desmond Tutu, *No Future Without Forgiveness* (New York: Doubleday, 1999).

26. Hannah Arendt, "Irreversibility and the Power to Forgive," in *The Human Condition*, 2nd ed. (Chicago: University of Chicago Press, 2018), 236–43.

27. My notion of civic grace is developed in my essay "Memory, Multiculturalism and the Sources of Solidarity," in *Interpreting Modernity: Essays on the Work of Charles Taylor*, ed. Daniel Weinstock, Jacob Levy, and Jocelyn Maclure, (Montreal: McGill-Queen's University Press, 2020). My notion builds on the concept of "political grace" defended by Geoffrey Scarre. See Scarre, "Political Reconciliation, Forgiveness

and Grace," *Studies in Christian Ethics* 24, no. 2 (2011): 171–82. Scarre defined grace as a general tendency and readiness to show "'good will,' 'benevolence,' 'magnanimity,' 'conciliation,' 'turning the other cheek'" and sometimes even forgiveness toward the other in response to their conduct (178–79). I conceive of civic grace as a distinctive extension of goodwill to the horizontal relationships we have with other citizens, especially (though not only) in a democracy. It is a *foundation* of democratic life, rather than a response to particular interactions—a central element of what I have described elsewhere as the democratic civic ethos.

28. E. B. White, "Wind the Clock: E. B. White to Mr. Nadeau," in *Letters of Note: An Eclectic Collection of Correspondence Deserving of a Wider Audience (Historical Nonfiction Letters, Letters from Famous People)*, comp. Shaun Usher (San Francisco: Chronicle, 2014), 10.

BIBLIOGRAPHY

Abramson, Kate. "Turning Up the Lights on Gaslighting." *Philosophical Perspectives* 28 (2014): 1–30.

Achen, Christopher H., and Larry M. Bartels. *Democracy for Realists: Why Elections Do Not Produce Responsive Government.* Princeton, N.J.: Princeton University Press, 2016.

Ackerman, Bruce. *We the People.* Vol. 3: *The Civil Rights Revolution.* Cambridge, Mass.: Harvard University Press, 2014.

Ackerman, Peter, and Jack Duvall. *A Force More Powerful: A Century of Non-Violent Conflict.* New York: St. Martin's, 2000.

Adichie, Chimamanda Ngozi. "The Danger of a Single Story." TED Talk, July 2009. https://www.ted.com/talks/chimamanda_ngozi_adichie_the_danger_of_a_single_story?language=en.

Alcoff, Linda Martin. *The Future of Whiteness.* Malden, Mass.: Polity, 2015.

Alexander, Michelle. *The New Jim Crow: Mass Incarceration in the Age of Color Blindness.* New York: New Press, 2010.

Allen, Danielle S. *Talking to Strangers: Anxieties of Citizenship Since Brown v. Board of Education.* Chicago: University of Chicago Press, 2004.

Anderson, Benedict. *Imagined Communities.* London: Verso, 2006.

Anderson, Elizabeth. "The Epistemology of Injustice." *Southern Journal of Philosophy* 58, no. 1 (2020): 6–29.

Anderson, Luvell. "Hermeneutical Impasses." *Philosophical Topics* 45, no. 2 (2017): 1–19.

Andrews, William L. "North American Slave Narratives: An Introduction to the Slave Narrative." Documenting the American South digital library.

University Library, University of North Carolina at Chapel Hill. https:// docsouth.unc.edu/neh/intro.html.

——. *To Tell a Free Story: The First Century of African American Autobiography, 1760–1865*. Urbana: University of Illinois Press, 1986.

Aquinas. *The Summa Theologica*, trans. Fathers of the English Dominican Province. Benziger Bros. edition, Thomistic Institute, 1947. https:// aquinas101.thomisticinstitute.org/st-index.

Arango, Tim, John Eligon, and Shaila Dewan. "How the Trial Over Floyd's Death Flipped the Script for Black Victims." *New York Times*, April 24, 2021. https://www.nytimes.com/2021/04/24/us/george-floyd-black-victims .html.

Araujo, Ana Lucia. "Toppling Monuments Is a Global Phenomenon." *Washington Post*, June 23, 2020. https://www.washingtonpost.com/outlook /2020/06/23.

Arendt, Hannah. *The Human Condition*. 2nd ed. Chicago: University of Chicago Press, 2018.

——. *On Violence*. New York: Houghton Mifflin Harcourt, 1970.

——. "Reflections on Little Rock." *Dissent Magazine* (Winter 1959). https:// www.dissentmagazine.org/article/reflections-on-little-rock/.

Atwood, Margaret. *The Handmaid's Tale*. New York: Houghton Mifflin Harcourt, 1986.

Averill, G. K., G. Catlin, and K. K. Chon. *Rules of Hope*. New York: Springer-Verlag, 1990.

Baker, Courtney. *Humane Insight: Looking at Images of African American Suffering and Death*. Urbana: University of Illinois Press, 2017.

Baldwin, James. *Collected Essays*. New York: Library of America, 1998.

Baptist, Edward. *The Half Has Never Been Told: Slavery and The Making of American Capitalism*. New York: Basic Books, 2014.

Benjamin, Walter. "The Work of Art in the Age of Mechanical Reproduction." 1935. In *Illuminations*, ed. Hannah Arendt, trans. Harry Zohn. New York: Schocken, 1997.

Bentham, Jeremy. *Introduction to the Principles of Morals and Legislation*. 1789. Reprint. New York: Hafner, 1948.

Berger, John. *Ways of Seeing*. London: Penguin and BBC, 1972.

Bingham, Clara, and Laura Leedy Gansler. *Class Action: The Landmark Case That Changed Sexual Harassment Law*. New York: Random House, 2002.

Blasingame, John W., ed. *Slave Testimony: Two Centuries of Letters, Speeches, Interviews, and Autobiographies.* Baton Rouge: Louisiana State University Press, 1977.

Blight, David. *Race and Reunion: The Civil War in American Memory.* Cambridge, Mass.: Harvard University Press, 2001.

Bloom, Joshua, and Waldo E. Martin, Jr. *Black Against Empire: The History and Politics of the Black Panther Party.* Oakland: University of California Press, 2016.

Boxill, Bernard. "Two Traditions in African American Political Philosophy." *Philosophical Forum* 24 (1992): 119–45.

Broad, C. D. *Five Types of Ethical Theory.* 1930. Reprint. London: Routledge and Kegan Paul. 1979.

Bruce, Dickson. "Politics and Political Philosophy in the Slave Narrative." In *Cambridge Companion to the African American Slave Narrative,* ed. Audrey Fisch, 28–43. Cambridge: Cambridge University Press, 2007.

Bruner, Jerome. "Life as Narrative." In "Reflections on the Self," special issue of *Social Research* 54, no. 1 (Spring 1987).

Burke, Kenneth. "Terministic Screens." *Proceedings of the American Catholic Philosophical Association* 39 (1965): 87–102.

Burns, Ken. *Thomas Jefferson—a Film by Ken Burns.* Episode 12. Public Broadcasting System.

Burrow, Rufus. "The Beloved Community: Martin Luther King Jr. and Josiah Royce." *Encounter* 73, no. 1 (2012): 37–64.

Butler, Judith. *Excitable Speech: A Politics of the Performance.* New York: Routledge, 1997.

——. *Notes Toward a Performative Theory of Assembly.* Cambridge, Mass.: Harvard University Press, 2017.

Calhoun, Cheshire. "Responsibility and Reproach." *Ethics* 99 (1989): 396–97.

Cameron, David. "State Multiculturalism Has Failed Says David Cameron." *BBC News,* February 11, 2011.

Campbell, Karlyn. "Agency: Promiscuous and Protean." *Communication and Critical/Cultural Studies* 2, no. 1 (2005): 1–19. doi:10.1080/1479142042000332134.

Cannady, Margot. *The Straight State: Sexuality and Citizenship in Twentieth-Century America.* Princeton, N.J.: Princeton University Press, 2011.

Capers, Bennett. "Rethinking the Fourth Amendment: Race, Citizenship and the Equality Principle." *Harvard Civil Rights–Civil Liberties Law Review* 46, no. 1 (2011): 1–50.

Cappelen, Herman, and David Plunkett, "A Guided Tour of Conceptual Engineering and Conceptual Ethics." In *Conceptual Engineering and Conceptual Ethics*, ed. Alexis Burgess, Herman Cappelen, and David Plunkett. Oxford: Oxford University Press, 2020.

Carlin, John. *Playing the Enemy: Nelson Mandela and the Game That Made a Nation*. New York: Penguin, 2009.

Castells, Manuel. *Networks of Outrage and Hope*. Cambridge: Polity, 2003.

Cerf, Juliette. "Thought Is the Courage of Hopelessness: An Interview with Philosopher Giorgio Agamben," trans. Jordan Fisher, June 2014. https://www.versobooks.com/blogs/1612-thought-is-the-courage-of-hopelessness-an-interview-with-philosopher-giorgio-agamben.

Chait, Jonathan. "Tom Cotton Calls Slavery 'Necessary Evil' to 'Development of Our Country.'" *New York Magazine*, July 27, 2020. https://nymag.com/intelligencer/2020/07/tom-cotton-slavery-necessary-evil-development-country-1619-project.html.

Chappell, David L. *A Stone of Hope: Prophetic Religion and the Death of Jim Crow*. Chapel Hill: University of North Carolina Press, 2004.

Charlton, Laura. "What Is the Great Replacement?" *New York Times*, August 6, 2019. https://www.nytimes.com/2019/08/06/us/politics/grand-replacement-explainer.html.

Chenoweth, Erica. *Civil Resistance: What Everyone Needs to Know©*. New York: Oxford University Press, 2021.

Chenoweth, Erica, and Maria Stephan. *Why Civil Resistance Works: The Strategic Logic of Non-Violent Conflict*. New York: Columbia University Press, 2011.

Cicero. *De Natura Deorum*, trans. H. Rackham. Loeb Classical Library. Cambridge, Mass.: Harvard University Press, 1951.

Cohn, Nate, and Kevin Quealy. "How Public Opinion Has Moved on Black Lives Matter." *New York Times*, June 10, 2020. https://www.nytimes.com/interactive/2020/06/10/upshot/black-lives-matter-attitudes.html.

Coles, Gregory. "The Exorcism of Language: Reclaimed Derogatory Terms and Their Limits." *College English* 78, no. 5 (2016): 424–46.

Cooper, David. "Moral Relativism." *Midwest Studies in Philosophy* 3 (1978). Special issue: *Studies in Ethical Theory*, ed. Peter French, Theodore Uehling, and Howard Wettstein.

Dean, Carolyn J. *The Fragility of Empathy After the Holocaust*. Ithaca, N.Y.: Cornell University, 2004.

Delmas, Candice. *The Duty to Resist: When Disobedience Should Be Uncivil*. Oxford: Oxford University Press, 2018.

Dennett, Daniel. *Elbow Room: The Varieties of Free Will Worth Wanting*. Cambridge, Mass.: MIT Press, 2015.

Devos, Thierry, Lisa A. Silver, Diane M. Mackie, and Eliot R. Smith. "Experiencing Intergroup Emotions." In *From Prejudice to Intergroup Emotions: Differentiated Reactions to Social Groups*, ed. Diane M. Mackie and Eliot R. Smith, 111–33. Philadelphia: Psychological Press, 2002.

Dewey, John. *Art as Experience*. New York: Berkeley, 1934.

——. "Creative Democracy: The Task Before Us." In *The Later Works*. Vol. 14: *1939–1941. Essays, Reviews and Miscellany*, ed. Jo Ann Boydston. Carbondale: Southern Illinois University Press, 1988.

Dewey, John, and James H. Tufts. *Ethics*. New York: Henry Holt, 1909.

Diamond, Cora. "The Difficulty of Reality and the Difficulty of Philosophy." In *Reading Cavell*, ed. Alice Crary and Stanford Shieh. London: Routledge, 2005.

Douglass, Frederick. "Capt. John Brown Not Insane." In *The Portable Frederick Douglass*, ed. John Stauffer and Henry Louis Gates, Jr. New York: Penguin, 2016.

——. "Men of Color, to Arms!" March 2, 1863. Reprinted in *Lay This Laurel*, by Lincoln Kirstein and Richard Benson. New York: Eakins, 1973.

——. *My Bondage and My Freedom*, intro. and notes by David Blight. 1855; New Haven, Conn.: Yale University Press, 2014.

——. "What to the Slave Is the Fourth of July?" 1855. In *The Portable Frederick Douglass*, ed. John Stauffer and Henry Louis Gates, Jr. New York: Penguin, 2016.

Du Bois, W. E. B. "The Criteria of Negro Art." *The Crisis* 32 (October 1925): 290–97. http://www.webdubois.org/dbCriteriaNArt.html.

Dworkin, Ronald. "On Not Prosecuting Civil Disobedience." *New York Review of Books*, June 6, 1968. https://www.nybooks.com/articles/1968/06/06/on-not-prosecuting-civil-disobedience/.

Ehrenberg, John. "What Can We Learn from Occupy's Failure?" *Palgrave Communications*, July 4, 2017. https://www.nature.com/articles/palco mms201762.

Eisenger, Jessie. "Why Only One Top Banker Went to Jail for the Financial Crisis." *New York Times*, April 30, 2014.

Ellison, Ralph. Interview, 1965. In *Who Speaks for the Negro?*, by Robert Penn Warren. New Haven, Conn.: Yale University Press, 1993.

Eyerman, Ron, and Andrew Jamison *Social Movements: A Cognitive Approach*. University Park: Pennsylvania State University Press, 1991.

Fanden, Nicholas. "Frustration and Fury as Rand Paul Holds Up Anti-Lynching Bill in the Senate." *New York Times*, June 5, 2020.

Fanon, Frantz. *Black Skin, White Masks*. New York: Grove, 1967.

Feinberg, Joel. *Doing and Deserving*. Princeton, N.J.: Princeton University Press, 1970.

Fishkin, James, and James Mansbridge, eds. "The Prospects and Limits of Deliberative Democracy." *Daedalus* (Summer 2017). https://www.amacad .org/daedalus/prospects-limits-deliberative-democracy.

Follett, Mary Parker. *Dynamic Administration: The Collected Papers of Mary Parker Follett*. Mansfield Center, Conn.: Martino, 2013.

Foster, Eugene A. F., et al. "Jefferson Fathered Slave's Last Child." *Nature*, November 5, 1998.

——. "Reply: The Thomas Jefferson Paternity Case." Letter to editor. *Nature*, January 7, 1999.

Fowler, Anne, Nicki Nichols Gamble, Frances X. Hogan, Melissa Kogut, Madeline McComish, and Barbara Thorp. "Talking with the Enemy." *Boston Globe*, January 28, 2001. https://www.feminist.com/resources /artspeech/genwom/talkingwith.html.

Francis, Pope. *Fratelli Tutti*, October 4, 2020. https://www.vatican.va /content/francesco/en/encyclicals/documents/papa-francesco_20201003 _enciclica-fratelli-tutti.html.

Frankl, Viktor. *Man's Search for Meaning*. Boston: Beacon, 2006.

French, Peter. *Responsibility Matters*. Lawrence: University of Kansas Press, 1992.

Fricker, Miranda. *Epistemic Injustice: Power and the Ethics of Knowing*. Oxford: Oxford University Press, 2007.

Fromm, Erich. *The Revolution of Hope*. Riverdale, N.Y.: American Mental Health Foundation, 1968.

Gadamer, Hans Georg. *Truth and Method*. Continuum Impacts. London: Bloomsbury, 1982.

Galanes, Philip. "Gretchen Carlson and Catherine MacKinnon Have a Few Things to Say." *New York Times*, March 17, 2018. https://www.nytimes.com/2018/03/17/business/catharine-mackinnon-gretchen-carlson.html.

Gandhi, M. K. *Mahatma Gandhi and Leo Tolstoy Letters*, ed. B. Srinivasa Murthy. Long Beach, Calif.: Long Beach Publications, 1987.

Ganz, Marshall. *Why David Sometimes Wins: Leadership, Organization, and Strategy in the California Farm Worker Movement*. New York: Oxford University Press, 2009.

Gatens, Moira, Justice Steinberg, Aurelia Armstrong, Susan James, and Martin Saar. "Critical Exchange—Spinoza: Thoughts on Hope in Our Political Present." *Contemporary Political Theory* 20 (2021): 200–231.

Gates, Henry Louis, Jr., ed. *The Classic Slave Narratives*. New York: New American Library, 1987.

Geyl, Pieter. *Napoleon For and Against*, trans. Olive Rentier. Harmondsworth, UK: Penguin, 1949. https://archive.org/stream/in.ernet.dli.2015.202235/2015.202235.Napoleon-For_djvu.txt.

Glover, Jonathan. *Humanity: A Moral History of the Twentieth Century*. New Haven, Conn.: Yale University Press, 2000.

Goodman, Nelson. "Twisted Tales." *Critical Inquiry* 7 (1980): 101–19.

Goodwin, Jeff, and James J. Jasper. "Editors' Introduction." In *The Social Movements Reader: Cases and Concepts*. 3rd ed. Oxford: Wiley-Blackwell, 2015.

Gordon-Reed, Annette. *Thomas Jefferson and Sally Hemings: An American Controversy*. Charlottesville: University of Virginia Press, 1997.

Graham, David. "The Bureaucrats Charged in Flint's Water Crisis." *Atlantic*, April 20, 2016.

Gutmann, Amy, and Dennis Thompson. *The Spirit of Compromise*. Princeton, N.J.: Princeton University Press, 2012.

Haines, Herbert H. "Black Radicalization and the Funding of Civil Rights." *Social Problems* 32, no. 1 (1984).

——. *Black Radicals and the Civil Rights Mainstream, 1954–1970*. Knoxville: University of Tennessee Press, 1988.

——. "Radical Flank Effect." In *The Wiley-Blackwell Encyclopedia of Social and Political Movements*, ed. David A. Snow, Donatella della Porta, Bern Klandermans, and Doug McAdam. Hoboken, N.J.: Wiley, 2013.

Halbertal, Moshe. *On Sacrifice*. Princeton, N.J.: Princeton University Press, 2012.

Haslanger, Sally. "Racism, Ideology, and Social Movements." *Res Philosophica* 94, no. 1 (2017): 1–22.

Havel, Vaclav. *Disturbing the Peace: A Conversation with Karel Huizdala*. New York: Vintage, 1990.

Heaney, Seamus. *The Cure at Troy: A Version of Sophocles' Philoctetes*. New York: Farrar, Straus and Giroux, 1991.

Herstein, Gary. "The Roycean Roots of the Beloved Community." *Pluralist* 4, no. 2 (2009): 92–107.

"Highlander Folk School." In *The Martin Luther King, Jr., Encyclopedia*. Stanford, Calif.: King Institute, 2008. https://kinginstitute.stanford.edu /encyclopedia/highlander-folk-school.

Hirschmann, Nancy. "Toward a Feminist Theory of Freedom." *Political Theory* 24, no. 1 (1996).

Hobbes, Thomas. *Leviathan*. Oxford: Oxford University Press, 2009.

Hochschild, Arlie. *Strangers in Their Own Land: Anger and Mourning on the American Right*. New York: New Press, 2016.

Honneth, Axl. "Recognition and Justice: Outline of a Plural Theory of Justice." *Acta Sociologica* 47, no. 4 (2004): 351–64.

hooks, bell. *Talking Back: Thinking Feminist, Thinking Black*. New York: Routledge, 2014.

Jacob, Ben S., and David Smith. "Trump Says If Ivanka Was Harassed at Work She Should 'Find Another Career.'" *Guardian*, August 1, 2016. https://www.theguardian.com/us-news/2016/aug/01/donald-trump -sexual-harassment-roger-ailes-fox.

"James Lawson." In *Martin Luther King, Jr. Encyclopedia*. Stanford, Calif.: King Institute, 2008. https://kinginstitute.stanford.edu/encyclopedia /lawson-james-m.

James, William. "Conversion," lecture 9. In *The Varieties of Religious Experience*, 271–30. Auckland: Floating, 2008.

——. "The Moral Philosopher and the Moral Life." In *Essays in Pragmatism*. New York: Hafner, 1948.

——. "Robert Gould Shaw: Oration by Professor William James." In *Essays in Religion and Morality*. Cambridge, Mass.: Harvard University Press, 1982.

Jarymowicz, Maria, and Daniel Bar-tal. "The Dominance of Fear Over Hope in the Life of Individuals and Collectives." *European Journal of Social Psychology* 36, no. 3 (May 2006): 367–92.

Jasper, James M. *The Art of Moral Protest: Culture, Biography and Creativity in Social Movements*. Chicago: University of Chicago Press, 1997.

Johnson, David Kyle. *The Lavender Scare: Cold War Persecution of Gay and Lesbians in the Federal Government*. Chicago: University of Chicago Press, 2004.

Johnson, Mark. *Moral Imagination: Implications of Cognitive Science for Ethics*. University of Chicago Press, 1994.

Johnson, Shaun. "Seamus Heaney: Hope Is Something That Is There to Be Worked For." *Independent*, October 31, 2002.

Joseph, Peniel E. *The Sword and the Shield: The Revolutionary Lives of Malcolm X and Martin Luther King, Jr.* New York: Basic Books, 2020.

Jowett, Garth, and Victoria O'Donnell *Propaganda and Persuasion*. 5th ed. Thousand Oaks, Calif.: Sage, 2012.

Kant, Immanuel. *Groundwork of the Metaphysics of Morals*, trans. H. J. Paton. 1785. Reprint. New York: Harper and Row, 1964.

Kind, Amy. "The Heterogeneity of Imagination." *Erkenntnis* 78 (2013): 141–59.

Kind, Amy, and Peter Kung. *Knowledge Through Imagination*. Oxford: Oxford University Press, 2016.

King, Martin Luther, Jr. "The Birth of a New Nation: Sermon Delivered at Dexter Avenue Baptist Church," April 7, 1957. King Papers, Martin Luther King, Jr., Research Institute. https://kinginstitute.stanford.edu/king-papers/documents/birth-new-nation-sermon-delivered-dexter-avenue-baptist-church.

——. *A Testament of Hope: The Essential Writings and Speeches of Martin Luther King, Jr.*, ed. James M. Washington. New York: Harper Collins, 1991.

Kirkland, Frank. "Enslavement, Moral Suasion, and Struggles for Recognition: Frederick Douglass's Answer to the Question—'What Is Enlightenment?'" In *Frederick Douglass: A Critical Reader*, ed. Bill E. Lawson and Frank M. Kirkland, 247. Malden, Mass.: Blackwell, 1999.

Kymlicka, Will, and Allen Patten. *Language Rights and Political Theory*. Oxford: Oxford University Press, 2003.

Lander, Eric S., and Joseph J. Ellis, "Founding Father." *Nature*, November 5, 1998.

Landrieu, Mitch. *In the Shadow of Statues: A White Southerner Confronts History*. New York: Penguin, 2018.

——. "Speech on the Removal of Confederate Monuments in New Orleans." *New York Times*, May 23, 2017. https://www.nytimes.com/2017/05/23/opinion/mitch-landrieus-speech-transcript.html.

Lawler, Andrew. "Pulling Down Statues? It's a Tradition That Dates Back to U.S. Independence." *National Geographic Magazine*, July 1, 2020.

Lear, Jonathan. *Radical Hope*. Cambridge, Mass.: Harvard University Press, 2006.

Le Bon, Gustave. *The Crowd: A Study of the Popular Mind*. 1895. Reprint. Digireads, 2009.

LeBron, Christopher. *The Making of Black Lives Matter: A Brief History of an Idea*. Oxford: Oxford University Press, 2017.

Lederach, John Paul. *The Moral Imagination: The Art and Soul of Building Peace*. Oxford University Press, 2010.

LeDoux, Joseph. "Coming to Terms with Fear." *Proceedings of the National Academy of Science* 111, no, 5 (February 2014): 2871–78.

Lemkin, Raphael. *Axis Rule in Occupied Europe: Laws of Occupation, Analysis of Government, Proposals for Redress*. Washington, D.C.: Carnegie Endowment for International Peace, 1944.

Lenhardt, Robin A. "Understanding the Mark: Race, Stigma, and Equality in Context." *New York University Law Review* 79 (2004): 803–930.

Lerner, Steve. *Sacrifice Zones*. Cambridge, Mass.: MIT Press, 2010.

Lewis, Michael. *The Big Short: Inside the Doomsday Machine*. New York: Norton, 2010.

Lichfield, Gordon. "All the Names for the New Digital Economy and Why None of Them Fits." *Quartz*, November 12, 2015. https://qz.com/548137/all-the-names-for-the-new-digital-economy-and-why-none-of-them-fits//.

Lilla, Mark. "The End of Identity Liberalism." *New York Times*, November 18, 2016. https://www.nytimes.com/2016/11/20/opinion/sunday/the-end-of-identity-liberalism.html.

——. *The Once and Future Liberal*. New York: Harper, 2017.

Lipsky, Michael. "Protest as a Political Resource." *American Political Science Review* 62, no. 4 (1968), 1144–58.

Lowe, Guy. "The Model Minority Narrative and Its Effect on Asian American Identity and Social Status." In *Modern Societal Impacts of the Model Minority Stereotype*, ed. Nicholas Daniel Hartlep, 323–50. Hershey, Pa.: IGI Global, 2015.

Lyons, David, "Moral Judgment, Historical Reality and Civil Disobedience." *Philosophy & Public Affairs* 27, no. 1 (1998): 31–49.

Machado, Antonio. *Border of a Dream: Selected Poems*, trans. Willis Barnstone. Port Townsend, Wash.: Copper Canyon, 2004.

——. *Selected Poems*, trans. Alan S. Trueblood. Cambridge, Mass.: Harvard University Press, 1988.

MacIntyre, Alasdair. *After Virtue*. 3rd ed. Notre Dame, Ind.: University of Notre Dame Press, 2007.

Macintyre, Stuart. "The History Wars." *Sydney Papers* (Winter/Spring 2003): 76–83. http://www.kooriweb.org/foley/resources/pdfs/198.pdf.

MacKinnon, Catharine A. *Feminism Unmodified: Discourses on Life and Law*. Cambridge, Mass.: Harvard University Press, 1987.

——. *Only Words*. Cambridge, Mass.: Harvard University Press, 1993.

——. "Where #Me Too Came From and Where It's *Going*." *Atlantic*, March 24, 2019.

Mallinson, Christine. "Language and Its Everyday Revolution Potential: Feminist Linguistic Activism in the United States." In *The Oxford Handbook of U.S. Women's Activism*, ed. Holly J. McCammon, Vera Taylor, Jo Reger, and Rachel L. Einwohner, 419–39. Oxford: Oxford University Press, 2017.

Mandela, Nelson. *Long Walk to Freedom: The Autobiography of Nelson Mandela*. New York: Little, Brown, 1994.

Mandelbaum, Maurice. "Some Neglected Philosophic Problems Regarding History." *Journal of Philosophy* 49, no. 10 (1952): 317–29.

Martin, Adrienne. *How We Hope*. Princeton, N.J.: Princeton University Press, 2014.

Masri, Safwan. *Tunisia: An Arab Anomaly*. New York: Columbia University Press, 2017.

McCarthy, Thomas. "Coming to Terms with Our Past. Part II: On the Morality and Politics of Reparations for Slavery." *Political Theory* 32, no. 6 (December 2004): 750–72.

McClelland, John S. *The Crowd, and the Mob: From Plato to Canetti*. Oxford: Routledge. 1989.

McGeer, Victoria. "The Art of Good Hope." In "Hope, Power and Governance." Special issue of *Annals of the American Academy of Political and Social Science* 592 (2004): 100–127.

Medina, José. *The Epistemology of Resistance: Gender and Racial Oppression, Epistemic Injustice, and the Social Imagination*. Oxford: Oxford University Press, 2013.

Méheut, Constant. "Groups Put French State on Legal Notice Over Police Racism." *New York Times*, January 27, 2021. https://www.nytimes.com /2021/01/27/world/europe/france-police-racism.html.

Metzl, Jonathan. *Dying of Whiteness: How the Politics of Racial Resentment Is Killing America's Heartland*. New York: Basic Books, 2019.

Mill, John Stuart. *On Liberty in Utilitarianism and On Liberty: Including Mill's "Essay on Bentham" and Selections from the Writings of Jeremy Bentham and John Austin*, ed. Mary Warnock. 2nd ed. Oxford: Wiley-Blackwell, 2003.

Miller, David, *On Nationality*. Oxford: Oxford University Press, 1997.

Mills, Charles. "Black Radical Kantianism." *Res Philosophica* 95, no. 1 (January 2018): 1–33.

——. "Theorizing Racial Justice." Tanner Lecture on Human Values, University of Michigan, February 12, 2020.

Mobley, Mamie Till, and Christopher Benson. *The Death of Innocence: The Story of the Hate Crime That Changed America*. New York: One World, 2003.

Mohai, Paul. "Environmental Justice and the Flint Water Crisis." *Michigan Sociological Review* 32 (Fall 2018): 1–41.

Moody-Adams, Michele. "Culture, Responsibility and Affected Ignorance," *Ethics* 104, no. 2 (January 1994): 291–309.

——. "Democracy, Identity and Politics. *Res Philosophica* 95, no. 2 (April 2018): 199–218.

——. "Democratic Conflict and the Political Morality of Compromise." *Nomos* 59 (2018): 186–219. https://www.jstor.org/stable/26786040.

——. *Fieldwork in Familiar Places: Morality, Culture and Philosophy*. Cambridge, Mass.: Harvard University Press, 1997.

——. "The Idea of Moral Progress." *Metaphilosophy* 30, no. 3 (July 1999): 171–72.

——. Memory, Multiculturalism and the Sources of Solidarity." In *Interpreting Modernity: Essays on the Work of Charles Taylor*, ed. Daniel M.

Weinstock, Jacob T. Levy, and Jocelyn MacClure. Montreal: McGill-Queens University Press, 2020.

———. "Moral Progress and Human Agency." In "Moral Progress." Special issue of *Ethical Theory and Moral Practice* 20, no. 1 (February 2017): 153–68.

———. "The Path of Conscientious Citizenship." In *To Shape a New World*, ed. Tommie Shelby and Brandon Terry. Cambridge, Mass.: Harvard University Press, 2018.

———. "Philosophy and the Art of Human Flourishing." In *Philosophy and Flourishing*, ed. John J. Stuhr and James Pawelski. Oxford: Oxford University Press, forthcoming.

———. "Reflections on Rawls and Racial Justice." Commentary on Charles Mills's Tanner Lecture on Human Values, University of Michigan, February 2020.

———. "What's So Special About Academic Freedom?" In *Who's Afraid of Academic Freedom*, ed. Akeel Bilgrami and Jonathan R. Cole, 97–122. New York: Columbia University Press, 2015.

Morris, Aldon. *The Origins of the Civil Rights Movement*. New York: Simon and Schuster, 1984.

Morrison, Toni. Nobel Prize Lecture, December 7, 1993. https://www.nobelprize.org/prizes/literature/1993/morrison/lecture/.

Moser, Whet. "What Martin Luther King Wanted for Chicago in 1966." *Chicago Magazine*, January 19, 2015. https://www.chicagomag.com/city-life/january-2015/martin-luther-king-jrs-policy-ideas-for-chicago-circa-1966/.

Mumford, Lewis. "The Death of the Monument." In *Circle: International Survey of Constructive Art*, 263–70. London: Faber and Faber, 1937.

Murdoch, Iris. *Existentialist and Mystics: Writings on Philosophy and Literature*. New York: Penguin, 1999.

Mutz, Diana C. "Status Threat, Not Economic Hardship, Explains the 2016 Presidential Vote." *Proceedings of the National Academy of Sciences* 115, no. 19 (May 8, 2018): E4330–39.

Neiman, Susan. *Learning from the Germans: Race and the Memory of Evil*. New York: Farrar, Straus and Giroux, 2019.

Nemy, Enid. "Women Begin to Speak Out Against Sexual Harassment at Work." *New York Times*, August 19, 1975. https://www.nytimes.com/1975

/08/19/archives/women-begin-to-speak-out-against-sexual-harassment
-at-work.html.

Neu, Jerome. "To Understand All Is to Forgive All—or Is It?" In *Before Forgiving—Cautionary Views of Forgiveness in Psychotherapy*, ed. Sharon Lamb and Jeffrie G. Murphy, 17–50. Oxford: Oxford University Press, 2002.

Nussbaum, Martha. *Cultivating Humanity: A Classical Defense of Reform in Liberal Education*. Cambridge, Mass.: Harvard University Press, 1997.

——. *Love's Knowledge: Essays on Philosophy and Literature*. Oxford: Oxford University Press, 1990.

Orwell, George. *All Art Is Propaganda: Critical Essays*. Boston: Mariner, 2009.

Page, Clarence. "Ron Paul's Harsh Definition of Freedom." *Chicago Tribune*, September 18, 2011.

Painter, Nell. "How We Think About the Term 'Enslaved' Matters." *Guardian*, August 14, 2019. https://www.theguardian.com/us-news/2019/aug/14/slavery-in-america-1619-first-ships-jamestown.

Patterson, Orlando. *Slavery and Social Death: A Comparative Study*. Cambridge, Mass.: Harvard University Press, 1982.

——. "Toward a Future That Has No Past: Reflections on the Fate of Blacks in the Americas." *Public Interest* (Spring 1972): 35–68.

Pauwels, Anne. "Linguistic Sexism and Feminist Linguistic Activism." In *The Handbook of Language and Gender*, ed. Janet Holmes and Miriam Meyerhoff, 550–70. Oxford: Blackwell, 2003.

Petersen, Michael, Mathias Osmundsen, and Kevin Arceneaux. "The 'Need for Chaos' and Motivations to Share Hostile Political Rumors." *PsyArxIV*, September 1, 2018. https://psyarxiv.com/6m4ts/.

Petit, Phillip. "Hope and Its Place in Mind." In "Hope, Power and Governance." Special issue of *Annals of the American Academy of Political and Social Science* 592 (March 2004): 152–65.

Philip Randolph Institute. *A "Freedom Budget" for All Americans: Budgeting Our Resources, 1966–1975, to Achieve "Freedom from Want."* New York: Philip Randolph Institute, 1966.

Phillips, Ulrich B. *Life and Labor in the Old South*. 1929. Reprint. Columbia: University of South Carolina Press, 2007.

Pinker, Steven. "One Thing to Change: Anecdotes Aren't Data." *Harvard Gazette*, June 21, 2019. https://news.harvard.edu/gazette/story/2019/06

/focal-point-harvard-professor-steven-pinker-says-the-truth-lies-in -the-data/.

Platts, Mark. "Moral Reality." In *Essays on Moral Realism*, ed. Geoffrey Sayre-McCord. Ithaca, N.Y.: Cornell University Press, 1988.

Polkinghorne, Donald E. *Narrative Knowing and the Human Sciences.* Albany, N.Y.: SUNY Press, 1988.

Polletta, Francesca, and Pang Chen "Narrative and Social Movements." In *The Oxford Handbook of Cultural Sociology*, ed. Jeffrey Alexander, Rob Jacobs, and Phillip Smith, 487–506. Oxford: Oxford University Press, 2012.

Posner, Richard. "The Problematics of Moral and Legal Theory." *Harvard Law Review* 111, no. 7 (May 1998): 1638–1709.

Powers, Samantha. *A Problem from Hell: America and the Age of Genocide.* New York: Basic Books, 2013.

Ravitch, Diane. "Multiculturalism: E Pluribus Plures." *American Scholar* 49, no. 3 (Summer 1990): 337–54.

Rawls, John. *Political Liberalism.* Exp. ed. New York: Columbia University Press, 2005.

——. *A Theory of Justice.* Rev. ed. Cambridge, Mass.: Harvard University Press, 1987.

Reisel, Daniel. "Neuroscience of Restorative Justice." TED Talk, March 18, 2014. ttps://www.youtube.com/watch?v=tzJYY2p0QIc/.

Renan, Ernst. *What Is a Nation and Other Writings*, trans. and ed. M. F. N. Giglioli. New York: Columbia University Press, 2018.

Ricoeur, Paul. "Narrative Time." In "On Narrative." Special issue, *Critical Inquiry* 7, no. 1, (Autumn 1980): 169–90.

Roberts, Adam, and Timothy Garton Ash. *Civil Resistance and Power Politics: The Experience of Non-Violent Action from Gandhi to the Present.* Oxford: Oxford University Press, 2011.

Roosevelt, Franklin Delano. "First Inaugural Address," Washington, D.C., March 4, 1933. In *Franklin Delano Roosevelt: Great Speeches*, ed. John Grafton, 28–33. Mineola, N.Y.: Dover, 1999.

——. "Second Inaugural Address," Washington D.C., January 20, 1937. In *Franklin Delano Roosevelt: Great Speeches* ed. John Grafton, 57–62. Mineola, N.Y.: Dover, 1999.

Rorty, Richard. *Achieving Our Country: Leftist Thought in Twentieth Century America.* Cambridge, Mass.: Harvard University Press, 1998.

——. *Contingency, Irony and Solidarity*. Cambridge: Cambridge University Press, 1989.

——. "Feminism and Pragmatism." Tanner Lectures on Human Values, University of Michigan, December 7, 1990. https://tannerlectures.utah .edu/_resources/documents/a-to-z/r/rorty92.pdf.

——. "Is Philosophy Relevant to Applied Ethics?" *Business Ethics Quarterly* 16, no. 3: 369–80 (2006).

——. *Objectivity, Relativism and Truth*. Cambridge: Cambridge University Press, 1990.

Rosetti, Christina. *The Complete Poems*. London: Penguin, 2001.

Ruquet, Camille. "The Legacy of American Photojournalism in Ken Burns' Vietnam War Documentary Series." *Images/Memoires* 41 (2019). https:// journals.openedition.org/interfaces/647.

Rustin, Bayard. "From Protest to Politics: The Future of the Civil Rights Movement." *Commentary* 39, no. 2 (February 1965). https://www .commentarymagazine.com/articles/bayard-rustin-2/from-protest-to -politics-the-future-of-the-civil-rights-movement/.

Sartwell, Crispin. *Political Aesthetics*. Ithaca, N.Y.: Cornell University Press, 2010.

Savage, Kirk. *Monument Wars: Washington, D.C., the National Mall, and the Transformation of the Memorial Landscape*. Berkeley: University of California Press, 2009.

——. *Standing Soldiers, Kneeling Slaves: Race, War and Monuments in Nineteenth Century America*. Princeton, N.J.: Princeton University Press, 1997.

Scarre, Geoffrey. "Political Reconciliation, Forgiveness and Grace." *Studies in Christian Ethics* 24, no. 2 (2011): 171–82.

Scheffler, Samuel. *Boundaries and Allegiances: Problems of Justice and Responsibility in Liberal Thought*. Oxford: Oxford University Press, 2003.

Schlesinger, Arthur M. *The Disuniting of America: Reflections on a Multicultural Society*. New York: Norton, 1991.

Sharp, Gene. *From Dictatorship to Democracy: A Conceptual Framework for Liberation*. New York: New Press, 1994.

Shea, Andrea. "16 Statues and Memorials Were Damaged During Sunday's Protests, Including One Dedicated to African American Soldiers." *NPR*, June 3, 2020. https://www.wbur.org/artery/2020/06/03/16-statues -memorials-damaged.

Shklar, Judith. *The Faces of Injustice*. New Haven, Conn.: Yale University Press, 1990.

Siegel, Reva. "A Short History of Sexual Harassment." In *Directions in Sexual Harassment Law*, ed. Catherine Mackinnon and Reva B. Siegel, 2–28. New Haven, Conn.: Yale University Press, 2003.

Sinha, Manisha. *The Slave's Cause: A History of Abolition*. New Haven, Conn.: Yale University Press, 2016.

Slote, Michael. "Is Virtue Possible?" *Analysis* 42, no. 2 (March 1982): 70–76.

Smith, Adam. *The Theory of Moral Sentiments*, ed. D. D. Raphael and A. L. Macfie. Indianapolis, Ind.: Liberty Fund, 1982.

Smith, David Livingstone. *Less than Human: Why We Demean, Enslave and Exterminate Others*. New York: St. Martin's Griffin, 2012.

Smith, Mitch. "Flint Water Prosecutors Drop Criminal Charges." *New York Times*, June 13, 2019. https://www.nytimes.com/2019/06/13/us/flint-water-crisis-charges-dropped.html.

Snyder, Charles R. *Handbook of Hope*. San Diego, Calif.: Academic, 2000.

Sontag, Susan. *On Photography*. New York: Picador, 1973.

——. *Regarding the Pain of Others*. New York: Picador, 2003.

Spinoza, Baruch. *Ethics: Proved in Geometrical Order*, ed. Matthew J. Kisner. Cambridge: Cambridge University Press, 2018.

——. *Treatise Theological-Political*, trans. Jonathan Israel. Cambridge: Cambridge University Press, 2007.

Staples, Brent. "The Perils of Growing Comfortable with Evil." *New York Times*, April 9, 2000. https://www.nytimes.com/2000/04/09/opinion/editorial-observer-the-perils-of-growing-comfortable-with-evil.html.

Stevenson, Leslie. "Twelve Conceptions of Imagination." *British Journal of Aesthetics* 45, no. 3 (July 2003): 238–58.

Stob, Paul. "'Terministic Screens,' Social Constructionism, and the Language of Experience: Kenneth Burke's Utilization of William James." *Philosophy & Rhetoric* 41, no. 2 (2008): 130–52.

Stone, Christopher D. *Should Trees Have Standing? Law, Morality, and the Environment*. Oxford: Oxford University Press, 1972.

Storing, Herbert. "The Case Against Civil Disobedience" (1978). In *Civil Disobedience in Focus*, ed. Hugo Adam Bedau, 85–102. London: Routledge, 1991.

Strawson, Peter. "Imagination and Perception." In *Experience and Theory*, ed. L. Foster and J. W. Swanson, 31–54. Amherst: University of Massachusetts Press, 1994.

Sullivan, Stacey. "War Rape Victims Sue Karadzic for Damages in the US. *Guardian*, August 6, 2000. https://www.theguardian.com/world/2000 /aug/06/warcrimes.theobserver.

Taylor, Charles. *Dilemmas and Connections*. Cambridge, Mass.: Harvard University Press, 2014.

——. "The Dynamics of Democratic Exclusion." *Journal of Democracy* 8, no. 4 (1998): 143–56.

——. *Modern Social Imaginaries*. Durham, N.C.: Duke University Press, 2003.

Tilly, Charles, Ernesto Castañeda, and Lesley J. Wood. *Social Movements, 1768–2018*. 4th ed. New York: Routledge, 2020.

Tilly, Charles, and Sidney Tarrow. *Contentious Politics*. 2nd ed. Oxford: Oxford University Press, 2015.

Torpey, John. *Making Whole What Has Been Smashed: On Reparations Politics*. Cambridge, Mass.: Harvard University Press, 2006.

Treuer, David. *The Heartbeat of Wounded Knee: Native America from 1890 to the Present*. London: Riverhead, 2019.

——. "Return the National Parks to the Tribes." *Atlantic* (May 2021): 30–45.

——. *Rez Life: An Indian's Journey Through Reservation Life*. New York: Grove, 2013.

Tufecki, Zeynep. *Twitter and Teargas: The Power and Fragility of Networked Protest*. New Haven, Conn.: Yale University Press, 2017.

Tutu, Desmond. *No Future Without Forgiveness*. New Yok: Doubleday, 1999.

Tversky, Amos, and Daniel Kahneman "Prospect Theory: An Analysis of Decision Under Risk." *Econometrica* 46, no. 4 (1979): 263–91.

Tyson, Timothy B. *The Blood of Emmett Till*. New York: Simon and Schuster, 2017.

UNESCO. *Atlas of the World's Languages in Danger*. UNESCO, 2017. http:// www.unesco.org/languages-atlas/en/statistics.html.

Van Parjis, Philippe. *Linguistic Justice for Europe and the World*. Oxford: Oxford University Press, 2011.

Waldman, Katy. "How Climate-Change Fiction, or 'Cli-Fi,' Forces Us to Confront the Incipient Death of the Planet." *New Yorker*, November 9, 2018. https://www.newyorker.com/books/page-turner/how-climate

-change-fiction-or-cli-fi-forces-us-to-confront-the-incipient-death-of
-the-planet.

Waldron, Jeremy. *The Harm in Hate Speech*. Cambridge, Mass.: Harvard University Press, 2014.

——. "Superseding Historic Injustice." *Ethics* 103, no. 1 (October 1992): 4–28.

Walzer, Michael. *Interpretation and Social Criticism*. Cambridge, Mass.: Harvard University Press, 1987.

——. *Thick and Thin: Moral Argument at Home and Abroad*. Notre Dame, Ind.: University of Notre Dame Press, 1994.

Werhane, Patricia. *Moral Imagination and Management Decision*. Oxford: Oxford University Press, 1999.

White, Elwyn B. "Wind the Clock: E. B. White to Mr. Nadeau." In *Letters of Note: An Eclectic Collection of Correspondence Deserving of a Wider Audience (Historical Nonfiction Letters, Letters from Famous People)*, comp. Shaun Usher. San Francisco: Chronicle 2014.

White, Jonathan W., and Scott Sandage. "What Frederick Douglass Had to Say About Monuments." *Smithsonian Magazine*, June 30, 2020. https://www.smithsonianmag.com/history/what-frederick-douglass-had-say-about-monuments.

Wnuk-Lipinski, Edmund. "Civil Society and Democratization." *The Oxford Handbook of Political Behavior*, ed Russell J. Dalton and Hans-Dieter Klingemann, 9–302. Oxford: Oxford University Press, 2007.

Wolff, Tobias. "The Art of Fiction No. 183." Interviewed by Jack Livings in *Paris Review*, no. 171 (Fall 2004). https://www.theparisreview.org/interviews/5391/the-art-of-fiction-no-183-tobias-wolff.

Woodward, C. Vann. "The Case of the Louisiana Traveler." In *Quarrels That Have Shaped the Constitution*, ed. John A. Garaty, 157–74. New York: Harper, 1987.

Wright, Robert. "Race Relations: The Police Battle to Regain Trust Among Black Britons." *Financial Times*, January 6, 2021. https://www.ft.com/content/56e9b6cd-2672-48b5-be7f-673270e8346e.

Yang, Guobin. "Narrative Agency in Hashtag Activism: The Case of #BlackLivesMatter." *Media and Communication* 4, no. 4 (2016): 13–17.

Yates, Michael, and Paul LeBlanc. *A Freedom Budget for All Americans Recapturing the Promise of the Civil Rights Movement in the Struggle for Economic Justice Today*. New York: Monthly Review, 2013.

Young, Iris. *Inclusion and Democracy*. Oxford: Oxford University Press, 2002.

——. *Justice and the Politics of Difference*. Princeton, N.J.: Princeton University Press, 1990.

——. "Polity and Group Difference: A Critique of the Ideal of Universal Citizenship." *Ethics* 99, no. 2 (January 1989): 250–74.

——. "Toward a Critical Theory of Justice." *Social Theory and Practice* 7, no. 3 (1981): 279–302.

Zaki, Jamil. *The War for Kindness: Building Empathy in a Fractured World*. New York: Crown, 2019.

Žižek, Slavoj. "Slavoj Žižek on Greece: The Courage of Hopelessness." *New Statesman*, September 2, 2021. https://www.newstatesman.com/world -affairs/2015/07/slavoj-i-ek-greece-courage-hopelessness.

INDEX

abolitionism: historical boundaries and, 42–43; slave narratives, 57, 70, 196–97, 202–8, 281n15, 299–300n29; violence/nonviolence and, 204–6. *See also* racial justice movements

accountability, 100–2, 106–7, 288n50

Achieving Our Country (Rorty), 72–74

"Action and Responsibility" (Feinberg), 176

Adichie, Chimamanda Ngozi, 143, 187, 189

aesthetic activism, 118, 138, 145. *See also* political iconoclasm

aesthetic imagination, 131, 225

affected ignorance, 88, 286n24

affective orientation, 230

affirming narratives, 188–89; humane regard and, 190–91, 196, 198–99, 202, 206–7; political agency and, 55, 57–58, 192; public discussion norms and, 62–65, 70; reframing and, 189–91, 192; slave narratives, 57, 70, 196–97, 202–8, 281n15, 299–300n29

After Virtue (MacIntyre), 55, 187

Agamben, Giorgio, 256

agape, 20–21

Alcoff, Linda, 33

Alexander, Michelle, 101

Alinsky, Saul, 52

Allen, Danielle, 121

alternative facts, 132, 136–37

American Revolution, 118

Anderson, Benedict, 119–21, 122, 123, 127

Anderson, Elizabeth, 206

Anderson, Luvell, 220, 227

Anderson, Marian, 147, 150

Andrews, William L., 202

animal rights movements, 26–27

anti-Apartheid movement, 46, 48, 117, 138, 143, 150, 206

Aquinas, Thomas, 84, 88, 286n24

Arab Spring, 50, 64–65

Arceneaux, Kevin, 249

Arendt, Hannah, 17, 76, 188, 272

Aristotle, 83

Art of Moral Protest, The (Jasper), 34

arts, 135–36, 137, 246–47. *See also* civic
art of remembrance; fiction

Asian Americans, 190–91

Atwood, Margaret, 246

Austin, J. L., 140, 228

*Axis Rule in Occupied Europe: Laws
of Occupation, Analysis of
Government, Proposals for
Redress* (Lemkin), 168–69

Baker, Courtney, 91–92

Baldwin, James, 74–75, 79, 87,
212–13, 264, 269

Baptist, Edward, 165–66

beloved community, 37, 38, 258–60

Benjamin, Walter, 154

Bentham, Jeremy, 80

Berger, John, 91, 134–35

Black Codes, 141

Black History Month, 213

Black Jeremiad, 75, 244–45

Black Lives Matter movement:
imagination and, 138;
membership, 43–44; moral
standing and value and, 32–34;
sacrifice and, 21–22

Black Panther Party, 183, 192, 252

Black Power movement, 252

"Black Radical Kantianism"
(Mills), 93–94

Black Skin, White Masks (Fanon),
263

Blasingame, John W., 203

Blight, David, 139, 151

Boston Memorial to Robert Gould
Shaw and the 54th Regiment,
146, 148–50, 207

Boxill, Bernard, 205

Brexit, 231

Broad, C. D., 81

Brown, Dee, 300n36

Brown, John, 205–6

Brown v. Board of Education, 40, 183

Bruce, Dickson, 299–300n29

Buber, Martin, 56

Bujak, Zbygniew, 53–54

Burke, Kenneth, 158–59, 160, 161,
197

Butler, Judith, 167

butterfly effect, 64, 282n26

Calhoun, Cheshire, 84

California Agricultural Labor
Relations Act (1975), 29–30

Cameron, David, 123

Capers, Bennett, 142

Carlson, Gretchen, 180

Carmichael, Stokely, 252

Carson, Rachel, 104

"Case Against Civil Disobedience,
The" (Storing), 34–36, 41

Castañeda, Ernesto, 24

Castells, Manuel, 64–65

Cesaire, Aime, 263

Charleston church shooting (2015),
140

Chavez, Cesar, 17, 35, 173

Chen, Pang, 208–9

Chenoweth, Erica, 17

Chicago Freedom Movement, 183

Christianity, 16, 20–21

Churchill, Winston, 169

citizenship: citizenship movements, 34–35; civil disobedience and, 35–36, 39–41, 280n52; conscientious, 37–38, 41, 47, 48; duty to face injustice and, 88; epistemic injustice and, 110; harms to, 142–43, 293n42; nonviolence and, 48; obligations of, 37, 39; public reason and, 69–70; universal, 4, 23, 275n7

civic art of remembrance, 145–53; discrimination and, 139–40, 141–42; reparations politics and, 262; stigmatizing narratives and, 118, 138, 139, 143, 153–54; transformation and, 143–44, 150–51, 154. *See also* Confederate monuments; political iconoclasm

civic grace, 273–74, 307–8n27

civil disobedience, 19, 34–36, 37–38, 39–41, 266, 280n52. *See also* Civil Rights Movement

Civil Rights Act (1964), 35, 69

Civil Rights Movement: as citizenship movement, 34–35, 41, 42; compromise in, 29; discrimination and, 56; duty to face injustice and, 87; economic justice and, 109–10; historical boundaries of, 43; humane regard and, 56, 96–97; legislative outcomes, 15, 35, 36, 69; narrative and, 65; nonviolence in, 16, 17, 18, 55;

political agency and, 51–53, 54–55, 192; political hope and, 240, 256; prevention of domination and, 99–100; public reason and, 20; radical flank effects and, 18, 252; social collaboration and, 77; social movements as socially constructive and, 15–17, 276n7

civil society, 50, 54–55, 250

Civil War: Black soldiers in, 70, 146, 148–50, 207, 300n31; Gettysburg Address, 66, 147, 244; King on, 38; Lost Cause and, 139–40, 141

Clark, Kenneth, 183

Clark, Mamie, 183

cli-fi, 27, 136, 246

climate change activism, 136

cognitive biases, 132, 136, 137

Cohen, Leonard, 255, 274

COINTELPRO, 192

compromise, 28–29

conceptual engineering, 134, 170, 175

Confederate monuments: citizenship and, 142–43, 293n42; discrimination and, 139–40, 141–42; number of, 293n41; stigmatizing narratives and, 118, 138, 139, 143; total expressive situation of, 140–41; transformation and, 143–44, 150–51. *See also* political iconoclasm

conflicts of interest, 27–30

conscientious citizenship, 37–38, 41, 47, 48

consciousness raising, 57, 133, 163
"Constructive Conflict" (Follett),
    28–29
constructive imagination, 46, 250
contentious politics: conflicts of
    interest and, 27–30; definition
    of social movements and, 24–25;
    democracy and, 15; interest
    assertion and, 25–27, 278nn31–
    32; moral standing and value
    and, 25, 26–27, 30–34; political
    hope and, 235
Contingency, Irony and Solidarity
    (Rorty), 162
Cotton, Tom, 218
courage, 257
"Creative Democracy: The Task
    Before Us" (Dewey), 49
Crowd, The: A Study of the Popular
    Mind (Le Bon), 14
crowd, the, 13–15, 16, 23, 249, 250,
    276n7
Cultivating Humanity (Nussbaum),
    193
culture wars, 213–14
Cure at Troy, The (Heaney), 253

Daughters of Bilitis, 57
Dean, Carolyn J., 90
Death of Innocence: The Story of the
    Hate Crime That Changed
    America (Mobley), 92
deep story, 229–31, 247–48
"Defence of Poetry, The" (Shelley),
    243
de Klerk, F. W., 48

deliberative democracy, 59–60, 67
Delmas, Candace, 3, 37, 39
democracy: appeal of, 71, 283n38;
    breakdown of, 71–74, 109, 136;
    citizenship and, 49–50, 279n48;
    civic art of remembrance and,
    146–47; civil disobedience and,
    19; commemorative projects in,
    141; contentious politics as
    source of, 15; deliberative,
    59–60, 67; humane regard and,
    49; political community and,
    120, 121–22, 123, 124, 126–27;
    prevention of domination and,
    100, 288n50; public discussion
    norms and, 58–59, 62, 71; public
    reason and, 67–68, 70. See also
    citizenship; revolutionary
    democratic movements
de Pareja, Juan, 149
despair, 75
Dewey, John, 2, 47, 49, 74, 95, 135,
    146–47, 250
Diamond, Cora, 198
digital activism, 62–65
discrimination: civic art of
    remembrance and, 139–40,
    141–42; historical reclamation
    and, 220; political agency and,
    56–57; public acknowledgment
    and, 61–62
distributive justice, 22, 97, 266
Disturbing the Peace (Havel), 235–36
domination, 28, 29, 98–99, 288n50
Douglass, Frederick, 1, 5, 70, 146,
    151, 204–5, 212, 259

Du Bois, W. E. B., 95, 135, 153
Duchamp, Marcel, 141, 143, 149–50
duty to face injustice, 86–96;
    affected ignorance and, 88,
    286n24; humane regard and,
    91–95; photography and, 89–91,
    95–96, 286n28
*Duty to Resist, A: When Disobedience
    Should Be Uncivil* (Delmas), 37
Dworkin, Andrea, 44
Dworkin, Ronald, 39–40
dystopian narratives: civic grace
    and, 273–74; fear and, 75;
    historical reclamation and,
    219–21; King on, 255–56;
    political hope and, 231–32,
    247–51

Eastern European revolutions
    (1989): accountability and, 101;
    democracy and, 50, 280–81n4;
    moral inquiry and, 80, 82,
    285n17; narrative activism and,
    192; political agency and, 53–54,
    55–56; political iconoclasm and,
    138; prevention of domination
    and, 99; transformation of civic
    art and, 144
economic justice, 108–13, 189–90
Ellison, Ralph, 188
Emancipation Memorial, 146,
    150–51
emancipatory narrative activism,
    202–12; fiction and, 70, 135,
    211–12; Native Americans and,
    210–11, 300n36; slave narratives,

57, 70, 196–97, 202–8, 281n15,
    299–300n29; women's
    movement, 208–9
empire of affect, 230
environmental justice movement,
    87, 103–6, 285n21
environmental movement:
    imagination and, 136; interest
    assertion and, 25, 26, 27, 278n31.
    See also climate change activism;
    environmental justice
    movement
epistemic imagination, 130, 131,
    133–34, 159, 225, 250
epistemic injustice, 110–11
Ethics (Dewey and Tufts), 2
Ethics (Spinoza), 234
expressive harm, 141–42
Eyerman, Ron, 2–3

Faces of Injustice, The (Shklar), 76,
    88
Fanon, Frantz, 263
Farm Workers Movement. *See*
    United Farm Workers
    Movement
fascism, 15
Faulkner, William, 200
fear, 75, 232–33, 234–35, 243
Feinberg, Joel, 176, 214, 301n47
Feminine Mystique, The (Friedan),
    163
feminist movement. *See* women's
    movement
fiction, 27, 70, 135, 136, 211–12, 246
filter bubbles, 120

Fire Next Time, The (Baldwin), 74
Flint water crisis, 104–6
Floyd, George, 21, 62, 93, 267
Foa, Robert, 71
Follett, Mary Parker, 28–29
forgiveness, 76, 272. *See also* reconciliation
Francis (Pope), 123
Frankl, Viktor, 166, 239
Franklin, John Hope, 215, 301*n*47
Fratelli Tutti (Francis), 123
Freedom Budget, 109–10
French Revolution, 13–14, 257
Fricker, Miranda, 110, 134
Friedan, Betty, 163
Fromm, Erich, 238

Gadamer, Hans, 216
Gandhi, Mohandas: agape and, 20–21; Civil Rights Movement and, 16, 55, 276*n*7; moral inquiry and, 80, 173; nonviolence and, 17; social movements as socially constructive and, 15
Garrison, William Lloyd, 205
Gates, Henry Louis, 204
Gay Liberation Movement. *See* LGBTQ rights movement
genocide, 157, 168–72, 174
Gettysburg Address (Lincoln), 66, 147, 244
Geyl, Pieter, 217
Ginsburg, Ruth Bader, 85
Glory, 148
Glover, Jonathan, 93
Goffman, Erving, 165

Goodman, Nelson, 199–200
Gordon-Reed, Annette, 215, 216, 268
Gramsci, Antonio, 80, 182
greetings, 59–60
Griswold, Charles, 152–53
Guernica (Picasso), 135
Gutmann, Amy, 59

Habermas, Jurgen, 59
Haley, Nikki, 140
Half Has Never Been Told, The: Slavery and the Makings of American Capitalism (Baptist), 165–66
Hampton, Fred, 252
Handmaid's Tale, The (Atwood), 246
Hart, H. L. A., 102–3
hashtag activism, 62. *See also* digital activism
Haslanger, Sally, 3
Havel, Vaclav: language activism and, 167; moral inquiry and, 80; on political agency, 53–54, 55–56, 192; on political hope, 232, 235–36, 238, 257
Heaney, Seamus, 253, 257, 265
Heartbeat of Wounded Knee, The: Native America from 1890 to the Present (Treuer), 210
Heg, Hans Christian, 146, 151–52
Heirlooms and Accessories (Marshall), 95, 102
Hemings, Sally, 215–17
hermeneutical divides, 227–28, 247–48. *See also* dystopian narratives

Heroic Slave, The (Douglass), 212
high confidence view of
  imagination, 127–28
Highlander Folk School, 54–55
Hirschmann, Nancy, 57, 163
historical reclamation, 212–21;
  dystopian narratives and, 219–21;
  legitimacy of of, 213–17, 301n47;
  perspectival order and, 217–18
history, coming to terms with,
  264–70; humane regard and,
  266–67; narrative activism and,
  268–69; reparations politics
  and, 260–65. *See also* historical
  reclamation
Hitler, Adolf, 174
Hobbes, Thomas, 232, 290n7
Hochschild, Arlie, 229–31, 247
Holiday, Billie, 135
Holocaust, 90, 166, 168–71, 261,
  269–70
Honneth, Axel, 97
hooks, bell, 166, 167
hope, 234–53, 270–74. *See also*
  political hope
Horton, Myles, 55
Huerta, Dolores, 17
humane regard: accountability and,
  101; affirming narratives and,
  190–91, 196, 198–99, 202, 206–7;
  coming to terms with history
  and, 266–67; components of,
  4–5; democracy and, 49;
  distributive justice paradigm
  and, 97; duty to face injustice
  and, 91–95; environmental

justice movement and, 105;
  justice as, 96–98, 112; perceptual
  bias and, 135; physical security
  and, 103; political agency and,
  56; reparations politics and, 262.
  See also sympathetic
  imagination
*Humanity: A Moral History of the
  20th Century* (Glover), 93
human rights movement. *See*
  international human rights
  movement
Hungarian Revolution (1956–57),
  280n4

iconoclasm. *See* political
  iconoclasm
identity politics, 72, 123
"I Have a Dream" (King), 66,
  241–42, 244, 256
imagination: aesthetic, 131, 225;
  epistemic, 130, 131, 133–34, 159,
  225, 250; heterogeneity of,
  128–31; high confidence view of,
  127–28; humane regard and, 5;
  moral, 128, 270; narrative, 131,
  193, 225, 229; political
  community and, 119–27, 138,
  290n7; political hope and, 226;
  resistance to facts and, 132–38;
  sacrifice and, 121–22;
  sympathetic, 27, 131, 134, 135, 159,
  250; visionary leadership and, 46.
  See also political iconoclasm
"Imagination and Perception"
  (Strawson), 129

Imagined Communities (Anderson), 119–21
Inclusion and Democracy (Young), 22, 59, 241
integrative consensus, 29
interests: assertion of, 25–27, 30–31, 278*n*n31–32; conflicts of, 27–30; morally defensible/indefensible, 31–33; moral standing and value and, 30–32
internal goods, 53–54. *See also* political agency
international human rights movement, 87, 168–72, 174
Interpretation and Social Criticism (Walzer), 1–2

James, William, 3, 80, 148, 228
Jamison, Andrew, 2–3
Jasper, James, 34
Jefferson, Thomas, 215–17, 268
Jenson v. Eveleth Taconite Co., 22
Jim Crow segregation. *See* Civil Rights Movement; racial justice movements
Jowett, Garth, 153
Joyce, James, 200
Jungle, The (Lewis), 212
justice: economic, 108–13, 189–90; environmental safety and, 103–6; as humane regard, 96–98, 112; physical security and, 102–3; prevention of domination and, 98–100, 288*n*50; as removal of disabling constraints, 22–23, 98–99; social

movements as praxis for, 2–3; structural injustice and, 106–8
Justice and the Politics of Difference (Young), 22, 88

Kahneman, Daniel, 248
Kameny, Frank, 58
Kant, Immanuel, 67, 80–81, 94, 270
Kennedy, Robert F., 35
Khmer Rouge, 257
Kind, Amy, 129
King, Martin Luther, Jr.: on agape, 20–21; assassination of, 183, 252; on collective nature of social movements, 45; on compromise, 29; on conscientious citizenship, 37–38, 41, 47; on dystopian narratives, 255–56; economic justice and, 110; evolution of thought and, 271; humane regard and, 56, 96–97; language activism and, 167; moral inquiry and, 80, 172, 173; narrative and, 65; on nonviolence, 16, 17, 36, 38, 48, 252; political agency and, 52–53, 192; on political cooperation, 77; on political hope, 75, 226, 232, 240, 256, 257; radical flank effects and, 252; on reconciliation, 36, 38, 47, 258–60, 272; rhetoric and, 66, 241–42, 244, 259; slave narratives and, 204–5; United Farm Workers Movement and, 35; on Vietnam War, 38, 42, 259; as visionary leader, 46

Kingdom of God Is Within You, The: Christianity Not as a Mystic Religion but as a New Theory of Life (Tolstoy), 21
Kirkland, Frank, 205

labor movement, 45. *See also* United Farm Workers Movement
Lacan, Jacques, 91–92
Landrieu, Mitch, 139, 140, 142
language activism, 155–83; attention filtering and, 158–61, 168; effects of injustice and, 175–80; linguistic diversity and, 156–57; moral inquiry and, 173–75; oppressive language and, 180–83; reclamation projects, 156; reductive claims and, 161–65; resistance and, 165–67; unnamed wrongs and, 168–73
Lawson, James, 55
Lear, Jonathan, 239
Learning from the Germans: Race and the Memory of Evil (Neiman), 269–70
Le Bon, Gustave, 14, 23, 249, 276n7
Lebron, Chris, 3
Lee, Harper, 257
legislative outcomes, 15, 28, 29–30, 35, 69
Lemkin, Raphael, 157, 168–72
Lenhardt, Robin A., 142, 293n42
Lerner, Steve, 87
"Letter From Birmingham Jail, A" (King), 29, 56, 266
Leviathan (Hobbes), 232

Levinas, Emmanuel, 60
Lewis, Sinclair, 212
LGBTQ rights movement, 45, 57–58, 87
libertarianism, 111–12
Lichfield, Gordon, 160
Life and Labor in the Old South (Phillips), 203
Lilla, Mark, 72
Lincoln, Abraham, 46, 66, 147, 150, 151, 244, 300n31
Lincoln Memorial, 147
linguistic relativism, 161–62
Lipsky, Michael, 52
Locke, John, 290n7
Long Walk to Freedom (Mandela), 46, 239
Lorenz, Edward, 282n26
Lost Cause, 139–40, 141
Love Canal, 285n21
lynching, 86–87, 88, 90, 91, 95–96, 102, 304n27. *See also* racial justice movements
Lyons, David, 3, 36, 265–66

McCarthy, Thomas, 262–63
McClelland, J. S., 14
Machado, Antonio, 13, 28
MacIntyre, Alasdair, 55, 187, 188
MacKinnon, Catherine: duty to face injustice and, 89; humane regard and, 103; language activism and, 163, 180; moral inquiry and, 80, 84–85, 172; public discussion norms and, 64; radical flank effects and, 44

Mandela, Nelson: civic grace and, 273–74; narrative activism and, 206; political hope and, 226, 232, 239, 245, 253, 257; reconciliation and, 48, 261; reparations politics and, 261; transformation of civic art and, 143, 150; as visionary leader, 46

Mandelbaum, Maurice, 267–68

Man's Search for Meaning (Frankl), 166, 239

Marshall, Kerry James, 95, 102

Martin Luther King, Jr. Memorial, 152

Marx, Karl, 271

Masri, Safwan, 65

Mattachine Society, 57, 58

Meritor Savings Bank v. Vinson, 85, 178

#MeToo Movement, 63–64, 180, 209

Metzl, Jonathan, 174, 248

Mill, John Stuart, 60, 84, 270

Miller, David, 119

Mills, Charles, 93–94, 265–66, 286n24

Minersville School District v. Gobitis, 39

Mobley, Mamie Till, 87, 91, 96

model minority narrative, 190–91

Modern Social Imaginaries (Taylor), 126

Montgomery bus boycott (1955–56), 15, 16, 41, 53, 55, 65, 182, 259–60

monument removal project. *See* political iconoclasm

moral entitlements, 25

moral entrepreneurs, 173, 174

moral inquiry, 3, 79–86, 172, 173–75, 285n17

morality: imagination and, 128, 270; language activism and, 172; moral inquiry, 3, 79–86, 172, 173–75, 285n17; moral standing and value, 30–34. *See also* duty to face injustice

moral standing and value, 30–34

moral suasion, 205

Moro, RoseAnn, 112

Morrison, Toni, 155, 159, 180

Mounk, Yascha, 71–72

Moynihan, Patrick, 266

Mumford, Lewis, 154

Murdoch, Iris, 198

muscular liberalism, 123, 290n12

Mutz, Diana C., 248

My Bondage and My Freedom (Douglass), 204

narrative: deep story and, 229–31, 247–48; features of, 193–95; perspectival order in, 197–98, 199; public discussion norms and, 62–65, 70, 194–95; situated knowledge and, 199, 202; as source of meaning and value, 195–202; twisting of time in, 199–201. *See also* affirming narratives; dystopian narratives; narrative activism; stigmatizing narratives

narrative activism, 188–92, 201–21; coming to terms with history and, 268–69; fiction and, 70, 135, 211–12; Native Americans and, 210–11, 300n36; resentment and, 219–20; risks of, 207–8; slave narratives, 57, 70, 196–97, 202–8, 281n15, 299–300n29; women's movement, 208–9. *See also* historical reclamation

narrative imagination, 131, 193, 225, 229

Narrative Knowing and the Human Sciences (Polkinghorne), 194

National Nurses United (NNU), 112

Native Americans, 197–98, 210–11, 300n36

Nazi Germany, 138, 144, 166, 168–71, 197

Nazism, 15

"Negro Family, The: The Case of National Action" (Moynihan), 266

Negro History Week, 213

Neiman, Susan, 269–70

Neu, Jerome, 228

Niagara Movement, 40, 43, 182

Nietzsche, Friedrich, 217

nonviolence: abolitionism and, 205–6; King on, 16, 17, 36, 38, 48, 252; political agency and, 55; social movements as socially constructive and and, 15, 16–18

Notes on the State of Virginia (Jefferson), 216

Notes Toward a Performative Theory of Assembly (Butler), 167

Nussbaum, Martha C., 167, 193, 198, 227, 229

Obama, Barack, 183–84

Occupy Wall Street Movement, 108

O'Donnell, Victoria, 153

On Liberty (Mill), 84

"On Not Prosecuting Disobedience" (Dworkin), 39

On Photography (Sontag), 90

"On Violence" (Arendt), 17

oppression, 98

ordinary emotions, 230

organic intellectuals, 80

Orwell, George, 153

Osmundsen, Matthias, 249

Painter, Nell, 218

Pankhurst, Emmeline, 44

Parks, Rosa, 55

Patterson, Orlando, 165, 263–64

Paul, Ron, 111, 112

perceptual biases, 132, 134–35

perspectival order, 197–98, 199, 217–18

Peterson, Michael, 249

Phillips, Ulrich, 203

"Philosopher and the Moral Life, The" (James), 80

philosophical humility, 2, 3

photography, 89–91, 95–96, 286n28

Picasso, Pablo, 135

Pinker, Steven, 132

Plato, 2, 13, 16, 19, 65, 83, 90, 95, 270

Platts, Mark, 81

Plessy v. Ferguson, 40, 149, 181–82, 183, 184
police violence: accountability and, 101, 102; coming to terms with history and, 267; duty to face injustice and, 93; moral inquiry and, 83; political iconoclasm and, 152; public discussion norms and, 62; sacrifice and, 21–22. *See also* racial justice movements
political agency, 51–58; Civil Rights Movement and, 51–53, 54–55, 192; discrimination and, 56–57; narrative and, 55, 57–58, 192; Solidarity and, 53–54
political community, 119–27, 138, 290n7
political cooperation. *See* social collaboration
political hope, 226–54; affective responses and, 230, 236–37; Baldwin on, 74–75; collective pathways to, 233–34; contentious politics and, 235; courage and, 257; deep story and, 229–31; definitions of, 237; dystopian narratives and, 231–32, 247–51; fear and, 232–33, 234–35, 243; Havel on, 232, 235–36, 238, 257; hermeneutical divides and, 227–28, 247–48; history and, 265; hopelessness and, 256–57; King on, 75, 226, 232, 240, 256, 257; optimism and, 288–89; radical hope, 239–40; rhetoric and, 241–47;

social change and, 235–36; understanding and, 227–29; varieties of, 236–38; visionary leadership and, 46, 241
political iconoclasm, 117–19; haphazard approach to, 144–45; misguided targets of, 145–46, 151–52; stigmatizing narratives and, 118, 138, 139, 143; transformation and, 143–44
Political Liberalism (Rawls), 67, 124, 125
political obligation, 120–21, 125, 290n7
Politics (Plato), 83
Polkinghorne, Donald, 194, 196, 198
Polletta, Francesca, 208–9
pornography, 89
positional hope, 230, 240, 243, 257
Posner, Richard, 173, 174, 175
postmodernism, 162
"Power of the Powerless, The" (Havel), 53–54, 192
pragmatism, 2
prejudice. *See* perceptual bias
"Protest as a Political Resource" (Lipsky), 52
provocative proposals, 59–61
public acknowledgment, 59–62
public discussion norms, 58–66; democracy and, 58–59, 62, 71; deterioration of, 70–71; narrative and, 62–65, 70, 194–95; public acknowledgment and, 59–62; rhetoric and, 65–66, 70
public reason, 20–21, 67–70

Race and Reunion: The Civil War in National Memory (Blight), 139

racial justice movements: accountability and, 102; Black Jeremiad and, 75, 244–45; civic art of remembrance and, 147, 148–51; civil disobedience and, 34–36, 40, 266; Civil War and, 146, 148–50, 207, 300*n*31; collective nature of, 45; coming to terms with history and, 265–67; current struggles, 183–85; duty to face injustice and, 86–87, 89, 91–93; economic justice and, 109–10; environmental justice movement and, 106; historical boundaries and, 43; historical reclamation and, 213, 215–17, 218–19; humane regard and, 56, 95–97; imagination and, 117–19, 138–45; model minority narrative and, 190–91; moral inquiry and, 83; morally defensible/indefensible interests and, 31–34; moral standing and value and, 32–34; narrative activism and, 192–93; narrative and, 57, 70, 190–91, 281*n*15; nonviolence/violence and, 16, 17, 36, 38, 48, 252; oppressive language and, 181–83; public acknowledgment and, 62; public reason and, 68–70; radical flank effects and, 18, 252; reparations politics and, 262–64; rhetoric

and, 66, 70, 244–45, 259; sacrifice and, 188. *See also* political iconoclasm

radical flank effects, 18, 44, 252

radical hope, 239–40

Rawls, John, 3, 19–20, 22, 36, 39, 41, 59, 67–69, 82, 124–25, 127, 265–67, 270

reclamation projects, 156, 295*n*3

reconciliation: King on, 36, 38, 47, 258–60, 272; Mandela and, 48, 261; rhetoric and, 226, 245, 252; self-righteousness and, 76

"Reflections on Little Rock" (Arendt), 188

Regarding the Pain of Others (Sontag), 89–90

Renan, Ernst, 121

reparations politics, 260–65

Republic (Plato), 2, 13, 90

resentment. *See* dystopian narratives

respect, 4–5

Reveille for Radicals (Alinsky), 52

revolutionary democratic movements: accountability and, 101; challenges to, 283*n*29; democracy and, 50–51, 280–81*n*4; moral inquiry and, 80, 82, 285*n*17; narrative activism and, 192; political agency and, 53–54, 55–56; political iconoclasm and, 138; prevention of domination and, 99; public discussion norms and, 64–65; transformation of civic art and, 144

Rez Life: An Indian's Journey Through Reservation Life (Treuer), 210–11
rhetoric: political hope and, 241–47; protest and, 259; public discussion norms and, 65–66, 70; reconciliation and, 226, 245, 252
"Rhodes Must Fall" movement (2015), 117, 138, 143
Robben Island prison, 143, 150
Room of One's Own, A (Woolf), 201
Roosevelt, Franklin D., 46, 66, 242–43, 304*n*27
Rorty, Richard, 72–74, 75, 162–65, 166, 167, 208, 244, 270
Rossetti, Christina, 225, 234

sacrifice, 21–22; moral inquiry and, 174–75; narrative and, 188; political community and, 121–22, 125, 126–27
Saint-Gaudens, Augustus, 148–49
Santayana, George, 265
satyagraha, 15, 20–21, 55, 276*n*7. *See also* Gandhi, Mohandas
Savage, Kirk, 148
Scheffler, Samuel, 124
science fiction, 27, 136, 246
self-righteousness, 76–77
"separate but equal," 181–82
sexual assault, 61–62, 63–64
sexual harassment, 84–85, 133–34, 164, 176–79, 209
Sexual Harassment of Working Women (MacKinnon), 84–85
Sharp, Gene, 17–18, 51, 280–81*n*4
Shaw, Robert Gould, 146, 148

Shelley, Percy Bysshe, 243
Shklar, Judith, 76, 88, 100, 101
Siegal, Reva, 178, 179
Silent Spring (Carson), 104
Sinha, Manisha, 42–43, 57, 281*n*15
situated knowledge, 199, 202
1619 project, 218–19
slave narratives, 57, 70, 196–97, 202–8, 281*n*15, 299–300*n*29
slavery: civic art of remembrance and, 139, 146; historical reclamation and, 215–17, 218, 301*n*47; language activism and, 165–66; moral inquiry and, 83–84; reparations politics and, 262–64. *See also* abolitionism; racial justice movements; slave narratives
Slavery and Social Death (Patterson), 165
Slave's Cause, The: A History of Abolition (Sinha), 42–43
Slote, Michael, 83
Smith, Adam, 27
Smith, David Livingstone, 93
Snyder, C. R., 236
social collaboration, 77
social connection model, 107
social constructionism, strong, 161–62
social justice. *See* justice
social movements: as citizenship movements, 34–35; as cognitive praxis, 2–3; collective nature of, 44–45; complexity of, 42–46; conflicts of interest and, 27–30; defined, 23–25; democratic

breakdown and, 73–74; despair and, 75; evolution of, 271–72; goals of, 3, 22–23, 25–26, 275n7; historical boundaries of, 42–43; interest assertion and, 25–27, 278nn31–32; measurements of success, 28; membership, 43–44; as moral inquiry, 79–86; organic intellectuals and, 80; political agency and, 51–58; political cooperation and, 77; public discussion norms and, 58–66; public reason and, 20–21, 67–72; radical flank effects and, 18, 44, 252; as rational, 17; Rawls on, 19–20; sacrifice and, 21–22; self-righteousness and, 76–77; as socially constructive, 15–17, 276n7; tasks of, 5; and "the crowd," 13–15, 16, 23, 276n7; visionary leadership and, 45–46, 168, 171; Young on, 22–23. *See also* contentious politics; morality

Socrates, 173. *See also* Plato

Solidarity, 53–54, 192, 280–81n4. *See also* Eastern European revolutions

Sontag, Susan, 89–90

South Africa. *See* anti-Apartheid movement; Mandela, Nelson

Southern Poverty Law Center, 139–40, 293n41

Spinoza, Baruch, 234–35

Stalinism, 257

Staples, Brent, 90

status quo bias, 136

Stephan, Maria, 17

Stevenson, Leslie, 128–29

stigmatizing narratives, 187–88; civic art of remembrance and, 118, 138, 139, 143, 153–54; discrimination and, 56–57; economic justice and, 111–13; narrative activism and, 188–89, 191–93; perspectival order in, 197–98; public discussion norms and, 194–95; sacrifice and, 188; social roles and, 187–88; as source of meaning and value, 196–97

Storing, Herbert, 34–36, 41

Stowe, Harriet Beecher, 70, 135, 212

Strange Fruit, 135

Strangers in their Own Land: Anger and Mourning on the American Right (Hochschild), 229–31

"Strategy of Protest, The: Problems of Negro Civic Action" (Wilson), 51–52

Strawson, P. F., 129

Stride Toward Freedom (King), 53, 65, 192

structural injustice, 106–8

Subjection of Women, The (Mill), 84

suffering. *See* sacrifice

sympathetic imagination, 27, 131, 134, 135, 159, 250

Talking Back: Thinking Feminist, Thinking Black (hooks), 166

Talking to Strangers: Anxieties of Citizenship Since Brown v. Board of Education (Allen), 121

Taylor, Charles, 122, 126, 127, 189
"Terministic Screens" (Burke),
    158–59
Theory of Justice, A (Rawls), 82, 125,
    267
Theory of Moral Sentiments, The
    (Smith), 27
*Thomas Jefferson and Sally Hemings:
    An American Controversy*
    (Gordon-Reed), 215
Thompson, Dennis, 59
Thoreau, Henry David, 103–4
Till, Emmett, 86–87, 92–93, 96,
    269
Tilly, Charles, 15, 24
"Time To Break Silence, A"
    (King), 38, 110, 259
To Kill a Mockingbird (Lee), 257
Tolstoy, Leo, 21
Torpey, John, 264
total expressive situation, 140–41
Treatise Theological-Political
    (Spinoza), 234–35
Treuer, David, 197–98, 210, 300n36
Truth and Method (Gadamer), 216
Truth and Reconciliation
    Commission (South Africa), 261
Tubman, Harriet, 70
Tufecki, Zeynep, 65
Tufts, James, 2
Tutu, Desmond, 272
Tversky, Amos, 248
Twain, Mark, 117, 132
*Twitter and Teargas: The Power and
    Fragility of Networked Protest*
    (Tufecki), 65

Uncle Tom's Cabin (Stowe), 70, 135,
    212
*UN Convention on the Punishment
    and Prevention of Genocide*, 171,
    174
understanding, 227–29
"undeserving poor" narrative, 111
United Farm Workers Movement,
    17, 25, 29–30, 35–36
Unite the Right rally
    (Charlottesville, 2017), 140
universal citizenship, 4, 23, 275n7
utilitarianism, 80, 83, 94

Varieties of Religious Experience, The
    (James), 228
Velasquez, Diego, 149
Velvet Revolution (1989), 50, 82, 99,
    101, 285n17
Vietnam Veterans Memorial,
    152–53, 262
Vietnam War: civic art of
    remembrance and, 152–53, 262;
    conscientious citizenship and,
    38, 42; duty to face injustice
    and, 90, 286n28; economic
    justice and, 110; protest and, 259
volitional attitudes and
    dispositions, 230
Voting Rights Act (1965), 15, 35,
    36, 69

Walden Pond (Thoreau), 103–4
Waldron, Jeremy, 264
Walzer, Michael, 1–2, 45, 82, 99,
    170, 285n17

Ways of Seeing (Berger), 91

West Virginia State Board of Education v. Barnett, 39

"What Is a Nation?" (Renan), 121

"What Is Enlightenment?" (Kant), 67

"What to the Slave Is the Fourth of July?" (Douglass), 5, 259

White, E. B., 274

Wilson, James Q., 51–52

Wittgenstein, Ludwig, 95

Wolff, Tobias, 212

women's movement: epistemic imagination and, 133–34; humane regard and, 96, 103; language activism and, 163–64, 176–78, 180; moral inquiry and, 84–85; moral standing and value and, 31; narrative and, 57, 201, 208–9; public discussion norms and, 61–62, 63–64; public reason

and, 20; radical flank effects and, 44; reframing and, 189–90

Women's Social and Political Union (WSPU), 44

Wood, Lesley J., 24

Woodson, Carter G., 213

Woodward, C. Vann, 149, 181

Woolf, Virginia, 200, 201

World Justice Project, 288n50

Wounded Knee massacre (1890), 198, 300n36

X, Malcolm, 35, 252, 259

Yang, Guobin, 63

Young, Iris, 3, 19, 22–23, 58–60, 62–63, 64, 65–66, 67, 70–71, 88, 97, 98, 107, 147, 194, 199, 209, 241, 258, 275n7, 288n49

Žižek, Slavoj, 256, 257